Filling in the Gaps

Kelley Christopher

University of West Georgia

Kendall Hunt
publishing company

Kendall Hunt
publishing company

www.kendallhunt.com
Send all inquiries to:
4050 Westmark Drive
Dubuque, IA 52004-1840

Dedication

For Birdie, Jesse, Steve, and my little Zarek~
                              Life, made possible~
For my Mother, Joy~ who, every day, lives up to her name.
For my enormously lovable siblings, Michelle, Brian, and Robin.
And for both my Fathers in heaven.

A special thanks to my colleague and mentor, Dr. David Jenks,
whose guidance and support have been invaluable~
And for Tiffany Parsons, my treasured confidant.

Kelley Christopher holds graduate degrees in Post-Secondary Education, Public Administration, and Sociology. She currently teaches in the Department of Criminology at the University of West Georgia in Carrollton, Georgia.

Table of Contents

CHAPTER ONE
Female Offenders

TRENDS IN WOMEN'S CRIME

Meda Chesney-Lind and Lisa Pasko

Women's crime, like girls' crime, is deeply affected by women's place. As a result, women's contribution to serious and violent crime—like that of girls—is minor. Of those adults arrested for serious crimes of violence in 2001 (murder, forcible rape, robbery, and aggravated assault), only 17% were female. Indeed, women constituted only 21.4% of all arrests during that year (FBI, 2002, p. 239). This also means that adult women are an even smaller percentage of those arrested than their girl counterparts (who now comprise more than one out of four juvenile arrests).

Moreover, the majority of adult women offenders, like girls, are arrested and tried for relatively minor offenses. In 2001, women were most likely to be arrested for larceny theft (which alone accounted for 12.1% of all adult women's arrests), followed by drug abuse violations (10.1%). This means that more than a fifth of all the women arrested in the United States that year were arrested for one of these two offenses. Women's offenses, then, are concentrated in just a few criminal categories, just as women's employment in the mainstream economy is concentrated in a few job categories. Furthermore, these offenses, as we shall see, are closely tied to women's economic marginality and the ways women attempt to cope with poverty.

UNRULY WOMEN: A BRIEF HISTORY OF WOMEN'S OFFENSES

Women's concentration in petty offenses is not restricted to the present. A study of women's crime in 14th-century England (Hanawalt, 1982) and descriptions of the backgrounds of the women who were forcibly transported to Australia several centuries later (Beddoe, 1979) document the astonishing stability in patterns of women's lawbreaking.

The women who were transported to Australia, for example, were servants, maids, or laundresses convicted of petty theft (stealing, shoplifting, and picking pockets) or prostitution. The number of women transported for these trivial offenses is sobering. Between 1787 and 1852, no less than 24,960 women, fully a third of whom were first offenders, were sent to relieve the "shortage" of women in the colonies. Shipped in rat-infested holds, the women were systematically raped and sexually abused by the ships' officers and sailors, and the death rate in the early years was as high as one in three. Their arrival in Australia was also a nightmare; no provision was made for the women and many were forced to turn to prostitution to survive (Beddoe, 1979, pp. 11-21).

Other studies add different but important dimensions to the picture. For example, Bynum's (1992) research on "unruly" women in antebellum North Carolina adds the vital dimension of race to the picture. She notes that the marginalized members of society, particularly "free black and unmarried poor white women" were most often likely both to break social and sexual taboos and to face punishment by the courts. Indeed, she observes that "if North Carolina lawmakers could have done so legally, they would have rid society altogether" of these women (p. 10). As it was, they harshly enforced laws against fornication, bastardy, and prostitution in an attempt to affect these women and their progeny.

The role of urbanization and class is further explored in Feeley and Little's (1991) research on criminal cases appearing in London courts between 1687 and 1912, and Boritch and Hagan's (1990) research on arrests in Toronto between 1859 and 1955. Both of these studies examine the effect of industrialization and women's economic roles (or economic marginalization) on women's offenses. Both works present evidence that women were drawn to urban areas, where they were employed in extremely low-paid work, As a result, this forced many into forms of offending, including disorderly conduct, drunkenness, and petty thievery. Boritch and Hagan make special note of the large numbers of women arrested for property offenses, "drunkenness," and "vagrancy," which can be seen as historical counterparts to modern drug offenses. But what of women who committed "serious" offenses such as murder? Jones's (1980) study of early women murderers in the United States reveals that many of America's early women murderers were indentured servants [Raped by calculating masters who understood that giving birth to a "bastard" would add 1 to 2 years to a woman's term of service, these desperate women hid their pregnancies and then committed infanticide. Jones also provides numerous historical and contemporary examples of desperate women murdering their brutal "lovers" or husbands. The less dramatic links between forced marriage, women's circumscribed options, and women's decisions to kill, often by poison, characterized the Victorian murderesses. These women, though rare, haunted the turn of the century, in part because women's participation in the methodical violence involved in arsenic poisoning was considered unthinkable (Hartman, 1977).]

In short, research on the history of women's offenses, and particularly women's violence, is a valuable resource for its information on the level and character of women's crime and as a way to understand the relationship between women's crime and women's lives. Whenever a woman commits murder, particularly if she is accused of murdering a family member, people immediately ask, "How could she do that?" Given the enormous costs of being born female, that may well be the wrong question. The real question, as a review of the history of women's crime illustrates, is not why women murder but rather why so few murder.

Take a look at some facts. Every 15 seconds, a woman is beaten in her own home (Bureau of Justice Statistics, 1989). One in every three women report having been physically attacked by an intimate partner some time in her life (Wilt & Olson, 1996). In 1999, women were three times more likely to be killed by their intimate partners than were men and accounted for 85% of all victims of domestic violence (Rennison, 2001, p. 1), A National Institute of Mental Health study (based on urban area hospitals) estimated that 21% of all women using emergency surgical services had been injured in a domestic violence incident; that half of all injuries presented by women to emergency surgical services occurred in the context of partner abuse; and that over half of all rapes of women over the age of 30 had been perpetrated by an intimate partner (Stark et al., 1981). In addition, other studies have shown that marital rape is often more violent and repetitive than other forms of sexual assault and is often not reported (Richie, 2000, p. 4). In the United States, for example, former Surgeon General C. Everett Koop (1989) estimated that 3 to 4 million women are battered each year; roughly half of them are single, separated, or divorced (Rennison). According to the National Crime Victimization Survey, women separated from their husbands are victimized at higher rates than married, divorced, or single women, with females aged 16 to 24 experiencing the highest rate of intimate partner violence—151 per 1,000 women (Rennison, p. 5). Battering also tends to escalate and become more severe over time. Almost half of all batterers beat their partners at least three times a year (Straus, Gelles, & Steinmetz, 1980). This description of victimization doesn't address other forms of women's abuse, such as incest and sexual assault, which have rates as alarmingly high (see Center for Policy Studies, 1991).

The real question is why so few women resort to violence in the face of such horrendous victimization—even to save their lives. In 2001, in the United States, only 14.2% of those arrested for murder were women—meaning that murder, like other forms of violent crime, is almost exclusively a male activity. In fact, women murderers, as both Jones and Hartman document, are interesting precisely because of their rarity. The large number of women arrested for trivial property and moral offenses, coupled with the virtual absence of women from those arrested for serious property crimes and violent crimes, provides clear evidence that women's crime parallels their assigned role in the rest of society (Klein & Kress, 1976). In essence, women's place in the legitimate economy largely relegates them to jobs that pay poorly and are highly sex segregated (such as secretarial and sales jobs). Likewise, in the illicit or criminal world, they occupy fewer roles and roles that do not "pay" as well as men's crime. There is, however, little understanding of why this is the case and, until recently, little scholarship devoted to explaining this pattern. This chapter attempts to address both the reality of women's crime and the fascination with the atypical woman offender who is violent and defies her "conventional role" in both the mainstream and the criminal world.

TRENDS IN WOMEN'S ARRESTS

Over the years, women have typically been arrested for larceny theft, drunk driving, fraud (the bulk of which is welfare fraud and naive check forgery), drug abuse violations, and buffer charges for prostitution (such as disorderly conduct and a variety of petty offenses that fall under the broad category of "other offenses"; Steffensmeier, 1980; Steffensmeier & Allan, 1995; see Table 5.1).

Arrest data certainly suggest that the "war on drugs" has translated into a war on women. Between 1992 and 2001, arrests of adult women for drug abuse violations increased by 42.3%, compared to 31.4% for men (FBI, 2002, p. 239). The past decade (1992–2001) has also seen increases in arrests of women for "other assaults" (up 57.7%)—not unlike the pattern seen in girls' arrests. Arrest rates show much the same pattern. In the past decade, arrests of women for drug offenses and other assaults have replaced fraud and disorderly conduct as the most common offenses for which adult women are arrested.

These figures, however, should not be used to support notions of dramatic increases in women's crime. As an example, although the number of adult women arrested between 1992 and 2001 did increase by 15%, that increase followed a slight decline in women's arrests between 1992 and 1993; and by 1997, the overall arrest rate for women has been steadily declining (FBI, 1994, p. 226; 1995, p. 226; 2002, p. 241).

The arrests of women for Part One or Index offenses (murder, rape, aggravated assault, robbery, burglary, larceny theft, motor vehicle theft, and arson) decreased by 9.1% (compared to a decrease in male arrests of 22%) between 1992 and 2001 (FBI, 2002, p. 239; see Table 5.1). Much of this decrease in both women's and men's overall crime index is due to decreases in larceny theft arrests.

Moreover, looking at these offenses differently reveals a picture of stability rather than change over the past decade. Women's share of these arrests (as a proportion of all those arrested for these offenses) rose from 23% to 26% between 1992 and 2001. Women's share of arrests for serious violent offenses rose from 12.4% to 17% during the same period (FBI, 2002, p. 239). This increase is not a result of more murder or robbery arrests, but rather, it is due to aggravated assault. At the other extreme is the pattern found in arrests for prostitution—the only crime among the 29 offense categories tracked by the FBI for which arrests of women account for the majority (63.2%) of all arrests.

Overall, the increase in women's official arrest statistics is largely accounted for by a similar pattern noticed in their juvenile counterparts—increases in other assaults (up 57.7%), drug abuse violations (up by 42.3%), and property offenses, such as check forgery (forgery/counterfeiting, which was up 37.7%) and embezzlement (which was up 78.9%; FBI, 2002, p. 239). Despite an increase in aggravated and other assaults, women's crime is mostly nonviolent in nature—one fifth of all women offenders are arrested for some type of property crime (compared to 8% of men). Here, both property and drug violation arrests are real, because the base numbers are large and, as a result, these offenses make up a large portion of women's official deviance. Whether the increase in other assaults and drug violations arrests (coupled with a consistently large number of arrests for property offenses) are the product of actual changes in women's behavior over the past decade or changes in law enforcement practices is an important question, and one to which we now turn.

HOW COULD SHE? THE NATURE AND CAUSES OF WOMEN'S CRIME

In summary, adult women have been, and continue to be, arrested for minor crimes (generally shoplifting and welfare fraud) and what might be called "deportment" offenses (prostitution, disorderly conduct, and, arguably, "driving under the influence"). Their younger counterparts are arrested for essentially the same crimes, in addition to status offenses (running away from home, incorrigibility, truancy, and other noncriminal offenses for which only minors can be taken into custody). Arrests of adult women, like arrests of girls, have increased for both aggravated and other assaults. Finally, and most important, adult women's arrests for drug offenses have soared.

Table 1.1   Adult 10-Year Trends by Sex, 1992–2001

Offense Charged	Men	1992 % Change	Women	1992 % Change
Total	4,829,151	−2.6	1,318,566	+15.0
Index Offenses:				
Murder and nonnegligent manslaughter	5,223	−32.0	865	−4.0
Forcible rape	11,726	−29.0	143	−22.0
Robbery	38,524	−24.8	4,592	−9.4
Aggravated assault	182,362	−8.7	43,668	+33.3
Burglary	62,001	−55.3	16,070	−0.01
Larceny-theft	284,265	−25.3	160,003	−18.2
Motor vehicle theft	41,673	−18.9	8,010	+38.5
Arson	4,159	−10.1	993	+22.6
Total violent crime	237,835	−13.6	49,268	+26.6
Total property crime	424,369	−26.2	185,076	−15.2
Other Offenses:				
Other assaults	445,832	+8.2	124,704	+57.7
Forgery and counterfeiting	36,603	+12.2	24,688	+37.7
Fraud	90,496	−16.3	78,085	−15.8
Stolen property: buying, receiving, possessing	43,052	−23.2	9,063	+3.0
Offenses against family	58,271	+16.7	15,547	+84.6
Prostitution, vice	13,484	−21.0	23,118	−18.5
Embezzlement	5,186	+18.3	5,359	+78.9
Vandalism	72,936	−11.0	15,888	+23,0
Weapons (carrying, etc.)	62,745	−31,5	5,136	−30.3
Drug abuse violations	585,206	+31.4	133,006	+42.3
Gambling	2,344	−55.9	405	−48.8
Liquor law violations	206,040	+18.6	55,951	+55.5
Driving under the influence	653,307	−18.7	130,832	+2.8
Drunkenness	302,378	−29.2	46,878	−9.9
Disorderly conduct	177,931	−23.0	51,400	−7.3
Vagrancy	10,585	+3.0	2,903	+57.5
All other offenses	1,364,173	+23,8	358,412	+52.3
Suspicion	1,003	−66.1	232	−53.0

Source: Federal Bureau of Investigation. (2002b). 2001 *Uniform Crime Reports* (p. 239), Washington, DC: Author.

Where there have been increases in women's arrests for offenses that sound nontraditional, such as embezzlement, careful examination reveals the connections between these offenses and women's place.

Embezzlement

In the case of embezzlement, for which women's arrests increased by 78.9% in the past decade, careful research disputes the notion of women moving firmly into the ranks of big-time, white-collar offenders. Because women are concentrated in low-paying clerical, sales, and service occupations (Renzetti & Curran, 1995), they are "not in a position to steal hundreds of thousands of dollars but they [are] in a position to pocket smaller amounts" (Simon & Landis, 1991, p. 56). Moreover, their motives for such theft often involve family responsibilities rather than a desire for personal gain (Daly, 1989; Zietz, 1981).

Daly's (1989) analysis of gender differences in white-collar crime is particularly useful. In a review of federal "white-collar" crime cases in seven federal districts (which included people convicted of bank embezzlement, income tax fraud, postal fraud, etc.), she found that gender played a substantial role in the differences between men's and women's offenses. For example, of those arrested for bank embezzlement, 60% of the women were tellers and 90% were in some sort of clerical position. By contrast, about half of the men charged with embezzlement held professional and managerial positions (bank officers and financial managers). Therefore, it is no surprise that for each embezzlement offense, men's attempted economic gain was 10 times higher than women's (Daly). In commenting on this pattern, Daly notes, "the women's socio-economic profile, coupled with the nature of their crimes, makes one wonder if 'white collar' aptly described them or their illegalities" (p. 790).

Embezzlement is a particularly interesting offense to "unpack" because it is one of the offenses for which, if present trends continue, women may comprise about half of those charged (Renzetti & Curran, 1995, p. 310). In fact, women composed about half of those charged with embezzlement in 2001 (FBI, 2002, p. 239). Yet these increases cannot be laid at the door of women breaking into traditionally "male" offense patterns. Women's increased share of arrests for embezzlement is probably an artifact of their presence in low-level positions that make them more vulnerable to frequent checking and hence more vulnerable to detection (Steffensmeier & Allan, 1995). Combining this with these women's lack of access to resources to "cover" their thefts prompts Steffensmeier and Allan to draw a parallel between modem women's involvement in embezzlement and increases in thefts by women in domestic service a century ago.

Driving Under the Influence

Arrests of women driving under the influence (DUI) account for almost 1 arrest in 10 of women (FBI, 2002, p. 239). One study (Wells-Parker, Pang, Anderson, McMillen, & Miller, 1991) found that women arrested for DUI tended to be older than men (with nearly half of the men but less than a third of the women under 30), more likely to be "alone, divorced or separated," and to have fewer serious drinking problems and fewer extensive prior arrests for DUI or "public drunkenness" (Wells-Parker et al., 1991, p. 144). Historically, women were arrested for DUI only if "the DUI involved a traffic accident or physical/verbal abuse of a police officer" (Coles, 1991, p. 5). These patterns have probably eroded in recent years because of public outrage over drinking and driving and an increased use of roadblocks. Changes in police practices, rather than changes in women's drinking, could easily explain the prominence of this offense in women's official crime patterns.

Women tend to drink alone and deny treatment (Coles, 1991). Also, in contrast to men, they tend to drink for "escapism and psychological comfort" (Wells-Parker et al., 1991, p. 146). For these reasons, intervention programs that attempt to force women to examine their lives and the quality of relationships, which tend to work for male DUI offenders, are not successful with women. Indeed, these interventions could "exacerbate a sense of distress, helplessness and hopelessness" that could, in turn, trigger more drinking (Wells-Parker et al., p. 146).

Larceny Theft/Shoplifting

Women's arrests for larceny theft are composed largely of arrests for shoplifting. Steffensmeier (1980) estimates that perhaps as many as four fifths of all arrests on larceny charges are for shoplifting. Cameron's (1953) early study of shoplifting in Chicago explains that women's prominence among those arrested for shoplifting may not reflect greater female involvement in the offense but rather differences in the ways men and women shoplift. Her research revealed that women tend to steal more items than men, to steal items from several stores, and to steal items of lesser value. Store detectives explained this pattern by saying that people tended to "steal the same way they buy" (Cameron, p. 159). Men came to the store with one item in mind. They saw it, took it, and left the store. Women, on the other hand, shopped around. Because the chance of being arrested increases with each item stolen, Cameron felt that the stores probably underestimated the level of men's shoplifting.

Although women stole more items than men, the median value of adult male theft was significantly higher than that of women's (Cameron, 1953, p. 62). In addition, more men than women were defined as "commercial shoplifters" (people who stole merchandise for possible resale).

Perhaps as a result of women's shopping and shoplifting patterns, studies done later (Lindquist, 1988) have found that women constitute 58% of those caught shoplifting. Steffensmeier and Allan (1995) go so far as to suggest that shoplifting may be regarded as a prototypically female offense. Shopping is, after all, part of women's "second shift" of household management, housework, and child care responsibilities (Hochschild, 1989). Shoplifting can be seen as a criminal extension of expected and familiar women's work.

Even the reasons for shoplifting are gendered. Men, particularly young men, tend to view stealing as part of a broader pattern of masculine display of "badness" and steal items that are of no particular use to them (Steffensmeier & Allan, 1995). At the other extreme, they may be professional thieves and thus more likely to escape detection (Cameron, 1953).

Girls and women, on the other hand, tend to steal items that they either need or feel they need but cannot afford. As a result, they tend to steal from stores and to take things such as clothing, cosmetics, and jewelry. Campbell (1981) notes that women—young and old—are the targets of enormously expensive advertising campaigns for a vast array of personal products. These messages, coupled with the temptations implicit in long hours spent "shopping," lead to many arrests of women for these offenses.

Despite some contentions that women actually shoplift more than men, self-report data in fact show few gender differences in the prevalence of the behavior (see Chesney-Lind & Shelden, 1992, for a review of these studies). What appears to be happening is that girls and women shoplift in different ways than men. In addition, they are more often apprehended because store detectives expect women to shoplift more than men and thus watch women more closely (Morris, 1987).

BIG TIME/SMALL TIME

English (1993) approached the issue of women's crime by analyzing detailed self-report surveys she administered to a sample of 128 female and 872 male inmates in Colorado. She examined both "participation rates" and "crime frequency" figures for a wide array of different offenses. She found few differences in the participation rates of men and women, with the exception of three property crimes. Men were more likely than women to report participation in burglary, whereas women were more likely than men to have participated in theft and forgery. Exploring these differences further, she found that women "lack the specific knowledge needed to carry out a burglary" (p. 366).

Women were far more likely than men to be involved in "forgery" (it was the most common crime for women and fifth out of eight for men). Follow-up research on a subsample of "high crime"-rate female respondents revealed that many had worked in retail establishments and therefore "knew how much time they had" between stealing the checks or credit cards and having them reported (English, 1993, p. 370). The women said that they would target "strip malls" where credit cards and bank checks could be stolen easily and used in nearby retail establishments. The women reported that their high-frequency theft was motivated by a "big haul," which meant a purse with several hundred dollars in it, in addition to cards and checks. English concludes that "women's over representation in low-paying, low status jobs" increases their involvement in these property crimes (p. 171).

English's (1993) findings with regard to two other offenses, for which gender differences did not appear in participation rates, are worth exploring here. She found no difference in the "participation rates" of women and men in drug sales and assault. However, when examining the frequency data, English found that women in prison reported making significantly more drug sales than men but not because they were engaged in big-time drug selling. Instead, their high number of drug sales occurred because women's drug sales were "concentrated in the small trades (i.e., transactions of less than $10)" (p. 372). Because they made so little money, English found that 20% of the active women dealers reported making 20 or more drug deals per day (p. 372).

A reverse of the same pattern was found when English (1993) examined women's participation in assault. Here, slightly more (27.8%) women than men (23.4%) reported assaulting someone in the past year. However, most of these women reported making only one assault during the study period (65.4%), compared to only about a third of the men (37.5%).

English (1993) found that "economic disadvantage" played a role in both women's and men's criminal careers. Beyond this, however, gender played an important role in shaping women's and men's response to poverty. Specifically, women's criminal careers reflect "gender differences in legitimate and illegitimate opportunity structures, in personal networks, and in family obligations" (p. 374).

PATHWAYS TO WOMEN'S CRIME

As with girls, the links between adult women's victimization and crimes are increasingly clear. As was noted in earlier chapters, the backgrounds of adult women offenders hint at links between childhood victimization and adult offending. Experiencing gender and racial oppression, those groups of women who are most socially marginalized are particularly vulnerable to both problems—abuse/victimization and involvement in illegal activity (Richie, 2000), For example, a 1996 survey of women in prison reported that at least half of them experienced sexual abuse before their incarceration—a much higher rate than what is reported in the general population (Richie, p. 5). Other studies have documented the link between women's experiences with physical and/or sexual violence and their involvement with illegal drugs (Harlow, 1999).

Widom (2000) demonstrates in her work the importance of understanding women's experiences of abuse and neglect during childhood and their entrance into criminal activity. Abused and neglected girls are nearly twice as likely to be arrested as juveniles, twice as likely to be arrested as adults, and 2.4 times more likely to be arrested for violent crimes (p. 29). They are "more likely to use alcohol and other drugs and turn to criminal and violent behaviors when coping with stressful life events" (p. 33). Widom explains (and as previously mentioned in Chapter 2) victimization prompts girls' entry into delinquency as they try and flee their abusive environments. With deficits in cognitive abilities and achievement and few positive relationships or social controls, these girls end up on the streets with hardly any legitimate survival skills (p. 30). Their experiences with victimization and violence may result in lowered self-esteem, a lack of sense of control over one's life, and behavioral inclinations for crime and violence. Consequently, they become women with few social or psychological resources for successful adult development.

Family problems and violence—such as death, disruption, abuse and neglect, poverty, and drug/alcohol addiction—produce gendered effects for boys and girls. Although both boys and girls who grow up in family environments riddled with crime and violence have higher propensities to model such behavior (Widom, 2000), girls must also negotiate gender oppression. Such oppression confines girls and women to a dichotomous characterization: weak and dependent as well as sexually uncontrollable (Gelsthorpe, 1989; Girschick, 1999). Girschick (p. 30), in her stories of women in prison, points out an important consequence: Abused females are the least likely to have been affected in a positive way by the challenge of the women's movement to traditional gender roles and expectations. In a desperate need to have someone close to them, they often feel powerless, have limited options for change, and meet with continued abuse and violence. These women are trapped by patriarchy (and for women of color, racial and ethnic discrimination), their gender identity, their loyalty to their partners, and the violence itself (Girschick, p. 58; Richie, 1996).

Other studies have also demonstrated this important link between childhood trauma and adult criminality. Gilfus (1992) interviewed 20 incarcerated women and documented how such childhood injuries were linked to adult crimes in women. Gilfus extends the work of Miller (1986) and Chesney-Lind and Rodriguez (1983) on the ways in which women's backgrounds color their childhoods and ultimately their adulthoods. She conducted in-depth interviews in 1985 and 1986 with the women in a Northeastern women's facility that, at the time, served as both a jail and a prison. From these lengthy interviews, she reconstructed "life event histories" for each of the women, The group had a mean age of 30 (ranging from 20 to 41 years of age), and included 8 African American and 12 white women. All of the women had life histories of what Gilfus characterized as "street crimes"—by which she meant prostitution, shoplifting, check or credit card fraud, and drug law violations. Their current offenses included assault and battery; accessory to rape; breaking and entering; and multiple charges of drug possession, larceny, and prostitution (Gilfus, p. 68). Sentence lengths ranged, for this group, from 3 months to 20 years.

Most of the women were single mothers, three-quarters were intravenous drug users, and almost all (17) had histories of prostitution (7 of the women had begun as teenage prostitutes). Most of these women had grown up with violence; 13 of the 20 reported childhood sexual abuse, and 15 had experienced "severe child abuse" (Gilfus, 1992, p. 70). There were no differences in the levels of abuse reported by black and white respondents, although African American women grew up in families that were more economically marginalized than their white counterparts. Although some women's childhood memories were totally colored by their sexual abuse, for most of the women in Gilfus's sample, coping with and surviving multiple victimization was the more normal pattern. In the words of one of these women, "I just got hit a lot. . . . 'Cause they would both drink and they wouldn't know the difference. Mmm, picked up, thrown against walls, everything, you name it" (p. 72).

Despite the abuse and violence, these women recall spending time trying to care for and protect others, especially younger siblings, and attempting to do housework and even care for their abusive and drug or alcohol dependent parents. They also recall teachers who ignored signs of abuse and who, in the case of African American girls, were hostile and racist. Ultimately, 16 out of the 20 dropped out of high school (Gilfus, 1992, p. 69). The failure of the schools to be responsive to these young women's problems meant that the girls could perceive no particular future for themselves. Given the violence in their lives, drugs provided these girls with a solace found nowhere else.

Many (13) ran away from home as girls. "Rape, assault, and even attempted murder" were reported by 16 of the 20, with an average of three "rape or violent rape attempts" per woman; many of these occurred in the context of prostitution but when the women attempted to report the assault, the police simply "ridiculed" the women or threatened to arrest them. In some cases, the police would demand sexual services for not arresting the woman (Gilfus, 1992, p. 79).

Violence also characterized these women's relationships with adult men; 15 of the 20 had lived with violent men. The women were expected to bring in money, generally through prostitution and shoplifting. These men functioned as the women's pimps but also sold drugs, committed robberies, or fenced the goods shoplifted by the women. Thirteen of the women had become pregnant as girls but only four kept their first baby. Most of the women had subsequent children whom they attempted to mother despite their worsening addictions, and they tended to rely on their mothers (not their boyfriends) to take care of their children while in prison. The women continued to see their criminal roles as forms of caretaking, taking care of their children and of their abusive boyfriends. As Gilfus (1992) puts it, "the women in this study consider their illegal activities to be form of work which is undertaken primarily from economic necessity to support partners, children, and addictions" (p. 86). Gilfus further speculates that violence "may socialize women to adopt a tenacious commitment to caring for anyone who promises love, material success, and acceptance" (p. 86), which, in turn, places them at risk for further exploitation and abuse.

The interviews Arnold (1995) conducted, based on this same hypothesis, with 50 African American women serving sentences in a city jail and 10 additional interviews with African American women in prison are an important addition to the work of Gilfus (1992). Arnold notes that African American girls are not only sexually victimized but are also the victims of "class oppression." Specifically, she notes that "to be young, Black, poor and female is to be in a high-risk category for victimization and stigmatization on many levels" (p. 139). Growing up in extreme poverty means that African American girls may turn earlier to deviant behavior, particularly stealing, to help themselves and their families. One young woman told Arnold that "my father beat my mother and neglected his children. . . . I began stealing when I was 12. I hustled to help feed and clothes the other [12] kids and help pay the rent" (p. 139).

Thus, the caretaking role noted in women's pathways to crime is accentuated in African American families because of extreme poverty, Arnold (1995) also noted that economic need interfered with young black girls' ability to concentrate on schoolwork and attend school. Finally, Arnold (p. 140) noted, as had Gilfus (1992), that African American girls were "victimized" by the school system; one of her respondents said that "some [of the teachers] were prejudiced, and one had the nerve to tell the whole class he didn't like black people" (p. 140). Most of her respondents said that even if they went to school every day, they did not learn anything. Finally, despite their desperate desire to "hold on . . . to conventional roles in society," the girls were ultimately pushed out of these, onto the streets, and into petty crime (p. 141),

The mechanics of surviving parental abuse and educational neglect were particularly hard on young African American girls, forcing them to drop out of school, on to the streets, and into permanent "structural dislocation" (Arnold, 1995, p. 143). Having no marketable skills and little education, many resorted to "prostitution and stealing" while further immersing themselves in drug addiction.

Mothers Behind Bars

Of the 869,600 women under some form of criminal justice surveillance, over 70% have children under the age of 18; this accounts for over 1.3 million children (Bureau of Justice Statistics, 1999; see Table 7.6). Many of these women will never see their children if this and other national studies (see Bloom & Steinhart, 1993) are accurate. Snell and Morton (1994) found that 52.2% of the women with children under 18 had never been visited by their children. Most of the women who were able to be visited by their children saw them "less than once a month" or "once a month." More women were able to send mail to or phone their children, but even here, one in five never sent or received mail from their children, and one in four never talked on the phone with their children. This is despite the fact that many of these women, prior to their incarceration, were taking care of their children (unlike their male counterparts).

According to Snell and Morton (1994), just under three quarters of the women with children had lived with them before going to prison, compared to only slightly over half (52.9%) of the male prisoners. Moreover, because women's work is never done, it is more often the imprisoned woman's mother (the child's grandmother) who takes care of her children, whereas male inmates are more likely (89.7%) to be able to count on the children's mother to care of the child (Snell & Morton, p. 6).

These patterns are particularly pronounced among African American and 'Hispanic women. White female inmates more often report access to husbands as primary caretakers of their children, whereas African American women do not identify this as an option (Enos, 2001, p. 55). Although black women and Hispanic women are more likely to share caretaking responsibilities with other family members and are less likely to rely upon foster care services, the ability of the family to effectively respond, both financially and emotionally, to the incarceration of a female family member with children is dependent upon social and economic status (Enos). This becomes highly problematic for women of color, because poverty and race are intertwined and families often have few resources to extend.

Table 1.2   Children of Women Under Correctional Supervision, 1998

	Women Offenders	Women Offenders With Children Under Age 18	Number of Minor Children
Probation	721,400	516,200	1,067,200
Jail	63,800	44,700	105,300
State prisons	75,200	49,200	117,100
Federal prisons	9,200	5,400	11,200
Total	869,600	615,500	1,300,800

Source: Bureau of Justice Statistics. (1999). *Women Offenders* (p. 7). Washington, DC: Department of Justice.

WOMEN'S PATHWAYS TO CRIME: LINKING VICTIMIZATION AND CRIMINALIZATION

Leanne Fiftal Alarid and Paul Cromwell

To understand female criminality, it is important to begin with possible origins or sources that led to criminal acts or a pattern of law-violating behaviors. Criminologists have called these origins "pathways to felony court" (Daly 1992), "routes of entry" (Gilfus 1992), "paths to crime" (Richie 1996), and "pathways to imprisonment" (Owen 1998). These routes make two important assumptions. First, that we live in a patriarchal society that structurally devalues the status of women compared with men. Raising and socializing girls is, for most people, different than raising boys. Early childhood experiences in turn affect how young girls view themselves. This continues throughout adulthood and affects how women view their relationships with other people and with organizations and social systems outside the family.

There is not just one entry route that purports to explain all types of female criminality. Paths to crime are not neatly divided or clear-cut to explain each specific type of female crime. Instead, criminal behavior and paths to those crimes overlap, embedded like a spiderweb in women's lives. The readings in this section illustrate the process and types of victimization that many offending women experience, thus obscuring the boundaries between that of a victim and a criminal. Daly (1992) identified three main paths to crime: (1) survival; (2) resistance to oppressive relationships; and (3) economic and/or physical victimization. Gilfus (2002, 3) identified, a total of six paths and noted that

> the first three pathways best reflect the process of criminalization by which girls' and women's resources for escaping and surviving abuse are so limited that they must depend on illegal activity for income.

These pathways include abused and runaway girls, homeless women, and women addicted to drugs.
The next three pathways are

> . . . more reflective of the process of entrapment by which battered women are forced into crime by abusers and/or poverty and are forced into the criminal justice system by laws and practices that entrap battered women." (Gilfus 2002, 4)

These situations include women arrested for economic crimes who are coerced by batterers, women arrested for harm to children or abusers, and women affected by discriminatory and coercive welfare or immigration policies. However, criminalization and entrapment are influential in all six paths.

Women's criminal behavior may thus be seen as coping mechanisms or resistance to childhood sexual and physical victimization, childhood neglect, economic marginalization, and domestic violence. Still, a large percentage of women prisoners take responsibility for their actions that ultimately led to their incarceration (Owen 1998). **The first reading in this section, by Mary Gilfus,** is a classic, and it is included here because it accurately illustrates a broad overview of situations that precede lawbreaking behavior, such as poverty, childhood abuse, running away from home, and battering and other forms of intimate abuse. These themes form the basis of girls' and women's responses to victimization and are therefore discussed in more detail here.

CHILDHOOD ABUSE, INCEST, AND NEGLECT

Traumatic childhood experiences for many juvenile girls play a significant role in both female juvenile delinquency and, later, in various forms of adult lawbreaking behavior. Childhood abuse in the home, in the form of

---

In Her Own Words: Women Offender's Views on Crime and Victimization by Alarid and Cromwell (2004) pp. 1–3, 5–13, 93–101. By permission of Oxford University Press, USA.

sexual assault, incest, and/or parental neglect, is more likely to happen to juvenile girls than to boys (Belknap, Holsinger, and Dunn 1997). Longitudinal studies of girls who have been abused or neglected compared with girls who were not abused indicate that over 70 percent of abused and neglected girls do not become juvenile or adult offenders. However, of the girls who come to the attention of the juvenile justice and criminal justice system, abused and neglected girls are twice as likely as girls who have not been abused to be arrested as a juvenile or an adult, and over twice as likely to commit a violent crime (Widom 2000). Abused girls are more likely to run away from home, and they are also more likely to later be arrested for drug offenses and violent crimes as adults (Siegel and Williams 2000).

Childhood abuse and neglect has a negative impact within all socioeconomic classes. According to other studies, middle-class girls who engage in fighting at school are significantly more likely than assaultive boys and nonassaultive boys and girls to have been physically and sexually abused at home (Artz 1998). Other than this main difference, assaultive girls more closely resembled assaultive boys than they do girls who do not engage in violence, in terms of delinquent behavior, drug use, and other status offenses (e.g., gang membership, curfew, skipping school, petty theft, smoking cigarettes, underage drinking).

RUNNING AWAY

Most girls run away from home to escape childhood abuse or family problems. If picked up by police, many runaways are placed in an alternative living arrangement, such as extended family networks, foster care, or group homes. Underage girls who avoid being detected by police or are able to survive on the streets support themselves by criminal activities such as theft, shoplifting, or panhandling, or they are supported by another adult male, who may introduce them to drugs and prostitution. Although some young Latina women tend to be more insulated from involvement in prostitution, Latinas may later become involved in criminal networks through men. Thus, running away and drug use are two main routes to deviant networks (Miller 1986). It is no accident that arrest data show adult prostitution and juvenile runaways are the only two offenses for which there are more females than males that come to police attention (Federal Bureau of Investigation 2003).

LIMITED ECONOMIC OPPORTUNITIES

Another assumption of pathways to crime is that many women, particularly women of color in the inner city, have limited economic opportunities. Many impoverished and undereducated people find other sources of income or "hustles" to supplement their legitimate income to support their families. **The second reading, by Lisa Maher, Eloise Dunlap, and Bruce Johnson,** explains how drug dealing is a lucrative form of hustling as an alternative income source, mainly due to lack of legitimate job opportunities and recognition of social marginality. Early age immersion in neighborhood street life and relationships, to the exclusion of outside relationships and activities, seems to limit opportunities for mainstream exposure to educational and employment institutions that, in turn, would expand choices.

WOMEN AS VICTIMS OF VIOLENCE

Tied to the themes of childhood abuse and neglect and women's decreased economic opportunities is the theme of adult women as victims of violence. Across the country in one year, between 1 and 1.5 million adult women in the general population are victimized by a violent crime, which includes battering, assault, rape, robbery, and homicide (Tjaden and Thoennes 2000). Women who are young and have never been married, or who have recently separated or divorced, are more likely to be victimized by someone they know than are older and/or married women. Age and marital status are stronger predictors than socioeconomic status and race/ethnicity, particularly for intimate partner violence (Lauritsen and Schaum 2004). Women who lack social support networks, either from being a single female-head of household, being new to a community, or having gone through a recent divorce, are more likely to be targets for violent behavior. Violence against women is proportionately higher for women who are incarcerated in jail or prison—about half of imprisoned women were physically or sexually assaulted prior to their arrest (Harlow 1999). One reason may be that women who react to recurrent abuse with violence are criminalized. Another reason for this difference is that many incidences of victimization by violent crime go unreported, particularly by women who feel the need to protect their abuser, or who are themselves involved in illegal activity. Researchers have suggested the possibility of a stronger causal relationship between some forms of victimization and criminal behavior of marginalized women, whereby women view violence as a protective measure, a way to postpone a violent episode, or a way out of the abusive relationship (Richie 1996, 2000). Some women, even after imprisonment, return to abusive relationships because of "fear, familiarity, the desire not to be alone, or a sense of loyalty" (Henriques and Manatu-Rupert 2001, 16).

RESISTING VIOLENCE AND ABUSE

Elizabeth Comack's reading, the third selection, addresses various forms of female criminality that are a result of coping with or resisting an abusive or violent relationship. The prevalence of women who are abused crosses racial, educational, age, and class lines. Many adult women who remain in abusive relationships feel a sense of learned helplessness and powerlessness over their own actions. This learned helplessness creates an inability to make choices and feel in control of one's actions (Thornburg and Trunk 1992). Low self-esteem and learned helplessness are precisely the ways that abusers effectively control another person. The battered woman typically has fabricated her own ideas of what she believes a traditional family should be and will maintain this role or image at all costs. This initial belief—together with pressure to stay together from other family members (e.g., parents, children), threats of bodily harm (or even death) from her partner if she leaves the relationship, and lack of a solid escape plan—makes leaving an abusive relationship nearly impossible.

According to official statistics, women are significantly more likely to be killed by their male partner or spouse than men are to be killed by a female partner. Murder committed by female offenders has declined consistently over the last 45 years (Heimer 2000). When women kill, it is most often a result of being powerless. There is a distinct difference between women who kill their abusers and battered women who do *not* kill their abusers. In one study, battered women who killed their male abusers endured more physical injury and more frequent threats, and were more likely to be sexually assaulted. Male abusers who were killed were also more likely to use drugs or alcohol and to abuse both women and children (Browne 1987). Of course, battered and abused women rarely kill in response to their abuse. Of the battered women with a partner involved in crime, it is more likely that they may commit crimes under duress or agree to commit crimes as a show of loyalty or to delay the abuse.

Among women as a group, African-American women are arrested for crimes of violence at much greater and disproportionate rates than Caucasian women and women of other ethnic groups (Steffensmeier and Allan 1988). Various explanations have been proposed, including increased attention to violence by researchers, differences in socialization (Holsinger and Holsinger 2005), and a racially biased perception by police and prosecutors. A general correlation between economic inequality and violence exists for men and women. Applying this correlation to white and black women's rates of violence, women who are African-American are more likely to be members of the economic underclass. White women can mitigate their powerlessness in a sexist and racist system by attaching themselves to white men. Black women face both sexism and racism in their daily lives and cannot merely attach themselves to black men, who also face economic hardships and racism. Violence may be a form of gender resistance (Lorde 1988), in which women act to protect themselves from further victimization by men. However, most women who have had experiences with abuse, neglect, sexual assault, and economic marginality turn their frustration and despair inward, and this has a profound effect on their self-esteem and how they ultimately view themselves. The **final selection, by Brenda Geiger and Michael Fischer,** explains why women (when compared with men) have a more difficult time resisting stigmatizing criminal labels and empowering themselves to reconstruct a positive identity.

In summary, in this first section we wish to establish the link between women's victimization, their identity of themselves, and their involvement in lawbreaking behaviors. We also wish to emphasize that there is not just one pathway to crime but many overlapping, yet complicated reasons for women's involvement in criminal behavior.

From Victims to Survivors to Offenders
Women's Routes of Entry and Immersion Into Street Crime
Mary E. Gilfus

This study explores the patterns by which women enter into crime by drawing on in-depth life history interviews with a sample of 20 incarcerated women. The author constructs a conceptual framework for understanding the progression from victim to survivor to offender in the subjects' life histories. This framework shows that the best available options for escape from physical and sexual violence are often survival strategies that are criminal (i.e., running away from home, drug use, and the illegal street work required to survive as a runaway). The women's own narratives are used to illustrate their views of themselves as survivors, not as victims, and their commitments to important relationships in their lives that explain their entry into and commitments to criminal activities. Women's responses to victimization and women's relational identities are seen as factors that both motivate and restrain women's criminal activities. The term "immersion in street crime" is more accurate than "criminal career" in describing women's criminal histories.

Criminology literature has recently begun to focus on concepts such as "criminal career" and "career offended" suggesting that there may be discernible patterns in the criminal histories of offenders (Gottfredson & Hirschi, 1986; Gottfredson & Hirschi, 1988). Yet this literature, thus far, centers almost exclusively about *male* offenders. Little attention has been paid to questions such as *whether* there is such a thing *as a female* "criminal career" pattern and if so, how that career begins and what shapes its contours and how they define their commitments and identities in relation to criminality. This study will focus on women's personal accounts of the life events and socializing experiences which they perceive to be connected to their entry into and immersion in illegal activity. Special attention will be given to men's interpretation of sex roles and the role of victimization, as well as poverty and racism, in setting up the conditions which both compel and constrain women's criminal activities.

GENDER, RACE, AND CRIME

Women's patterns of criminal activity differ markedly from those of men both in the types and the amounts of crime they commit. A major gender difference is the very low rate of violent crime committed by women. The offenses for which women are arrested and incarcerated are primarily non-violent and minor property offenses: shoplifting, larceny, check or credit card fraud, prostitution, and drug possession. When women do commit acts of violence, it is most likely against family members and in a context of self defense. Women's arrest and incarceration rates vary by race. For example, women of color are somewhat more likely than white women to be arrested for crimes against persons and are more likely to be sentenced to jail or prison; resulting in minority group women representing more than half of the adult female inmate population nationwide. The majority of incarcerated women are young, poor, single mothers, and are disproportionately from minority groups (American Correctional Association, 1990). These groups of women are also disproportionately the *victims* of crime, particularly violent crimes such as rape. Economic, social, and political marginality, may well account for the overlap in membership in high-risk groups among women who are at risk of becoming both victims and offenders.

Daly and Chesney-Lind (1988) argue that before we can address the question of what explains the gender gap in crime rates, and in order to understand race and class differences among women offenders, we need much more in-depth descriptive information about women who engage in crime. While in recent years there has been a burst of scholarly attention to women and crime, very few studies have been based on data obtained first hand from the women themselves in order to explore their own perceptions, experiences, and motivations for engaging in illegal activity. Nor have any studies focused specifically on women's criminal "careers," how women enter into illegal activities and what kind of progression occurs over time.

Miller (1986) concludes that economic marginality is strongly connected to women's motivations to enter illegal activity, and that black and white women enter illegal "street work" through somewhat different routes. She found family violence and runaway status more related to white women's entry patterns, while black women were more likely to be introduced to illegal activity through kin and neighborhood networks.

Miller (1986) and Romenesko and Miller (1989) document that once women become involved in street work, they become part of a highly gendered division of labor in the male-dominated world of street hustling. The male heads of the "pseudo-families" which are organized around street hustling activities keep women in subordinate positions by fostering competition among "their women," keeping the women economically dependent, and by physical and psychological abuse (Romenesko and Miller, 1989).

Chesney-Lind and Rodriguez's (1983) in-depth interviews with women incarcerated in Hawaii also reveal life histories which are characterized by high rates of victimization. Chesney-Lind and Rodriguez (1983; 62–63) conclude that victimization results in a "process of criminalization unique to women" in which

> young girls faced with violence and/or sexual abuse at home . . . became criminalized by their efforts to save themselves (by running away) from the abuse. . . . Once on the streets, the position afforded these women in the criminal world indicates that, again, it was not liberation but lack of formal education and genuine employment options that forced them to continue committing crimes.

Chesney-Lind (1989) argues that the criminalization of girls' survival strategies is the process by which young women who are victims of violence become transformed into offenders. This study illustrates that process of criminalization of girls' survival strategies and shows when and how a small sample of women entered into illegal activities. The study also explores how women's relational identities and socialization into nurturing and caretaking roles shape the ways in which women approach criminal activities.

CHILDHOOD: THEMES OF VIOLENCE AND CARING FOR OTHERS

Thematic coding of the childhood segments of the interviews were organized around the predominating themes by which each woman described her childhood memories. For most of the women the dominant themes were of violence, loss, and neglect with a strong sub-theme in which they portrayed themselves as caring for and protecting other family members.

Family Backgrounds

Four of the 20 women interviewed reported that they grew up in middle class families, 12 in working class families, and four in poor families which periodically received welfare benefits. The black women in the study were generally from more economically disadvantaged backgrounds than the white women.

Five women (two black and three white) reported growing up in families in which both parents were present throughout childhood but four of those five families were characterized by parental substance abuse and family violence. The remaining 15 women were from families disrupted during childhood by divorce, death, or desertion. Four women lost a parent during childhood due to death, two of those by suicide. Four of the eight black women had been cared for during some or all of their childhoods by grandparents or other members of their extended families, and two of the white women had spent some time in foster homes.

Eleven of the women felt that one or both parents (or guardians) had significant problems with drugs or alcohol, and ten women had seen their mothers battered by male family members. These patterns of family substance abuse and violence were similar for both the black and the white women.

Thirteen of the 20 women reported experiences of childhood sexual abuse. They reported an average of two different perpetrators each, with ten women reporting sexual abuse (incest) by a male family member. Fifteen of the women reported recurrent episodes of physical abuse by family members which resulted in bodily injuries and could be classified as severe child abuse. There were no differences between the black women and the white women either in the proportion who reported childhood physical and sexual abuse, or in the types of abuse reported.

Sexual Abuse and Incest

Five women's childhood memories were organized almost completely around sexual abuse experiences. These women explained their involvement in illegal activities as a direct result of childhood sexual abuse. For example, Janet, a 28-year-old, black woman incarcerated for breaking and entering, was sexually victimized repeatedly during childhood. Her first memory of sexual abuse was by a female babysitter around the age of three or four, then by a group of male and female cousins from age five to seven, then by her grandfather at the age of ten, by another male cousin at age twelve, and finally by her step-father from the age of twelve to fourteen. She never told anyone of these experiences. Janet left home at age 14 to escape her stepfather's sexual abuse and became involved in prostitution as a teenage runaway. The resulting drug addiction and abusive domination by her male partner kept Janet immersed in a variety of street crime activities.

Sarah, a 26-year-old white woman, was incarcerated for writing illegal prescriptions for drugs. She was sexually abused by her step-father from the age of nine to fifteen. Her step-father gave her drugs, money, and other gifts in order to secure her silence and cooperation in his sexual abuse. She became addicted to drugs while still living at home and being sexually abused by her stepfather. All of her criminal activity involved forging prescriptions in order to obtain drugs to maintain her habit.

Multiple Types of Abuse and Neglect

Ten other women organized their childhood memories around multiple forms of abuse and neglect. Marcia, a 28-year-old white woman, was one of ten children. Her parents were both alcoholics. Her father battered her mother, both parents battered the children and neglected their basic needs, and the two oldest sons sexually abused Marcia. She graphically portrayed herself as a "guinea pig," a "gopher," and "not human" in the following interview excerpts. At the same time, she minimized the extent of her parents' violence.

interviewer: Did either of your parents abuse you?

Marcia: No. As far as, what do you mean, sexually? No.

Interviewer: Physically or in any way.

Marcia: No, I just got hit a lot. 'Cause of the lies they used to tell. It was just like I was a guinea pig. You know, I was a gopher, out of ten kids, anything that used to happen, they said "she did it." I used to get beat up all the time from this one and that one.

Interviewer: So your parents both would hit you?

Marcia: 'Cause they both would drink and they wouldn't know the difference. Mmm, picked up, thrown against walls, everything. You name it

Interviewer: Did you ever have to go to a doctor or hospital for any injuries?

Marcia: No, never went. I always hid it. Bruises and welts all over me. Teachers used to ask me what's wrong with ya? I'd say I fell down.

Marcia, perhaps not unlike other abused children, protected her parents from discovery by covering up the signs of abuse. Next she described the neglect which accompanied the abuse. In doing so, she focused on the embarrassment she felt about going to school in dirty, ragged, and inappropriate clothing and described a number of strategies she used for coping with the neglect and the embarrassment: hiding, skipping school, daydreaming and fantasizing, and finally giving up.

Interviewer: Do you remember what it was like when you started school? How did it feel to you?

Marcia: Weird. 'Cause I wasn't dressed right or nothin', I didn't feel comfortable, I felt like a black sheep. Didn't have proper care. You know.

My mother would say "Go to school like you are, get your own clothes." You know odd socks, the whole bit. Oh god, I used to dread that.

So I never went, I hated it. Used to hide. Hated bein' laughed at. Teased. . . . Felt like I wasn't a human, like I was a creature or something all dirty and you know. . . . I don't know . . . just didn't like it. And I used to get hit for that too, and I didn't care. My father would hit me and say: "Why wasn't you in school today?" But he wouldn't find out until about six months later. 'Cause they never went to any events or anything like that.

I couldn't do home work, I couldn't concentrate, I couldn't do none of it. It was never quiet enough. And I had to sleep in a room with me and four brothers. . . .

I failed quite a few grades cause I used to day dream, and I didn't do the work. I didn't give a shit. I was in a fantasy land. I said: "I'm just going to be a movie star when I grow up, I don't need this homework shit." I didn't care. I didn't have nothin' to care about.

Caring for Others

In spite of the violence and neglect the women recalled in childhood, they often framed their presentations of themselves as protectors and caretakers of others. The following narrative by Denise, a 31-year-old black woman recalling events when she was ten years old, illustrates this point.

When my mother was going with this guy she really started drinking a lot and she started staying away from home a lot. So we had to get ourselves up for school, get ready, clean the house, fix ourselves something to eat. Me, my older sister and my brother, we looked out for the little ones. And we learned to cook, and we knew how to wash clothes with a rub board and a bucket. We used to get this stool and stand on it to reach the stove and cook. But we knew how to cook, we could cook anything.

And we didn't like to see her like that. She would be sick, and she would piss on herself and throw up on herself. And we used to clean her up, fix her hair, and try to get her to eat something. But she couldn't keep anything down, so we would get her some liquor, because we thought that would help her. Or if we refused to go get her some liquor, she would hit us. We would get mad at her and threaten to tell our father, but she threatened to flush our heads down the toilet, and we really believed that, so we never told, and we just did what we had to do.

In this narrative Denise recalled very actively trying to cope with her mother's alcoholism. She and her siblings took over all of the household tasks and began acting as parents toward their mother. They tried to intervene to stop their mother's drinking, but were eventually defeated by her threats and abusive behavior. Denise took pride in her ability to nurture the younger children and in spite of her anger at her mother, remained loyal to her and very lovingly cared for her. This sense of self as a caretaker of others was a positive part of Denise's identity, as it was for many of the other women interviewed. Yet this ability to care for others who are abusive and neglectful caused Denise much trouble throughout her life. The first man she fell in love with was a pimp and an addict who beat her and lived off of her earnings as a prostitute, yet her loyally to him allowed her to serve an earlier prison sentence for a crime which she now claims he had committed.

Educational Neglect and Racial Violence

Another set of themes in the childhood memories of many of the women, but particularly the black women and the white women who grew up in poor inner-city neighborhoods, were themes of educational neglect and racism. Many of the women attended public schools during the turbulent years of school desegregation.

Three of the black women directly experienced racial violence as children. Denise had seen her uncle murdered by two white men, Karen had been constantly taunted by white students in her school, and Tina had been insulted and slapped in school by white teachers. The remaining five black women attended predominantly black schools where they were not so directly exposed to white racism, but they were aware that they were receiving a segregated and inadequate education. Some of their parents spent scarce family resources sending the children to private Catholic schools, but the young women again encountered hostility and insult from students and teachers with low expectations and condescending attitudes toward black children. Many of the women recalled that they had once dreamed of going to college and entering professional careers, but had found no support for those aspirations.

Other complaints about school which were echoed by most of the women included teachers who failed to notice the signs of their abuse and the easy availability of drugs in the schools: Feeling like failures and misfits, unable to concentrate on school work, and their pain unacknowledged, the availability of drugs was too easy a temptation to turn down. Many of the young women found their first feeling of acceptance and belonging in the drug subculture of their schools.

ADOLESCENCE: SURVIVAL STRATEGIES AND DELINQUENCY

With the onset of adolescence themes of violence and caring for others, as well as the dreams for a successful future, gave way to questions of survival and escape.

Survival Strategies

Escape from an intolerable home situation may sometimes be the only sane solution for an abused child and the only way to end the violence. But when children or adolescents run away and seek sanctuary wherever they can find it, usually with "street people" and other runaways, they become delinquents in the eyes of law enforcement rather than children in need of protection from the recruiters for the sex and drug industries who prey on runaway children. This was exactly what happened during adolescence for many of the women interviewed.

Yvonne, a 20-year-old white woman incarcerated for drug possession, began running away from home at age 13 because she was being sexually molested by an uncle, occasionally physically abused by her mother, and emotionally taxed by her mother's episodes of depression and suicide attempts. On one of her first escapes from home she packed a suitcase full of stuffed animals and tried to hitchhike to where she thought a boyfriend lived, only to be picked up by the police and returned home. She continued to run away and was placed in several foster homes. She was raped by a foster brother in one of those homes, and while she was in foster care her mother gave away her dog. Feeling that she had nothing left to care about at home, she went to New York City with a boyfriend. She described the plight of a runaway with no money.

> The third night came, we had no more money. He said "get some money." I didn't understand what he was talking about. But be was talking about being a prostitute. . . . We didn't have a place to stay, we slept on trains. . . . I had to steal food, Times I went two, three days without eating, I'd have to steal something.

Yvonne began working as a prostitute and shoplifting to insure that she and her boyfriend had food and a place to stay.

Janet, who had been sexually abused multiple times as a child, engaged in a long narrative detailing the events leading up to the day she left home and the experiences which followed. At age 14 Janet felt pressured to have intercourse with her boyfriend in order to prove that she loved him. After their first sexual experience, her boyfriend left for summer camp. She described in great detail the day he returned from summer camp, and how she baked a cake for him and waited all day for him. He finally arrived at her house and announced that he was breaking up with her because she had not been a virgin for him. She was mortified that he had been able to tell that she was sexually "experienced" as a result of having forced intercourse with her stepfather.

After the rejection by her boyfriend she went to her father's nearby home and waited for him to return home from work. Just as he pulled into the driveway, teenage boys in a passing car yelled and waved at Janet, and she responded by waving back at them. Her father got out of his car, slapped her on the face and called her a "whore." Taking this as another rejection, Janet went home and tried to commit suicide by taking a bottle of aspirin. She slept for several hours and awoke to discover that no one had even noticed her suicide gesture, so she ran away. (Suicide was seriously considered as an escape by many of the women, and ten women made suicide attempts during adolescence).

Janet ran away to a nearby city where she was kidnapped, raped, and injected with drugs by a man who told her he was planning to sell her as a slave to a pimp. She escaped from her kidnapper and eventually returned home, but was once again faced with her stepfather's sexual demands and her mother's lack of concern. She ran away again and lied about her age in order to get a waitress job, only to be sexually harassed by her employer. This was the final straw for Janet; she decided that if everyone expected her to be a "whore" she might as well make some money at it. She went out on a street corner in the downtown prostitution district and tried soliciting customers on her own. Within minutes she was befriended by a man who offered to be her pimp, and she readily accepted. Janet had begun experimenting with drugs at age 12, began intravenous use of heroin shortly after entering prostitution, and reported that she was addicted by the age of 16 when she became pregnant with her first child.

Janet presented the above events as a way of explaining her entry into illegal street work, the best survival strategy she could find as a 14-year-old incest victim and runaway.

Onset of Delinquency

Chronologically the first "delinquent" event experienced by 13 of the 20 women was running away from home. When we consider the fact that most of the young women were being abused at home, running away seems to have been a sane and logical response. That logical act of self-protection, however, pushed the young women into finding illegal ways of supporting themselves.

Onset of drug use, truancy and stealing were closely associated with early runaway attempts. The women talked about how impossible it was to stay in school when on the run, sleeping in cars, parks, or "crash pads," and "hustling" money for food by panhandling and petty shoplifting. The first use of drugs or alcohol was reported at a mean age of 12.7 years old. The average age at leaving home for the whole sample was 16 years old, a very young age to be fending for oneself. Seven of the 17 women who had worked as prostitutes began as juvenile prostitutes, four of them having been coerced into prostitution while young runaways.

THE TRANSITION TO ADULTHOOD

Leaving home at an early age, often coupled with teenage pregnancy meant that adulthood began early for these women. Patterns of repeated victimization, drug addiction, street work, relationships with men involved in street crime, and the demands of mothering are the themes that mark their transitions from childhood to adulthood. The survival strategies which had helped the women escape from early victimization contributed to revictimization and their adult status as offenders. Yet, much like their childhood identities, the women presented themselves as adults committed to caring for others and organizing their lives around relational commitments. It was usually their relational commitments and their addiction to drugs which they described as creating the conditions which necessitated their continued involvement in criminal activity.

Street Work and Revictimization

Survival on the streets of any city is dangerous for a young woman. If she is too young to look for legal work or has too few skills to find work at a living wage, she has few choices other than to find a "hustle" which will generate income for food and a place to sleep. Whether looking for shelter, panhandling, shoplifting, selling drugs, or turning tricks, a young woman alone on the streets is often "fair game" for male violence (see Weisberg, 1985; Delacoste and Alexander, 1987). Rape, assault, and even attempted murder were experiences reported by 16 of the 20 women, with an average of three rapes or violent rape attempts per woman as adolescents or adults. Many of the rapes and assaults occurred while the women were working as prostitutes. A common scenario was for a trick to pick up the woman in his car, drive her to a remote location, rape and torture her, and leave her perhaps to die. The women who reported these crimes to the police were ridiculed and/or threatened with arrest for prostitution. Sometimes police officers would demand sexual services in exchange for not arresting the woman.

Battering Relationships

Sixteen of the women had been in battering relationships as adults, some as many as five different battering relationships. These were typically co-addict relationships in which the couple shared the activities of securing and injecting drugs, but had a gendered division of labor for illegally obtaining money for drugs. The female partner was often expected to supply money from her work as a prostitute and from shoplifting. Male partners, if they did any work other than pimping, were likely to commit robberies or did the fencing of the goods the women shoplifted. Severe battering episodes were likely to occur if the male partner felt the woman was using more than her "share" of the money on drugs, or if she was not producing "enough" income, or if he felt like punishing her for working as a prostitute.

Marcia, whose childhood narrative of abuse and neglect was presented above ran away at age 13 to the streets of a nearby city. There she met Charlie, a pimp for whom she worked from the age of 13 to 18, whenever she was not in juvenile detention halls. Charlie employed the techniques pimps often use to "season" young women into dependent and loyal prostitutes (Barry, 1984): isolation, physical violence, occasional indulgences of presents (usually drugs), and romantic vows of love. Marcia described being kept in darkened hotel rooms, heavily drugged, turning tricks, and being beaten periodically. At the time she was interviewed, Marcia had served a sentence for a crime which took place while Charlie was recruiting a new runaway to work for him, yet she still felt a strong bond of loyalty and affection for Charlie.

Addiction

Substance abuse has repeatedly been found to be one of the major long-term psychological effects of childhood sexual abuse (Briere & Runtz, 1988; Peters, 1988; Russell, Sherman, & Trocki, 1988; Stein et al, 1988). Nearly all of the 15 women who reported intravenous drug abuse histories began experimental drug or alcohol use prior to engaging in illegal activity (other than running away from home), on average by age 13. Accounts of why they started using drugs were strikingly similar, using terms such as "wanting to be obliterated" and describing their initial work as prostitutes as so "disgusting" that they "had to be high to do it." Additional reasons for beginning drug use included acceptance by peer groups and feelings of greater self-confidence when high. But the primary pattern of shifting from experimental use to intravenous use of opiates and/or cocaine typically occurred after entry into illegal activity, primarily prostitution. Many of the women attributed their continuing motivation for illegal activities to their deepening addiction to drugs. They also described numerous efforts to give up drugs, efforts which were often motivated by pregnancy or by the fear of losing custody of their children.

Mothering

Thirteen women became pregnant as teenagers; only four of them kept their first baby, struggling to survive as single teen parents. The nine women who miscarried, aborted, or gave their babies up for adoption deeply mourned the loss and felt that the loss had pushed them further into drug abuse and illegal activity. It was not long before some of the women became pregnant again and tried to keep their children in spite of their worsening addiction. Fifteen of the women had custody of their children prior to incarceration. All of the women whose mothers were still alive were in regular, nearly daily, contact with their mothers prior to incarceration, and most of the women had placed their children with their mothers while incarcerated. Even the mothers who had been physically and emotionally abusive toward them were entrusted with the care of their children. This arrangement was preferable to giving custody over to the state and risking permanent loss of one's children. One of the recurring themes expressed by the women was the pain and guilt they felt about their children. Most of the women saw themselves as good and loving mothers who tried very hard to protect their children from the negative effects of their own illegal activities, but who were increasingly torn between the competing demands of addiction, mothering, and hustling.

Relational Patterns of Entry and Immersion in Illegal Activities

Most of the women attributed some relational components to their reasons for entry into delinquent and illegal activity, either in response to childhood family violence, or death of a parent, or in response to adult marital or family issues. It should be noted that the women presented these connections not as excuses for their crimes, in fact, most of the women were quick to take responsibility for their actions, but rather as a constellation of problems which led them to "the street life."

Fourteen women had established patterns of serial relationships with men who shared and encouraged their drug abuse and illegal work and who used violence to keep the women "in line." Those 14 women presented themselves primarily in terms of their relational identities, organizing their legal work around caretaking responsibilities, and often *defining* their illegal work as a part of their caretaking roles. Thus these women had spent most of their adult years involved in a series of relationships in which mutual drug abuse and illegal activity were an integral part of the relationship. Interestingly, while the women defined their caretaking roles to include economic support of their partners, they did not define or expect their partners' roles to include childcare responsibilities. Seven women were currently incarcerated for offenses which they reported were committed with or by the male partner. All but one of the women who typically worked and lived in partnerships with men had been battered in those relationships.

Five women remained relatively independent of male partners after leaving their families of origin. One woman entered a long-term lesbian relationship, but was evasive about whether as a couple they shared a pattern of addiction and illegal activity. These five women seemed more independently committed to illegal activity and continued such activity whether or not they were in relationships with partners who supported or disapproved of their activity. Their illegal activity was still well within the traditional realm of women's street crimes: prostitution, petty drug trafficking, and shoplifting. What appeared to distinguish these women from the more traditional women was their obvious pride in their abilities at performing illegal work and the benefits which attracted them to it (fast money and the excitement and glamour of a "party" lifestyle). It is possible that these women were in fairly early stages of illegal street work, a time when the benefits appear to outweigh the risks and the costs (Rosenbaum, 1981; Romenesko and Miller, 1989). Three of these five women expressed a desire (without much optimism of successfully fulfilling it) to eventually marry, have children and leave behind their illegal work. Thus even the most independent of the women in this study were traditional in their views on women's roles and in the types of illegal activities in which they participated.

Caretaking Roles

A central theme in the ways the women presented themselves was as caretakers. Sometimes caretaking was a reason for initial entry into illegal work, other times illegal work was perceived as an integral component of a caretaking role.

Lois, a 37-year-old white woman, is an example of a woman who clearly defined her illegal work as one aspect of traditional female role responsibilities, Lois was violently abused as a child and sexually assaulted by her father at age 14. By age 17 she fell in love with a male addict and left home. She began using heroin just to be with him and continued using it, even though she disliked it, until she was also addicted. She had initially supplied the couple's drug money by stealing from her family, but when she could no longer get away with that, she took responsibility for finding a way to support their shared addiction. She described feeling especially nurturing toward her partner when he was experiencing withdrawal symptoms. She thought about her money-earning capabilities and options, realizing that she could not earn enough money through legal employment. She thought about robbery, but ruled this out on ethical grounds fearing that she might hurt someone. She then decided on prostitution thinking that "this way I was only hurting myself." At the age of 37 Lois was in her fifth addicted and battering relationship, again supplying money for her partner's drugs from her illegal work. By now she had abandoned her ethical stance and had resorted to breaking and entering because of her dwindling earning power as a prostitute. This caused her to begin examining the reasons for her vulnerability to abusive partners, and she had just begun to regain memories of being sexually assaulted by her father.

Ann, a 37-year-old black woman, was serving six months for disorderly conduct (a prostitution-related offense). Ann was violently abused by her stepfather from the ages of ten to 16. Whenever she had to be taken to the hospital for treatment of her injuries, her mother would lie about the source of the injuries, and Ann would collaborate in the lies, explaining: "I loved my mother, and I knew they would take me away from her if I told the truth." At age 16 she moved into her own apartment and worked for a year in a low-paying clerical job. That year she was raped by the first boyfriend she had ever dated. Feeling alone and betrayed, struggling economically, Ann was convinced by a girlfriend to go "downtown" to get a job as a go-go dancer. Ann enjoyed the money she began making and was enthralled by the glitter of "downtown" life. She soon met and fell in love with Joe, a flashy pimp who made no effort to conceal his plans for Ann. She readily agreed to work as a prostitute for him, explaining in retrospect: "I was a fool for love."

Joe already had a wife and children. Ann moved in with Joe, Carol, and the children. Both women took turns working as prostitutes for Joe and caring for the children. Joe battered both women regularly, but Ann felt that she was his "number one" woman since he beat Carol more severely. Ann described herself as the mother of the family, looking after Carol when she was injured or drug sick, making sure the children were properly clothed and fed, and serving as Joe's helpmate in his illegal operations. Ann bragged about obtaining a gun so she could return home periodically to threaten her stepfather that she would kill him if he ever hurt her mother or her younger sister. After 14 years in this family style arrangement, Joe replaced Ann with another "number one" woman, and Ann left. Ann had spent the last five years in what she described as an often-faltering effort to remain drug and arrest-free, going back to school, and living with a series of partners, but vowing not to fall in love again the way she had with Joe. Ann's narrative about her years with Joe focused heavily on the sense of fulfillment she derived from her caretaking roles which were rather androgynous: protector to her mother and sister, breadwinner and protector to Carol, and sometimes co-equal partner in crime with Joe, yet also stereotypically feminine in her nurturing, loyalty, and acceptance of Joe's domination in the family.

Some of the women interviewed began their illegal activities independently, usually as a means of obtaining drugs, but later organized their illegal work around their caretaking roles. Ellen, a 32-year-old white woman and mother of four young children, was serving a ten year sentence for distribution of narcotics, Ellen's father died when she was five years old; as an only child she grew up with a close bond with her mother who was severely depressed and abused prescription drugs. When Ellen was 18 years old her mother committed suicide, and Ellen began using heroin to deal with her own depression. She worked as a street prostitute and occasionally shoplifted to support her addiction. She eventually met Bill, a heroin addict, and they had four children together. Ellen tried from time to time to give up her heroin habit, but each time she was drug-free she became depressed and suicidal.

Ellen's identity revolved around her children, but unable to control her addiction, she organized her illegal work to accommodate her caretaking responsibilities. She did this by turning her home into a "shooting gallery," a place where other addicts could come to purchase and inject heroin. She described in careful detail the ways she managed her "business," operating only while the children were asleep or at school, so that her children would be sheltered from any knowledge of her activities. Of course this careful arrangement fell apart when she and Bill were arrested; the state took custody of their children and was petitioning for permanent adoptive homes for them. Ellen, having been unable to juggle the competing demands of her addiction and her mothering responsibilities, was seriously considering suicide if the state succeeded in removing her parental rights.

CONCLUSIONS AND IMPLICATIONS

The life histories examined here suggest that the nature of the violence to which some women have been exposed serves as a strong force in the "criminalization" of women, that is, the survival strategies selected by (or which are the only options available to) some women are the beginning of a process of transition from victim to offender.

The women in this study were victims of an overwhelming amount of violence as children and adults, yet they were on the whole committed to not harming others in their criminal activities. In spite of, or perhaps because of, those early experiences of violence, the women adopted roles and identities as caretakers and protectors, often remaining loyal to parents (and later to partners) who abused and exploited them. During adolescence the young women responded to those violations by striking out on their own, running away literally as well as symbolically through the use of drugs, but in doing so, their chances of achieving normative transitions to adult roles and responsibilities were derailed. What may have appeared to be the best available means of escape from violence meant that as young runaways they had to begin illegal "work" simply in order to survive, thus linking victimization to "criminalization" and blurring the boundaries between victim and offender. Those early experiences of violence may have had a strong socializing impact on the women's development of highly gender stereotyped identities centered around distorted notions of relational and caretaking obligations. Constant and repeated victimization by violence from early childhood into adulthood apparently seasons women well for the world of illegal street work where women's work is still highly exploited.

It is apparent that the women in this study consider their illegal activities to be a form of *work* which is undertaken primarily out of economic necessity to support partners, children, and addictions. Yet it is not so clear that terms such as "criminal careers" or "career criminals" are accurate descriptions of the women's activities or identities. At this stage of our thinking about women and crime, a more accurate conceptualization may be that of "immersion," a concept which takes into account the slide into criminality by way of survival strategies and which reflects the difficulty women have in extricating themselves from the relationships, addictions, and economic necessities which arise once they are immersed in "street work." However, further research is needed to test and elaborate upon the preliminary conceptualizations offered here.

The women studied here, similar to those studied by Romenesko and Miller (1989), Miller (1986), and Chesney-Lind and Rodriguez (1983), entered criminal activity which was itself highly sex-role stereotyped, suggesting that the division of labor remains highly sex-segregated whether in the world of legal or illegal work, and that such sex-segregation is enforced through physical and sexual violence. These findings also support the conclusions drawn by Chesney-Lind and Rodriguez (1983) that the process of criminalization for women is indeed intricately connected to women's subordinate position in society where victimization by violence coupled with economic marginality related to race, class, and gender all too often blur the boundaries between victims and offenders.

When women have been violated and exploited as harshly and as often as the women in this study, one must ask how those experiences of violence affect women's development and women's moral orientation to the world. When extreme victimization is accompanied by poverty and racial discrimination, women may have very few options for survival by legal avenues and may find a sense of belonging and relational commitment in the world of street crime when it is unattainable elsewhere.

Exposure to such extreme violence may socialize women to adopt a tenacious commitment to caring for anyone who promises love, material success, and acceptance, such that it represents an extreme liability for self survival and places some women at risk for becoming offenders. While women's moral orientation to caring (Gilligan, 1982), in the abstract, may appear to be an asset, in a social context of violence and an absence of the right to protection, the ethic of care (Gilligan, 1982) can be fatal. For the women in this study, the ethic of care appears to constrain them from initially engaging in more violent and serious crime, yet it is also that ethic coupled with the strength of women's commitment to relationships which seasons the women for recruitment and entrapment in illegal street work and ultimately leads to incarceration. Perhaps at later stages of their involvement in street work, the ethic of care gives way once again to questions of sheer survival, pushing some women into more serious forms of illegal activity. Future research should examine those later stages of women's immersion in street crime.

As we continue to investigate and understand the lives of women engaged in street crime, we can begin to call for criminal justice policies and programs which recognize the relationship between victimization and offending among women. We must begin to offer women realistic alternatives to illegal street work as a means of economic and emotional survival.

Women Who Have Killed Their Children

Susan M. Crimmins

Sandra C. Langley

Henry H. Brownstein

Barry J. Spunt

How do we understand homicides involving women who have killed their own children? Official records in the state of New York indicated that 86 out of a total of 443 women convicted for murder or manslaughter were incarcerated for the death of a child. Of those, 42 women (49 percent) participated in an interview. Findings from these 42 interviews are the focus of this chapter. The interview included life history questions concerning family, drug involvement and drug treatment, participation in illegal activities, and issues of violence in subjects' lives as both victims and perpetrators while growing up and as adults. In addition, subjects were asked detailed questions about the homicide for which they were convicted. Repeated experiences of damage to the self, including physical and sexual victimization, suicide attempts, and substance abuse, were evident throughout the lives of these women. This chapter discusses the extent to which these self-damage indicators interfered with the offender's ability to parent children.

The innocence and vulnerability of children, particularly of infants, typically arouse instincts of nurturance and protectiveness on a universal level. In addition, sociocultural expectations dictate that women are primary caretakers for the young. What then, would prompt a woman to kill an infant or child who is helpless and dependent upon her for survival?

Research shows that about two thirds of the victims of women who commit homicide are family members, with the most common event being the killing of a spouse or partner (Daly & Wilson, 1988; Jones, 1980). Research concerning women killing children is narrow in scope and often anecdotal in presentation due to small numbers. The paucity of reports on this topic may be related to truly low incidence of the crime, the underreporting or mistaken reporting of these crimes, or a combination of both. Crib deaths or Sudden Infant Death Syndrome (SIDS) overlap many times with the less socially acceptable report of infanticide (Asch, 1968; Nowak, 1993). Another complicating factor is the number of missing children reported each year, which may mask a more accurate count of child deaths by mothers. However, we do know that homicide remains one of the top five leading causes of death during early childhood in the United States (Abel, 1986).

Despite the relative infrequency of reports of child killing by mothers, as compared to the overall homicide rate, its seriousness and moral implications render it worthy of further examination to identify contributing factors as well as to reflect upon society's handling of such violence. Data derived from interviews with women convicted of killing children are presented in an attempt to understand the factors that contribute to committing such an exceptional crime.

LITERATURE REVIEW

Child killing has occurred throughout the ages, although the reasons given for its existence have varied. Malformation of the infant, economic distress, and social disgrace were all prevalent motives in dispensing with children, and killing was the most efficient method of ensuring that the burden was eliminated permanently (Friedman, 1993; Hoffer & Hull, 1981; Lyon, 1985; Piers, 1978; Weir, 1984). Additional literature has suggested that infant and child killing has also been influenced by complicating factors of jealousy and revenge, psychiatric conditions, and violence within families (Resnick, 1969; Scott, 1973a; Silverman & Kennedy, 1988).

The 1922 Infanticide Act and later, the Not Guilty by Reason of Insanity (NGRI) plea allowed the first opportunity to peer into the mind and intent of the mother who kills her child (see, e.g., Parker &

Good, 1981; Pasewark, Pantle, & Steadman, 1979). These legal concepts also set the stage for contro-versy and labeling in attempting to decipher if these mothers were "mad or bad" in their killings. "Mad" mothers were believed to be psychiatrically unstable and killed as a result of their mental illness, whereas "bad" mothers were considered intrinsically evil and killed because of this predisposition (Warren, 1989; Wilczynski, 1991).

Contemporary motives for killing children involve more psychological reasoning than having enough food to provide or being a victim of social disgrace. Revenge, sometimes referred to as the Medea Syndrome, involves the killing of children in an attempt to punish the husband or partner. Greek tragedy portrays Medea as the jealous, vengeful wife who gets back at her husband, Jason, by murdering their two children (Arboleda-Florez & Power, 1983). Although this drama may be sensationally appealing, it leaves us with the question of why angry wives choose this pathological means of revenge toward their husbands when there are many other options available to them.

In recent literature, additional motives or reasons for these killings fall under the rubric of: acute psycho-sis or gross mental pathology (Resnick, 1969; Scott, 1973a); unwanted child (Resnick, 1969; Scott, 1973a); mercy killing (d'Orban, 1979; Lomis, 1986; Resnick, 1969; Scott, 1973a); victim-precipitated (Daniel & Kashani, 1983; Scott, 1973a, 1973b); childhood maltreatment of women ("learned violence") (Korbin, 1986); and poverty, stress, "social disorganization" (Kaplun & Reich, 1976; Totman, 1978). Silverman and Kennedy (1988) distinguish between two different types of female child killers. The Type 1 mother com-mits infanticide due to severe psychological stress and is usually young, single, and immature. The Type 2 mother kills her child because she goes "too far" in physical abuse of the child, which may be the result of displaced anger, either conscious or unconscious. More often than not, she is married. The "goes too far" or Type 2 hypothesis is also proposed by Scott (1973a) who theorizes that killing is the result of learning or frustration for these women. Perhaps Daniel and Kashani (1983) advance this thinking by linking the theory of intergenerational violence within families as the basis for the killing. They suggest that a mother with a history of physical abuse and serious psychopathology is a strong candidate for murdering a child.

CHILD KILLING: A SELF-PSYCHOLOGY THEORETICAL CONSIDERATION

Consistent with examining the characteristics of women who have killed children and combining, as well as enhancing, some of the above-mentioned reasons for child killing is the self-psychological perspective, which suggests the woman's sense of self is too damaged for her to care about another human being. Self becomes damaged not simply because trauma occurs but also because an absence of social supports and an inability to rely upon others in times of need lays the foundation for the message that self is unimportant (Crimmins, 1995).

With this perspective in mind, when a woman kills a child, it may be that the child is not the literal object that she intends to destroy (similar to the Medea Syndrome), but rather that the child is representa-tive of some other object worthy of destruction. Often the impulse to destroy emanates from a feeling of rage. "Rage is associated with imagery of attacking whatever forces one can identify and hold responsible for the death and for one's own survivor pain" (Lifton, 1979, p. 148). The death may be real or imagined, physical or psychological. To clarify and simplify in the instances of women killing children, death may be perceived as synonymous with the terms *loss* and *threat* to the woman who is experiencing the rage.

Violence often emanates from the need to protect or preserve the self from an impending threat (Crimmins & Foley, 1989). The death threat loss is so powerful to the person who has a very fragile, damaged sense of self that the only possible means of gaining a balance of power is through physical force. Clearly an infant or small child does not pose a physical threat to a mother but may indeed represent a real threat to a shaky identity in a woman with little or no self-esteem. Horner (1989) wrote,

> Children, unbeknownst to them, often wield parental power over their own parents because of the kinds of conscious and unconscious attributions made by the parents to what the child does or says. Rejection by a son or daughter can have exactly the same emotional impact on the parent as did rejection by his or her mother or father in the past, evoking the same anxiety, rage, or depression. (pp. 20–2.1)

The threat, which may be manifested as rejection, is then introjected as an annihilation of self (death), a loss of self, and a wipe-out of power and identity due to the woman's unsuccessful separation from her own parents. As the result of poor object relations, object and self are fused together, so that the killing of the child may be viewed as a symbolic suicide. Because the message in the threat is "I am nothing," which is too painful for the mother to acknowledge, killing the child becomes an act of self-preservation. By killing the object of threat (the bad self), the true or core self is allowed to survive and the balance of power is restored.

Consistent with the thought that child killing is a result of going too far, Shengold (1989) takes the disturbed mother s thinking one step further by introducing the concept of soul murder. This is

> a dramatic term for circumstances that eventuate in crime—the deliberate attempt to eradicate or compromise the separate identity of another person . . . a crime most often committed by psychotic or psychopathic parents who treat the child as an extension of themselves or as an object with which to satisfy their desires. (pp. 2–3)

Because the mother identifies with the aggressors (her own parents), she unconsciously becomes intent upon carrying out punishment whenever the child exhibits willful statements or behaviors in an attempt to separate from her. Again, this may be manifested as the child merely behaving like his or her father would, and this would be sufficient for the mother to witness it as betrayal or defiance of her power.

Katz (1988) has suggested that a sense of "righteous slaughter" has been perceived by the woman who has determined that the child has, either realistically or symbolically, teased, dared, or defied the killer. In the killer's perception, she is acting in an attempt to "defend the Good." This subtle, slowly emerging phenomenon is often elusive to the general public, and it may escape others, who view the killing of a child as senseless or insane. However, the perpetrator's emotional and moral logic has developed to the extent that this path of action, killing, is the only possible way to defend and to preserve the integrity of self.

Katz outlines three essential components that characterize a righteously enraged slaughter: First, the killer interprets the victim (child) and his/her behaviors in a very particular way that is threatening to the value/livelihood of self and that "requires a last stand in defense of his (her) basic worth" (pp. 18–19), Second, an emotional process that is intense, all-consuming, and overwhelming has been initiated within the killer. Feelings of eternal humiliation, shame, and degradation are transformed into rage as the first step toward self-preservation. In a rage, the future can be discounted with an emphasis being placed on preserving the moral good. Finally, the perspective and posture outlined above must be maintained throughout the implementation of the entire situation. The punishment inflicted gives credence to the pain/anguish that the killer has withstood, and death of the child is then viewed as a sacrificial slaughter.

Given the perceptions and processes that the child killer embraces, it is emotionally logical to suppose that following the killing, the mother would feel a sense of relief, accomplishment, and peacefulness that self has been preserved. However, this is not an inevitable outcome. Post killing reality sets in and tampers with the trauma-based mind-set of the killer. Most mothers are remorseful about the killings but are unable to do more than acknowledge that it happened due to feelings of frustration or despair. It would appear that after the rage has been satiated, feelings return to or transform back into their homeostatic form of insecurity, self-doubt, and humiliation, so that a full cycle of victimization has been enacted with the only accomplishment being a greater entrenchment into feelings of despair. This dynamic may be reflective of the depression that overcomes mothers who kill their children and then become suicidal. If the killing was, indeed, supposed to remedy and preserve a true sense of self and this did not occur, the only available alternative is suicide (Katz, 1988).

One may ask how it is that there exists a need to defend the "righteous good" from threats to begin with. Why is it that everyone does not move toward violence when threatened? The answer is not monolithic in nature and may only be categorized as being a response to cumulative exposure of traumatic and unpredictable experiences that have injured one's sense of self. The formation of identity, or sense of self, is affected strongly by experiences that occur during our earliest years of life (Bowlby, 1973, 1988; Mahler, 1979; Zulueta, 1993). Feelings about self, also known as self-esteem or self-worth, are derived largely from a succession of interactions and experiences between significant others in the social environment and self. Mastery of social experiences builds positive self-worth, whereas a series of experiential failures contributes to frustration and a fragmented sense of self.

How you feel about yourself is largely influenced by how others conveyed they felt about you during your youngest years. During early childhood, a mother is usually the person upon whom you can rely for security, warmth, and feelings of comfort. An absence of nurturance by a primary caretaker will interfere with the ability to develop positive feelings about yourself or the ability to build positive social experiences, unless alternative social and emotional supports are in place. Without having a "secure base" from which to operate, one is unable to develop positive or healthy attachments with others (Bowlby, 1988). In situations where the mother may be emotionally unavailable to her child (e.g., mental illness, neglect) and other supports are absent, the child grows up with an impoverished emotional repertoire from which to gauge interpersonal relationships and an adequate sense of self-worth. When this child grows up and becomes a mother, she is then unable to give her own child a sense of warmth or security, for as a "motherless mother," she cannot give what she has not been given (Edelman, 1994; Zulueta, 1993).

There are several other areas of trauma that we know have deleterious effects upon the formation of personality or self in children who have early and prolonged exposure to them without the ameliorating benefits of social supports. Specifically, growing up in a family where alcohol and/or drugs are used on a regular basis or growing up where serious physical harm and sexual harm compromise a child's sense of safety and trust (Herman, 1992; Levin, 1987; Terr, 1990; Wood, 1987). Both of these scenarios are likely to result in the child developing a history of substance abuse to ward off feelings of psychic pain, as well as a plethora of mental health problems, including depression and suicidal behavior.

The influence of alcohol and drugs upon the formation of self have been well documented in the literature (e.g., Levin, 1987; Wood, 1987). From a self psychology perspective, people often ingest substances to replace or substitute an object or an object's love that they have lost or never had. Characteristically, there is a lack of predictability in the lives of families who abuse substances. All children need to be surrounded by caretakers who are predictable in their responses so that trust may be established and to ensure that a sense of safety may be developed. Substance abuse may be interpreted as an expression of yearning for a substitute to soothe or numb feelings of anxiety and/or pain and to block out unpleasant realities.

As part of a dissociative process, the child then learns to separate emotions from actions or events that are too painful. This coping mechanism is used frequently by trauma victims (Herman, 1992; Terr, 1990; Zulueta, 1993) and has characteristically been documented during times of war. The trauma victim often reports a "numbing" that occurs following the killing of another (Lifton, 1973). In situations of physical or sexual trauma by a parent or otherwise "trustworthy adult," this "disavow" of painful or distressing stimuli, also known as numbing, permits the child to collude with the parental perception that all is fine. The payoff for this distortion is the fantasy of parental love and security, which is guaranteed if the emotions are squelched. Disavowal becomes the developed defense against the meaning of an external perception. Reality is intact, but its meaning is not accepted (Basch, 1982). "For as long as you are not allowed to see something, you have no choice but to overlook it, to misunderstand it, to protect yourself against it in one way or another" (Miller, 1984, pp. 9–10).

What, then, are the experiences and sense of self held by women who kill children? Are they too damaged to care adequately for children? If so, what are the primary, damaging factors that so influenced their lives and development to the extent that they were rendered unable to care for and protect their children? Why did they resort to committing an act of lethal violence? These issues were examined via interviews with women who have been convicted of killing children.

FINDINGS AND DISCUSSION

Sociodemographic variables of race/ethnicity, age, education, and income status were examined for these 42 women with the following results: Race/ethnicity: 20 women of the 42 (48%) were Black, whereas 16(38%) were White, 3 (7%) were Hispanic, and 3 (7%) were from other racial/ethnic backgrounds. Age of the subjects at the time of the homicide ranged from 16 years to 42 years. The median age was 25.5 years. Education was measured as the highest grade completed. The median level of education was eleventh grade (range third grade to 2 years of college). An examination of income sources revealed that some subjects had more than one source of income at the time of the homicide, with the most frequently reported being welfare/public assistance for

13 women (31%), legitimate employment for 12 women (29%), and spouse/partner support for 12 women (29%). No more than three women reported each of the following sources of income: family, illegal means, unemployment, and social security benefits. One woman reported no income, and data for another woman was missing.

As mentioned before, the following variables are prominent self-damage indicators that are influential in personality development and thus in the shaping of a person's responses toward society: characteristics of "motherless mothering," drug/alcohol abuse in family of origin, self-drug history, serious childhood harm and serious adult harm (including physical and sexual harm by others), and self-harm. Examination of relevant interview data clearly indicates that many of these women were exposed to multiple experiences of damage that influenced their lives and their ability to parent children.

Twenty-seven of the women (64%) were categorized as being motherless mothers based upon their reports of early experiences with their own mothers. Several types of behaviors resulted in the subjects' mothers being unavailable to them: serious and prolonged verbal abuse, serious physical abuse, alcoholism, mental health problems, and absence due to neglect/death. More than a third of the women (38%) had alcoholic mothers, 19% experienced serious physical abuse by their mothers, and the mothers of 17% were absent. Almost a quarter of the women (24%) had mothers who had more than one characteristic that made them unavailable to these subjects during childhood.

Alma spoke about the immediate effects that being abused had upon her:

> I didn't have a family life. My mother used to sit on my head to make me still so she could beat me with a cord, belt, or anything she could get her hands on, and things got worse when she burned me with an iron, and she allowed certain relatives to have sex with me and get away with it. She sexually abused me too. . . . [All the abuse] made me feel less important and didn't care about myself too much.

Later in the interview, Alma also spoke about how her childhood abuse affected her parenting skills with her 4-year-old son.

> I was very scared cause I was pregnant and I was scared. I didn't know what to do because my daughter's father left me alone 'cause he got me pregnant and I was ready to move. I was packing up my stuff and my son was acting up and I didn't know what to do 'cause I don't understand nothing about disciplining a child cause I was raised by my own family, how they abused me and I didn't know what to do, so I took it out on my son and sent him to his room and I made him go to bed and he went to bed. I went near and he wasn't breathing, he stopped breathing, wouldn't breathe, I know he was sleeping and he didn't wake up. I hit him, I only hit him twice in the head with my hand. I don't know, with my shoe, my flat shoe in the head twice and that was it, and I sent him to his room cause I didn't want to hit him no more. . . . It was very hard for me 'cause I didn't know what to do. The only thing I knew was to take him to the doctor when he needed to go to the doctor and feed him and keep him clean, that was it. I didn't know how to love him, 'cause I didn't have, didn't love myself, I didn't know how to love him.

Abusive Partners and Motherless Mothers

Table 1.3 shows that slightly more than half (52%) of the women who killed children were motherless mothers who also had been involved with an abusive partner. A likely reason these women became involved with abusive partners was because their self-perceptions were damaged to the extent that they believed abuse was all they deserved. Only 12% of the women who were motherless mothers did not become involved with an abusive mate. An additional 26% were not characterized as motherless mothers but still became involved with an abusive partner. Although this group of women did not fit the description of being a motherless mother, they did have mothers who may be considered codependent in their behaviors. The possible impact this may have had upon the subjects' becoming involved with an abusive partner requires further research.

Table 1.3 Comparison of Having an Abusive Partner and Being a Motherless Mother (N = 42)

	Abusive Partner		
	Yes	No	Total
Motherless Mother			
Yes	22	5	27
	(52%)	(12%)	(64%)
No	11	4	15
	(26%)	(9%)	(36%)
Total	33	9	42
	(79%)	(21%)	(100%)

Substance Use in Family of Origin

Twenty-five of the 42 women (60%) reported that drugs/alcohol were used in their families of origin on a daily basis. Alcohol was overwhelmingly the most commonly used drug, as it was used on a daily basis in 24 of the families (57%). As previously mentioned, more than half of the 25 women were in families where the mother used alcohol on a regular basis. For these women, one can assume that their mothers were unavailable to them emotionally and were unable to provide them with the safety and comfort a child requires. Thus emotional abandonment was a common experience for these women, who, in turn, could not provide for their own children the safety and nurturance that they never had (Zulueta, 1993).

Subject Use of Alcohol and Drugs

In terms of their own usage, 27 women or 64% of the group described using drugs or alcohol on at least a regular basis. Regular basis was defined as using 3 or more days per week for a month or more. The most common drugs that were used regularly by the 27 women were marijuana (11 or 26%), alcohol (8 or 19%), and tranquilizers (7 or 17%). Eighteen respondents, or 43%, who reported growing up in families where alcohol or drugs were used on a regular basis also reported regular alcohol or drug usage in their own lives.

Serious Harm Witnessed by Subjects During Childhood

Serious physical harm, another self-damage indicator, was measured with a modified version of the Conflict Tactics Scales (Straus, Gelles, & Steinmetz, 1981). Behaviors such as kick, punch or bite, beat up, threaten with a weapon, and use of a weapon are included in the definition of serious physical harm. Sexual harm was added to the assessment of harm and was measured by two items: inappropriate sexual touching and forced sexual penetration. Subjects were asked about the incidence of these behaviors in their childhood (up to age 16) and in their adult years.

Three fourths (74%) of the women said they witnessed or experienced serious physical and/or sexual harm during childhood. Two thirds of the women witnessed or experienced serious physical harm, and half witnessed or experienced sexual harm. Most of the serious childhood physical harm was witnessed or experienced by the subjects equally with their mothers and with siblings (10 or 24%). On the other hand, most of the serious sexual harm during childhood was witnessed or experienced by the women with their father, stepfather or mother's boyfriend (9 or 21%), other relatives (i.e., male cousins, grandfathers), 8 or 19%, and then male siblings (6 or 14%). Thus an overwhelming majority of the harm witnessed or experienced by these women as children occurred in their own families among people they were supposed to trust or with whom they should have felt safe.

Serious Harm Experienced as an Adult The prevalence of serious harm during adulthood were experienced by 30 of 42 (71 %) women. All 13 of the women who experienced sexual harm were also victims of serious physical harm. Two thirds of the women (67%) were physically harmed by husbands or boyfriends. Another 11 women, or slightly more than one quarter of the sample (26%), reported that sexual harm toward them was committed by partners. Again, in relationships where a certain degree of intimacy and trust is expected, we see that these relationships are characterized by behavior that has rendered the woman unsafe. Lisa explained how the effects of being abused affected her self-esteem:

> When I was home from school one day and my mother had to go out for awhile, my older brother came in my room and forced me to have sex with him. I didn't want to, so he beat me up a little first and said he'd kill me if I told anyone. I can see now that I had very low self-esteem and would do anything for someone to love me.

Later in the interview, Lisa described how she ended up killing her own child to maintain the love of another and to preserve her own safety.

> I had gotten up, taken a shower and gotten dressed. Then I was walking down the street to catch the bus, and I missed the bus by 2 seconds. I walked back home and got my mother up and asked her to take me to work. She got up, got dressed, and had a cup of coffee and drove me to work. We hardly ever even speak. She didn't speak to anybody that day. When I got to work I went to the bathroom, got my things out of my locker, then went up and counted out my drawer. It was early in the morning that day so it was difficult. It was back and forth to the bathroom. [You were pregnant?] Yes. I was basically a robot that day just going through the motions and not really feeling anything. I was having pains and I wanted to go home, but I couldn't tell anyone I was pregnant. I just couldn't, [What month were you?] Ninth. [You weren't showing?] I guess to some people I was, but I basically wear big shirts to begin with so nobody knew. They may have suspected, but they didn't really know. I wasn't allowed to tell anybody that I was pregnant because the child's father threatened to kill me and that person I told it to. I took his threat very seriously. . . . I went out to lunch and the pains got worse. Came back to work. I wanted to leave so bad but I couldn't 'cause I wouldn't get relieved till 5 o'clock. I kept on checking out the customers and the pain got worse and worse and worse. I just wanted to go home and tell my mother to take me to the doctor but I couldn't. I went back into the bathroom and as I was sitting on the toilet, something came out. I don't really know what happened from there. It's still a blur, but all I remember is that I took a box cutter and cut his throat. Then I stuffed some toilet paper in his mouth so he wouldn't make no noise. [What did you do with the body?] I put it in the trash.

Self-inflicted Harm

In addition to experiencing harm at the hands of others with whom there should have been trust, 17 of the 42 women (41%) reported that they also inflicted harm upon themselves. It is striking that of the 17 women who reported that they tried to kill themselves, most of them (14) tried to kill themselves more than once. These figures were not significantly different from the rest of the sample. Of the women convicted of killing a child, 59% reported a history of emotional or mental health problems, compared to 37% of the other women in our sample. This difference was statistically significant ($\chi^2 = 6.42$, $p > .05$). The most common method of self-harm was overdose with various legal drugs (13 or 31 %), followed by cutting wrists (6 or 14%).

Seven of the 17 women who had attempted suicide made their first attempt before age 13. Another 7 women (17%) first tried to kill themselves during adolescence (13 to 19 years). Women were asked if their attempts to hurt themselves were related to others trying to hurt them. About 71% (12) stated that their self-harm attempts were related to others trying to hurt them. This sample of women who killed children had experienced severe damage to self during their formative years to the extent that life, at times, was perceived as no longer worth living. In fact, all of the 42 women experienced more than one self-damage indicator prior to killing a child. Given this shaky sense of self, it is not hard to imagine that for most of the women giving birth and raising a child under life conditions already considered stressful and harsh would be a most difficult feat to accomplish.

THE VICTIMS

Table 1.4 shows the ages of 45 victims who were killed by the 42 convicted women identified for this sample (one woman killed two children, another woman killed three). Slightly more than one third of the children (38%) were killed before age 1, and thus these cases can be considered cases of infanticide. Only about one

Table 1.4   Age of Homicide Victims (N = 45)

	n	Percentage
Birth to 6 months	12	27
7 to 12 months	5	11
1 to 3 years	17	38
4 to 8 years	10	22
Missing	1	2

quarter (22%) were older than 3 years at the time of their deaths. Thus these results support other findings that younger children and infants are considerably more at risk for being killed than older children.

Most of the women (75%) were the natural mothers of the children whom they killed. The remaining quarter killed their foster child or adopted child, a neighbor's child, or other relatives. Victims were slightly more likely to be male (*n* = 24), 55%, than female (*n* = 20), 45%. About 38% (16) of the 42 women reported that they had killed the child, whereas a slightly higher proportion, 41% (17 of 42), denied any involvement in the killing. Of the 17 women who denied killing children, 59%, or 10 of the women, reported that the child was killed by a partner/intimate, usually as a result of physical force. All of the women involved in neglect cases described a failure to protect their child, whereas the remaining 4 women either could not remember the incident or declined to discuss their role in it. Almost half of the victims (47%) were killed by physical force. This included shakings and beatings with hands or weapons (i.e., a shoe, a belt), as well as throwing out a window and shooting. The next most common method, asphyxiation, was used to kill almost a fifth of the victims. This was typically done by sticking materials in the child's mouth to block his/her air passage. Child neglect occurred in 13% of victims, manifested by children being starved or dehydrated, as well as medical conditions being ignored. Another 11 % were burned in fires purposely set, whereas 7% were drowned or scalded. For two children, method was unknown as these women declined to discuss the incident.

Motives for Killings

Although only 8 of the women (19%) had motives attributed to some type of psychological distress (e.g., depression, schizophrenia, "snapped"), almost twice as many women (14 or 33%) reported elsewhere in the interview that they were depressed at the time of the homicide. Similarly, an additional 4 women indicated mental health problems by stating that they were stressed, unable to cope with problems and had flashbacks at the time of the homicide. In fact, 59% of the women reported a history of emotional or mental health problems, compared to 37% of the other women in our sample. The paucity of internal resources that affected the women's ability to cope was overwhelming. Opportunities to engage external social supports were noticeably absent as these women admittedly felt isolated in their situations. Long ago, as children, they learned to "suffer in silence" with their pain, as no one was available then to provide them with comfort. It is of little surprise then that discipline of a child was also a common motive (19%) for killing. Circumstances of child killings were most commonly abuse (67%); neglect of children (21%) was the second most prevalent circumstance. In situations of child abuse, the parent often resorts to projective identification in the raising of children. This means that the disowned aspects of the parent's self are put onto the child, who is then expected to fulfill them or be "wiped out." The child then becomes the hated aspect of the parent, which then has to be corrected or disciplined (Zulueta, 1993, p. 118).

In addition to motive and circumstance, it is important to acknowledge that the women reported 13 of the child killings (31%) were drug-related. In 11 of these situations, the homicide was related to the mother using alcohol or other drugs, whereas in the other two situations, partners were using alcohol or other drugs. These women all indicated that the alcohol and drug usage seriously impaired their or their partner's judgment at the time of the homicide.

THE LINK TO LETHAL VIOLENCE

For the sample of women discussed herein, there was no single factor that led them into actions of lethal violence. Rather, their early years were characterized by various kinds of losses that were followed immediately by gross insensitivity to their emotional needs. This was typically the result of inadequate parenting and a paucity of social supports. Thus losses evolved into traumas that eroded their sense of self, and when self no longer exists, the roots of violence are born (Zulueta, 1993). Blatant disregard of these women's childhood needs was so profound that their voices were silenced and their spirits broken at very early ages. These women, too, were betrayed by those who should have protected them. Their voices, even when exercised, were to no avail. The learned, maladaptive methods of coping with harm and trauma (e.g., drug and alcohol abuse), in turn, exacerbated the women's difficulties and left them vulnerable to becoming involved in additional situations of harm. Pervasive social isolation, coupled with their learned silence, only serve to reinforce the cycle of poor self-esteem that had been initiated in their families of origin. Self was sacrificed in an attempt to remain connected to a larger social community called humanity. Factors that resulted in their resorting to lethal violence was built upon years of frustration, prior experiences of using violence as a means to "settle" disputes, and a desperate wish to alter their life situations, either immediately or long term.

Periodic expressions of rage became assertions of vitality in an attempt to keep self alive. Deprivation, loss, and abuse so depleted the self that defending itself becomes of paramount importance, whatever the cost to the Other (Zulueta, 1993, p. xii). As Miller (1984) stated, "If their psyche is killed, they will learn how to kill—the only question is who will be killed: oneself, others, or both" (p. 98). Kohut (1985) said that empathy involves others making an effort to understand self. Parents who are themselves deficient because of their own emotional deprivation are unable to offer empathy to their children's developing sense of self. When emotional needs are consistently unmet, attachments to others are disrupted and self-esteem does not develop in a healthy way. If empathy is an extension of self, then the child who has a poor sense of self is unable to feel compassion for others. When "self-objects," such as parents, lack empathy, the child often develops an insecure sense of self as a result of feeling low self-worth, isolation, and rejection. Such feelings often generate additional feelings of rage and despair that later erupt into violent, aggressive behaviors (Zulueta, 1993).

CONCLUSION AND RECOMMENDATIONS

Women who kill children are still somewhat of an enigma in the latter part of the 20th century, Whereas reasons and motives are complex, the literature still tends to focus upon these women as mad or bad. In an attempt to skirt further examination of this dichotomized thinking, attention has been diverted from the perpetrator and shifted onto the victims. Thus little is still known about those women who commit this crime.

The theoretical considerations raised here indicate that the mad or bad reductionistic thinking needs to be put aside in an attempt to understand better the intricacies of the process involved in child killing. There is a need for further research about women who kill children with an emphasis on exploring their own dilemmas as well as their reasoning. Findings presented here indicate they, too, are victims who have been unable to extricate themselves from this vicious cycle of self-damaging experiences, including suicide attempts, drug use, and physical and sexual victimization.

At the end of the interview, each woman was asked what type of advice or recommendations for programming she would give to women who found themselves in situations similar to her own. The emphasis of the women's suggestions points to rectifying those life situations and circumstances that have been outlined as self-damage indicators. Almost half (45%) of the women suggested that programs where their self-esteem could be developed were critical to their successful functioning. Low self-esteem, reliance upon a dysfunctional partner, and feelings of worthlessness characterized these women to the extent that their judgment about safety for themselves and their children was impaired. Due to the tremendous guilt feelings about their crime and to being ostracized within the prison system, as well as in society at large, these women hoped for a program that would help them deal with the loss of their children (Kaplan, 1988). Currently, there are no programs in prison for those who lost or killed a child. Women also wanted more parenting programs available to teach them about how to care for their children and identify their children's needs. Programs addressing domestic violence were also important to these women, who stated that they must first learn to care for themselves before they could adequately care for their children.

Acknowledging and identifying women who are perpetual victims is possible via day care centers, school programs, and child health care systems. However, outreach and subsequent education to prevent violence is a major effort that requires interest, skill, empathy, and resources. The findings here support the aggressive use of prevention and intervention services regarding the identification of parental needs and fulfillment of those needs. Self-esteem builders and self-care programs for new mothers should also be offered in communities while providing nursery care for newborns. If we can correct the deficits of living in those who give life, we stand a chance of breaking the cycle of abuse and offer a future to children who otherwise may have been robbed of one.

WOMEN

The number of women in prison, many of whom are incarcerated for drug offenses, has been increasing at a rate 50 percent higher than men since 1980. Women in prison often have significant histories of physical and sexual abuse, high rates of HIV, and substance abuse problems. Women's imprisonment in female-headed households leads to children who suffer from their mother's absence and breaks in family ties.

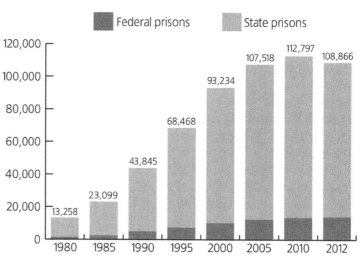

Number of Women in State and Federal Prisons, 1980-2012

Federal prisons   State prisons

- 1980: 13,258
- 1985: 23,099
- 1990: 43,845
- 1995: 68,468
- 2000: 93,234
- 2005: 107,518
- 2010: 112,797
- 2012: 108,866

Source: Carson, E.A., Golinelli, D. (2013). *Prisoners in 2012 – Advance Counts.* Washington, D.C.: Bureau of Justice Statistics.

Highest and Lowest State Incarceration Rates (per 100,000), 2012

Overall (National = 480)

State	Rate
HIGHEST	
Louisiana	893
Mississippi	717
Alabama	650
Oklahoma	648
Texas	601
LOWEST	
Maine	145
Minnesota	184
Rhode Island[b]	190
Massachusetts[c]	200
New Hampshire	211

Women (National = 63)

State	Rate
HIGHEST	
Oklahoma	127
Idaho	126
Kentucky	114
Arizona[a]	101
Louisiana	101
LOWEST	
Rhode Island[b]	15
Massachusetts[c]	15
Maine	20
New York	22
New Jersey	23

Men (National = 910)

State	Rate
HIGHEST	
Louisiana	1,720
Mississippi	1,370
Alabama	1,234
Texas	1,121
Oklahoma	1,178
LOWEST	
Maine	276
Minnesota	344
North Dakota	372
New Hampshire	396
Rhode Island[b]	376

a = Prison population is custody count.
b = Prisons and jails form one integrated system.
c = Includes persons sentenced to one year or more in prison and held in county jails.

Source: Carson, E.A., Golinelli, D. (2013). *Prisoners in 2012 - Advance Counts.* Washington, D.C.: Bureau of Justice Statistics.

LIVING IN PRISON

Joycelyn Pollock

It is clear that women acutely feel the deprivations imprisonment entails, especially the loss of their children and lack of emotional support. They feel isolated and surrounded by uncaring or hostile others, and the loss of their children is cause for pervasive worry and depression. Female inmates adapt to these deprivations in a variety of ways. Many attempt to remain aloof from the prisoner subculture; they find their niches in work, their cell, and other sanctuaries. Others participate fully in the "mix," the subcultural activities involving homosexuality, drugs, and fighting (Owen, 1998). In this chapter we will first describe and reiterate some of the deprivations of prison, and then explore prisoner adaptations. The prisoner subculture, including elements of leadership, argot roles, homosexual and pseudofamily relationships, and rule-breaking, will be discussed and compared to that in prisons for men.

THE DEPRIVATIONS OF IMPRISONMENT

Researchers have long engaged in a somewhat Kafkaesque inquiry into whether male or female prisoners suffer the pains of imprisonment more deeply. For instance, Ward and Kassebaum wrote: "The impact of imprisonment is, we believe, more severe for females than for males because it is more unusual. Female inmates generally have not come up through the 'sandlots of crime,' in that they are not as likely as men to have had experience in training schools or reformatories" (1965: 161).[1]

In their study of 832 women inmates, interviewing 45 of them, Ward and Kassebaum (1965) observed that women indicated that, although prison was not physically difficult, it was emotionally stressful, both because of a fear of the unknown and because of severed ties with children. Women expressed frustration at not being able to depend on staff for help and emotional support. This frustration marks a theme pervasive throughout the literature; women evidently expect and demand more from the correctional staff, whether or not they receive it. They do not adopt the social distance and isolation that characterize the relations between male inmates and officers but rather look to staff, as well as to one another, to provide support and nurturance (Ward and Kassebaum, 1965: 162).

A more recent attempt (Harris, 1993) used measures of prison elements and compared male and female inmate responses. The themes measured were: disorientation, lack of heterosexual activity, lack of emotional support, loss of self-esteem, loss of autonomy, loss of responsibility, lack of privacy, lack of security, and lack of property (derived from Toch, 1977). Harris concluded that women did not experience "greater deprivation" than men but noted that men and women experienced the deprivations of prison differently. Women identified relationship issues, and men did not.[2]

Although both men and women obviously share similar deprivations, they are touched in a different way by the prison experience. For women, prison is most painful because it cuts off ties to family and loved ones, especially children (Jones, 1993). Sex and companionship are needs of all humans, and women cite their absence as a painful aspect of imprisonment as well. Another pain of imprisonment is the inherent and unceasing boredom of prison life. One day follows the other in pretty much an endless succession.

Another pain felt by women is forced association and lack of privacy. Women must live together with others they scorn and despise. They must share their living space against their will and must learn to coexist with others with whom they would never associate outside prison. Privacy is nonexistent, since women must shower together and may be observed even when excreting or taking care of hygiene needs. In these times of overcrowding, this deprivation is exacerbated; rooms that were built to hold two women are often holding four. Many prisons today use a dormitory style of housing, providing even less privacy for women.

In addition to the need for affiliation, women must find a way to cope with the prison environment, which is cold, inconvenient, and unaccommodating. It is not as hostile as the prison for men, but there are dangers. Women report fears upon entry, and they learn to either isolate themselves as best they can or adapt to the prison social life. Whereas the prison for men seems to be a jungle, where the strong survive at the expense of the weak and the only option is to band together for mutual protection, the women's prison is marked by small pockets of friendship and allegiance. Although individuals must be constantly on guard against exploitation, there is less reason to fear physical harm and evidenly more opportunity to create bonds of love, however transitory.

There are isolated reports of violence in women's prisons. Women have been "raped" by other women inmates with bottes and fingers. At times this is done as punishment for perceived infractions of the informal code; at other times, it seems to be done for no other reason than because the woman thought she was "better" than other prisoners and "needed to be taught a lesson." In addition to these serious but extremely rare violent incidents, women often attempt exploitation through intimidation. One female inmate, during her first day in general population, was approached by an aggressive, "tough" woman prisoner. This woman said, "Give me your ring," and upon the refusal of the newcomer, the exploiter retorted, "Give me your ring, bitch, or I'll cut your finger off!" The newcomer continued to refuse to acquiesce to the demands of the other woman and eventually was left alone, but more often the "fish" may fear the threats sufficiently to submit to exploitation.

On the other hand, much less violence is reported in the women's prison than in prisons for men. Women are also less likely to manufacture or carry weapons. The relative lack of weapons may be partly due to the fact that there are no metal shops or other industries that provide appropriate materials for weapons. Women are probably also less skilled in the manufacture of weapons because of their backgrounds and life experiences. Some women do carry weapons, but the weapons are less sophisticated than those found in prisons for men, and less lethal. During an altercation, women pick up nearby objects—chairs, brooms, irons—to use as makeshift weapons, or they fight without weapons. Violence in a women's prison usually is between two people in a personal relationship or due to perceived thefts. Thus the violence is rarely impersonal and very infrequently results in serious injury. Faith (1993a) compares the relative lack of violence in women's prisons with the stereotypes portrayed in movies wherein violent "butches" victimize innocent feminine newcomers. Screenwriters utilize the fear and pervasive violence of men's prisons, and charge this mix with sexuality. While it may be titillating and popular with audiences, this depiction is far from the reality of life in women's prisons.

Another need prisoners experience in prison is for items that are taken for granted on the outside. Prisoners develop elaborate mechanisms for preserving such small freedoms as having a cup of coffee during the evening or a sandwich at midnight. Another species of contraband, of course, is drugs. The need for drugs may be physical or psychological. Drugs may serve as a release from the frustration and boredom of a prison day or be used to forget the experiences of a lifetime.

Although much of the research reported in this chapter comes from the 1960s, 1970s, and 1980s, there is little reason to believe that these early findings are substantially outdated today. The few researchers who study prison life today reiterate some of the descriptions found in much earlier studies. For instance, a recent writer reports that toughness and individual survival are more relevant themes in men's prisons, and affective relationships are more present in women's institutions (Rolison, 1993). Owen (1998: 4–5), writing about California prisons, notes that "much of women's prison culture has changed little. Personal relationships with other prisoners, both emotionally and physically intimate, connections to family and loved ones in the free community . . . and commitments to pre-prison identities continue to shape the core of prison culture among women." However, she does note that drugs have had a tremendous impact on female offenders and prison culture.

Rierden (1997) spent 18 months interviewing in Niantic, Connecticut's prison for women. She chronicled the changes that had taken place in Niantic, from the small, "homey" prison of the first part of the 20th century, surrounded by gardens and farmland, with litde social distance between officers and inmates, to a "state-of-the-art" confinement model of custody. Still, many of the issues brought out in the early studies remain the same—the importance of children, the wary nature of prison friendships, and the presence of homosexuality, among other issues. Girshick (1997) also provides us with a more current view of prison life. Her interviews also reinforce prior descriptive studies of prisons and prisoners.

ADAPTATIONS: THIS PRISONER SUBCULTURE

Individuals who are sentenced to prison must learn to adapt to the prison world: *prisonization* is the term used to describe the degree to which an individual inmate has adopted the prisoner subculture and its value system. The prisoner subculture is a subterranean culture that exists within but is distinct from the formal culture of the prison and society. It is the *sub rosa* culture of norms, values, and social roles, This system of power and interchange occurs among prisoners more or less outside the control or even knowledge of prison officials. The formal prison culture, on the other hand, is what is seen; it is the product of all the actors in the prison environment, including prison administrators, staff, and the prisoners themselves.

Elements of the Prisoner Subculture

Early researchers documented the subculture in prisons for men, describing elements of leadership, social roles, race, the role of violence, and the like (Berk, 1966; Carroll, 1974; Davidson, 1974; Hayner, 1961; Irwin, 1970; Irwin and Cressey, 1962; Schrag, 1944, 1954, 1966; Sykes, 1958; Sykes and Messinger, 1960). At least a few studied these elements in institutions for women (e.g., Giallombardo, 1966; Hartnagel and Gillan, 1980; Heffernan, 1972; Mahan, 1984a & b; Moyer, 1984; Ward and Kassebaum, 1965; Wilson, 1980, 1986). Researchers, unfortunately, merely compared the women's institution to the descriptions of men's institutions, rather than approach the women's world without preconceptions or expectations derived from prior research.

Every institution has a somewhat unique prisoner subculture. Each subculture is molded and constrained by several variables, such as the demographic characteristics of the prisoners, the level of custody, population size, physical layout, regional location, characteristics of the city from which the prisoners are drawn, average length of sentence, and a whole range of other elements. However, there are similarities and persistent themes that prevail across institutions. We will discuss the inmate "code " argot roles, and the role of snitches in prison before moving on to a fuller discussion of the patterns of social organization found in prison.

The "Inmate Code"   The "inmate code," a *Magna Carta* of prison life, was originally described by researchers studying prisons for men in the 1940s and 1950s. Interestingly, very little research has been done in the last 30 years; therefore, we do not know how different it is today from the descriptions provided to us many years ago. The major values the code has been described as endorsing are: "Don't interfere with inmate interests"; "Never rat on a con"; "Don't be nosy"; "Don't have a loose lip"; "Keep off a man's back"; "Don't put a guy on the spot"; "Be loyal to your class"; "Be cool"; "Do your own time"; and "Don't exploit inmates" (Sykes, 1958).

Female prisoners have never adhered to the code provisions in the same way as men (Hawkins, 1995). For instance, although one hears the statement that women should "do their own time," female prisoners seem to be more involved with each other and not shy about getting involved in other's business. Women's sexual involvements and latest breakups are known and discussed. Women will also become involved in an individual's confrontation with staff members, or intervene in someone's emotional crisis. Depression or suicidal tendencies sometimes have a contagious effect where one woman's pain will trigger a rash of emotional crises.

Women also do not have strong proscriptions regarding interaction with correctional officers (C.O.s). In a men's prison, inmates tend to avoid officers so as not to be labeled a "snitch." Thus, correctional officers and male inmates share very little and, except in certain settings, tend to limit interaction to formal exchanges regarding duties or needs. There is more casual and social interaction between women and C.O.s, even if it is, at times, rancorous. Some inmates believe that C.O.s should be avoided at all costs, but they have little control over other inmates' behavior.

Arguably, with changes brought about by the drug culture, a different racial mix, an altered demographic profile of offenders, and legal changes in the operation of the prison, the old system of values in men's prisons described by Sykes and others is probably quite different today. Because of differences in offender criminal background, gender differences, and different institutional features, including staff interactions and expectations, it should not be surprising that female prisoners have exhibited different values and a somewhat different inmate code from that found in prisons for men. Unfortunately, researchers have always used the male inmate code as the standard and have merely compared the women's subculture to this standard. Thus, we have had a somewhat distorted view of the inmate code for women; typically we have been told only what it is not (when it does not conform to men's). We do not have a comprehensive portrait of what it *is* because early studies merely compared the women's prison to the men's. We also do not have a comprehensive sense of what it *is* because, except for a few notable exceptions (see Owen, 1998), we have little information about what is occurring in women's prisons today.

Argot (Social) Roles   Argot (social) roles describe the behavior patterns, motivation, and place of the individual in the prison culture. Not all inmates can be categorized into a social role, but some are easily recognizable. The social roles present in male institutions have been the topic of many articles and debates among researchers. Sykes's classic work (1958) specified *rats, centermen, gorillas, merchants, wolves, ball busters, real men, toughs,* and *hipsters.* Hayner (1961) described *real men, racketeers, smoothies, politicians,* and *dings.* Schrag's typology, which is perhaps the best known, included *square johns, right guys, con politicians,* and *outlaws* (1961: 12).

The *real man* was the type who populated the "Big House" of earlier days. He was an honest thief and subscribed wholeheartedly to a criminal subculture. Neither the administration nor brutal guards could break him; he would maintain control through any and all attempts to belittle or humiliate him. The *square john* was the innocent among wolves. He held middle-class values and identified more closely with the guards than with fellow inmates. Consequendy, he was never trusted and often victimized. The *con politician,* because of verbal skills and intelligence, was the articulate manipulator, serving as liaison for the inmate body with the administration but ever watchful for opportunities to advance his own interests. The *outlaw* was the inmate others feared because he would use violence and force to take what he wanted, living outside the bounds of normal prison society. Finally, the *ding* was also feared, but because his violence was irrational and unpredictable. He was the inmate whose tenuous hold on sanity was destroyed by the hard edges of prison life, and he was shunned because of his unpredictable violence borne of fear and paranoia.

Apparently the social roles found in prisons for men and women were different, although there was some obvious overlap. Some roles were observed in both prisons (*squares, snitches,* and *homies*), and others were similar. For instance, Simmons (Moyer) described a type of female inmate who worked well with the administration and probably was a type of *politician* (1975: 103). She also mentioned women who used violence to get their way, and they may have represented a type of *outlaw* (Simmons, 1975: 108).

Interestingly, sometimes the same social role was explained in different terms. Giallombardo discussed the *homey* relationship found in the women's prison as one created to prevent gossipy women from spreading stories about one another on the outside. The woman befriended those who came from her neighborhood to guard against such "feminine" tendencies. Strangely, Giallombardo did not recognize that *homies* existed in men's prisons as well, and probably not merely to stem the flow of gossip (Giallombardo, 1966: 279). Giallombardo's social roles included *snitchers* (common to men's prisons), *inmate cops, squares* (a parallel to *square johns*), *jive bitches, rap buddies,* and *homies* (common to men's prisons), *boosters, pinners,* and the cluster of roles associated with homosexuality (1966: 105–123).

Real man was a term applied to old-style cons who possessed characteristics such as generosity, integrity, and stoicism in the face of provocation from guards. Giallombardo wrote that there were no corresponding *real women,* because female prisoners did not have the positive qualities associated with the role. Instead, they were described as "spiteful, deceitful and untrustworthy" (Giallombardo, 1966: 130). Heffernan (1972), however, described the *real woman,* who seemed to come fairly close to the concept of the *real man.* This inmate was described as one who was responsible, loyal, and willing to stand up for what she thought (1972: 158). Heffernan's *square, cool,* and *the life* corresponded almost identically to Irwin and Cressey's (1962) *square, thief,* and *con* subcultural roles.

These different subcultural adaptations within a prison also helped explain differential adherence to the inmate code. According to Heffernan (1972), the different normative orientations were more potent predictors of prison adaptation than length of prison sentence or other variables. They also had relevance, in the women's institution, to participation in homosexuality; those who were in *the life* subculture were involved most heavily in prison homosexuality.

These three subcultures were indicative of differential attitudes and adaptations to prison. Findings indicated that those women in *the life* were more comfortable in the prison environment. Only 22 percent of those women rejected prison, compared to 60 percent of those described as belonging to the *cool* subculture and 75 percent of those termed *square* (Heffernan, 1972: 67). Those in *the life* participated more often in the homosexual subculture and had more inmate friends. They totally immersed themselves in the prison life. This group also had the fewest contacts with the outside.

The *cool* type was described as the professional criminal. These women did their time with as little trouble as possible. They participated the least in prison programs, and they limited contacts with other prisoners. They adhered most strongly of all the groups to the inmate code. Although these results seem valid, some problems exist with Heffernan's work, including an arbitrariness in the way individuals were assigned to subcultures.[3]

Mahan (1984a) discussed several types of women inmates in her descriptions of prison life. These included the *junior C.O.s,* who were similar to Giallombardo's *inmate cops; inmates,* who were opportunistic and wanted to do easy time, and were similar to Heffernan's *cool* type; and *convicts*, who were the long termers and probably similar to *the life* type of Heffernan's research (1984a: 361). There are some differences, however, in that Mahan found that the *convicts* upheld some tenets of the inmate code, such as 'Don't rat," "Don't ask for protective custody," and "Take care of your people"—values that Heffernan (1972) and Irwin and Cressey (1962) identified with the *thief* or *cool* roles.

Recent ethnographies of women's prisons have not described these social roles. Owen (1998) has offered the most complete view, and she makes little mention of argot roles or the subcultural adaptations described previously, with the exception of her description of *the mix*. In her ethnography of a California prison, this phrase describes the social world in the prison that many women tried to avoid because it represented trouble. Homosexual activity, drugs, and fighting are the elements of *the mix*, and many of her interviewees reported that they avoided going to the yard for exercise or the dining hall in order to avoid it. Owen's "mix" can be compared to Heffernan's older definition of *the life*.

Snitches A large part of the inmate code is concerned with the proscription against "ratting," or in any way conveying information about inmate activities to prison officials. The importance of the "rat" in the prisoner subculture is made clear by the number of argot terms related to the person who informs on others, or even who is seen as overly friendly with staff. The common perception is that this concern is present in both prisons for men and prisons for women, but the rule against ratting is much more heavily enforced in male prisons.

Giallombardo (1966) believed that women showed greater propensity for snitching than men; however, this was probably a misperception. "Rats" exist in both prisons, and there is no shortage of male or female prisoners willing to talk for personal reasons or for profit. The sanctions employed against "rats" are sometimes more extreme in prisons for men. In both prisons, social isolation is used against individuals, but gossip is used in women's prisons, and sometimes violence, in the form of threats or pushing and shoving sessions. Serious violence, however, is extremely rare in women's prisons, although it does occur.

Several reasons can be suggested for these differences. The stakes involved are probably not as high in prisons for women. Specifically, women do not engage in the same large-scale drug trafficking that can be found in prisons for men. Because of the money involved and the potential risk of good time lost or new charges, sanctions against inmates who expose a drug-smuggling operation or black market activities are more extreme in men's prisons. Owen (1998) reinforces some of the earlier studies of women's prisons in finding that female inmates who are believed to be snitches are avoided and shunned, but do not suffer the extreme physical sanctions that might occur in men's prisons.

Social Organization

The social organization of men's prisons is shaped primarily by gang structures and other pseudopolitical units. In many prisons for men today, gangs are very powerful and control drugs and other types of contraband. Inmates must either join a gang or risk victimization, although some male inmates successfully isolate themselves from the gang structures, and a number of others are rejected by the gangs. Inmates also create clubs in conjunction with formal prison programs. These groups are not gangs but provide safety and order through numbers and a formal hierarchy of power. Men sometimes also bond together in *homey* relationships based on where they are from. Obviously men in prison do have friendships; however, by all accounts, prison life for men is an extremely anomic existence. Men rarely get close to one another, and most ties are based on racial or political allegiance. Male inmates share a subculture with a strict hierarchy of power; those who rule and those who are ruled live in uneasy alliance, marked by frequent battles.

The social organization of a women's prison is comprised of pseudofamilies (make-believe families), friendships, and homosexual liaisons. Instead of grouping in pseudopolitical organizations such as gangs, clubs, and associations, women are more likely to group in familial units, cliques, or dyads. Their allegiances are emotional and personal; their loyalty is to a few rather than to the many.

Hart (1995) found that women in prison had higher levels of social support, meaning "close" or "meaningful" friendships with other prisoners and outsiders. A statistical relationship between social support and psychological well-being existed for women, but not for male inmates. Hart noted that social support in general seems to be gender-related; many studies show women have same-sex friendships and relatives who provide emotional support in times of stress; studies also document the importance of the role of social support for psychological well-being and recovery from illness.

In this study, social support was measured by questions that measured the degree and frequency of intimate relationships. Other measures included those that addressed depression, anxiety, self-esteem, and identity integration as measures of psychological well-being. Significant differences were found between the extent of social support indicated by female prisoners and male prisoners. Interestingly, social support did not seem to be correlated with psychological health for men, as it was for women (Hart, 1995: 79).[4]

Racial Gangs Whereas racial gangs are common in men's prisons, race is not a predominant theme in prisons for women. Although a few reports have described women banding together in racial groupings and discussing racial tensions (Mahan, 1984a & b), most studies have found that integration is the norm. For instance, one study found that although African-American women felt that job placement and other staff treatment was racially discriminatory, there was a high degree of informal racial integration among inmates. According to Kruttschnitt (1983), 55 percent of white inmates had close ties with one or more African-American women, and 75 percent of African-American women had close ties with one or more white women (1983: 583).

Current writers, for the most part, reiterate the earlier finding that racial divisions are fairly unusual in women's prisons. Although Rierden (1997: 52) reported that gang affiliation (including the Latin Queens and The Nation) is flourishing in Niantic, Connecticut, Owen (1998: 73, 151) informed us that race is "deemphasized" and not "critical" to the inmate culture. Although some of Owen's respondents reported that they felt race was a factor and there was discrimination in the way job assignments were determined, most women felt that race was not an issue. Owen saw little evidence of racial gang affiliation, and the pseudofamilies and homosexual relationships she observed often crossed racial lines.

Resource Distribution/Black Market Living in prison involves making accommodations to an institutional environment. This means developing ways of acquiring needed or desired goods, whether or not the formal organization supplies such items. Whereas men tend to operate businesslike black market systems, complete with entrepreneurs and corporate mergers, women distribute contraband and goods through family ties, small cliques, and roommate relationships.

One consistent finding of all research is that female prisoners have less variety and quantity of contraband, including drugs, than male prisoners. One possible explanation for the women's smaller black market in street drugs is that they have less ability to obtain outside drugs, fewer resources, and no organization, all of which are needed to set up a distribution system. Another explanation, as one officer spelled out, is that women get relatively smaller amounts of street drugs because of their greater success in obtaining prescribed drugs from prison officials.

> I don't see as much drunkenness, for example, among women in prison. . . . An awful lot of people will tell you that psychotropic drugs are used more and they're used probably legally perhaps because the medical staff are more prone to give out Valium, probably the same way, you know, if you went into everybody's pocketbook on this floor you'd find a lot of Valium. Doctors seem to give it to the women and it's a drug that's very easily abused. (Pollock, 1981)

No information indicates that a sophisticated black market operates in women's prisons to the extent that it can be found in institutions for men. Although women may engage in petty theft, and contraband is distributed in informal circles, the degree of organization observed in prisons for men does not seem to be present in women's institutions. Women more often tend to share legitimate and contraband goods through informal social networks, such as pseudofamilies, friendships, or roommate groups.

Many inmates prefer to avoid eating in the dining hall. Foodstuffs are purchased, received through the mail, or stolen from the institution to make private meals. Owen's (1998) respondents discussed the range of food that can be cooked using shared food and minimal equipment.

> We have some of the most screaming food go through here you would not believe. . . . I had something the other night that could have come out of a Chinese restaurant. Our whole world revolves around boiled water. (1998: 107)

Food and other products can be bought in the prison commissary. Inmates may receive money from family and friends on the outside, which is held "on account" in the commissary and from which purchases are subtracted. Those who do not have family or friends who are willing or able to send money must find other ways to get resources. Some sell services (such as doing other inmates' laundry), some "sell" boxes (that is, they receive a box in their name for another inmate who has exceeded her allowance), and others have "johns" or "tricks" on the outside that they manipulate in order to receive money (Owen, 1998: 103). Assistance may also come from others in the institution, especially for "homegirls" (women who are from the same neighborhood) who are without resources. Owen (1998: 109) discusses how some inmates receive care packages from "homegirls." These packages are also called welcome wagon packages, and include clothing, hygiene supplies, and food.

Leadership Another aspect of social organization is the existence and power of inmate leaders. In a men's prison, leaders are connected with gangs. Leaders may also arise from formal organizations in the prison, but these individuals often have no real power in the inmate subculture. Leadership in a men's institution tends to be fragmented; no universal leaders emerge, although some men may gain notoriety through violence and intimidation. Leadership is a complicated concept. In a men's prison, leadership may be shown primarily through fear and threat—the gang leader may hold his place through fear rather than respect. Another component of leadership is respect. Some male inmates may gain the respect of numbers of prisoners through the force of their personalities or their interactions with administration; these leaders, however, may not hold formal roles or be connected with a particular gang or following.

Giallombardo (1966) postulated that leaders within the women's system were to be found only within the kinship system; the male or father figure was the unquestioned leader for that family, and to some extent "he" gained status in the eyes of those outside the family by virtue of "his" position. This implies that women value qualities in a leader that parallel the traditional male role in society. One study of leadership in women's prisons found that leadership as observed in a classroom situation bore no relation to age or race, and education was a more influential factor than male or female roles (van Wormer, 1976, 1979). Other studies found that leaders tended to be young, African American, and high interactors, and they were likely to be homosexually active (Moyer, 1980; Simmons, 1975).[5]

Moyer (Simmons) described the women leaders as high interactors and young, African American, narcotics offenders with prior felony records and prison incarcerations. They were part of *the life* and were oriented toward prison life. Possessing forceful characters, they were perceived as willing and able to fight. They might have been homosexual stud broads (Simmons, 1975: 5). Moyer (1980/Simmons, 1975) defined leaders as those who stood up for others and got what they wanted. She found a relationship between interaction and leadership and a somewhat less clear relationship between homosexuality and leadership.

Van Wormer (1976) used an ethological approach to study sex role behavior in several prison classrooms. She examined the relationships between leadership and qualities such as masculinity, homosexual involvement, age, race, and dominance. The author found no significant relationship between leadership and masculinity. Leadership was related to the violence of the crime (using the Mann-Whitney test); it was also related to homosexual involvement. Van Wormer found that education was more important than masculine/feminine (M/F) factors in determining leadership, and pseudofamily involvement bore little relationship to M/F scores.

No significant relationship showed up between leadership and age, race, or other variables.[6] Heffernan (1972) also discussed types of female leaders. The *real woman* was one who told people the truth regardless of consequences, never did anything spiteful, was loyal, and so on.

A recent description of a prison leader is provided by Owen (1998: 33) who met "Divine," a woman who acted as a gatekeeper in Owen's study. Because this woman was well respected and liked by other inmates, her endorsement ("cosigning") of Owen and her project ensured the cooperation of other inmates. Without such an endorsement, Owen may never have acquired the trust of her interviewees. "Divine" was a type of informal prison leader, and her leadership was based on respect and admiration. Owen also discussed "prison smarts" and the respect and reputation that comes with it. Women with "juice" were those who could get things done. Others came to them for help in navigating the unfamiliar world of the prison. Their status increased with their ability to get things done (1998: 170).

Women have been described (by correctional officers) as having difficulty organizing and cooperating with a leader: "Men are more organized than females. With the leaders they'll stand there and they'll face whatever's necessary" (Pollock, 1981). This perceived tendency of women to be resistant to organized leadership may relate to why there are fewer organized protests, fewer lawsuits, and a smaller number of formal inmate organizations in women's prisons.

More recent studies reiterate the belief that women are less likely to organize formally or follow inmate leaders; however, current explanations tend to offer a reason. Several observers have noted that women may be hesitant to oppose prison administrators because they fear being cut off from their children. Owen (1998: 73) quoted an inmate who observed that women will give up a protest or organized resistance because they are afraid of being sent to administrative segregation or losing their family visits. Other observers also have noted that women worry more about losing family visits and will not participate in formal protests because of this fear (Cook and Davies, 1999).

Homosexuality One of the first areas that attracted researchers to women's prisons was the pervasive homosexuality that seemed to characterize most adult women's institutions. The relationships of women in prison seemed to be defined as either familial or connubial; women formed pseudofamilies, with parental and sibling roles in an extended family system, or they entered lesbian liaisons, sometimes formalized by "marriages," complete with mock ministers and marriage certificates. Less permanent relationships existed in "romantic love affairs" accompanied by love notes, hand-holding, or kissing (Leger, 1987). Often one party to a relationship plays a masculine role, with stereotypical short hair, masculine clothing, and assumed authoritativeness and dictatorial behavior. For instance, a quote from Owen's (1998: 106) recent study illustrates this: "When I shared a room with my wife, she would cook for me. But when my wife ain't living with me, I'll have to carry it outside. . . . "A prison relationship also may be one in which neither party exhibits a masculine role or any public signs of affection.

Although it is true that early researchers seemed to be interested in the homosexuality of female prisoners to the exclusion of other issues, the importance these relationships play in a prison for women demands attention. According to most research and inmate accounts, only a portion of the women who engage in homosexual relationships in prison are committed to this orientation as a lifestyle. Prison homosexuality is thus a sociological phenomenon and a subcultural adaptation to a specific situation. Except for a small group whose sexual orientation was same-sex before prison, most women are "in the life" only during their prison stay and revert back to a primarily heterosexual lifestyle upon release. In fact, what might appear as a same-sex relationship may not include a sexual component. Rather, the women involved receive the affection and attention they need in a dyad with a sexual connotation.

While sex is often a commodity for men, it is more often an expression of attachment for women. As one officer explained:

> The homosexuality that is done in the male facilities is usually masked, and there is a percentage of rapes, but I think a lot more of it is permissive, it is sold and so forth. In the female facilities it's not sold, it's not rape, it's just an agreement between two people that they're going to participate and there is a lot of participation. In this facility of 420 people or 430, I would say that maybe 50 percent of the population tends to deal in homosexual acts. (Pollock, 1981)

An inmate echoes this viewpoint:

> [A] lot of women have relationships, which is something you won't find in a men's institution. I mean, [the men] have sex, but they don't have relationships. But these women, it's more than sex to them. It's a relationship. You can get a woman who comes in off the street that ain't never been gay and is crazy about men, and she'll end up having a relationship. But it's just a substitution, I think, for lack of emotional and, you know. It's one way to try to have your needs met. (cited in Girshick, 1999: 86)

Homosexuality in men's prisons may be the result of violent assaults or coercion; older inmates (wolves) offer protection to young men (punks) for sexual favors and commissary articles. It should be noted, however, that some evidence indicates that consensual and affectionate relationships may be more prevalent in men's prisons than believed (see, for instance, Cromwell, 1999). In women's prisons, homosexuality is consensual, and the majority of females (femmes) vie for the favors of the few who have assumed the male role (butches).

Since the early 1900s, when writers first exposed this form of subculture in the women's institution, the forms of the relationships seem to have remained fairly stable. One of the first descriptions of female inmate homosexuality was written more than 80 years ago. Otis (1913) described "unnatural" relationships between white and African-American female inmates. Even today, one of the most obvious differences between men and women is that there seems to be little racial disharmony in institutions for women. Indeed, many homosexual relationships cross racial boundaries. Although homosexuality in prisons for men may also cross racial lines, it is more likely to be an expression of domination rather than the consensual liaison found in women's prisons.

Selling (1931) described four types or stages of involvement, including lesbianism, pseudohomosexuality, mother-daughter relationships, and friendship. He observed that these relationships were a substitute for the natural family group the women had been deprived of by their imprisonment. Although he observed that homosexual involvement progressed in stages, this is no doubt a misconception, since there does not seem to be any progressive nature to the women's involvement in these relationships. Women may be in either make-believe family relationships or homosexual dyads, and may even play a male role in a pseudofamily system while abstaining from sexual relationships.

Other early works described the love notes of girls in juvenile institutions involved in romantic affairs, nicknames adopted by those participating in such relationships, and level of activity (Kosofsky and Ellis, 1958; Taylor, 1968). Halleck and Herski, 1962), using self-reports, found that more than half of the females in the sample participated in some form of homosexuality. The percentage differed, however, depending on the activity. While 69 percent reported they were involved in "girl stuff," 71 percent said they had only kissed; 11 percent said they had been involved in fondling; and only 5 percent had engaged in stimulation of genitals. Nine percent predicted they would continue to be involved (Halleck and Herski, 1962: 913).

Some of these early studies were done in institutions for adolescents and some in prisons for adults, and it would be wise to differentiate between the two because some differences do seem to show up between the involvements of females at different ages. For instance, juvenile institutions seem to manifest the most active pseudofamily systems, while adults seem to be more likely to be involved in active sexual relationships. This difference may result because different needs are being met by the relationships. Whereas adult women are more likely perhaps to need and seek sexual relationships, juveniles' needs are still predominantly for love, support, and excitement. The "girl stuff" reported in juvenile institutions may meet those needs. This difference may also explain the wide range in the estimates of homosexuality. Ward and Kassebaum (1965) reported that although official records indicated only 19 percent of women were involved, more than half the staff felt that 30 to 70 percent of women were involved. Most of the inmate respondents also reported wide ranges, between 30 and 70 percent. Although the authors described homosexuality as kissing and fondling of breasts, manual and/or oral stimulation of the clitoris, and simulation of intercourse, the respondents may have had different definitions of sexual involvement (Ward and Kassebaum, 1965: 167).

Mitchell (1975) also looked at the relationship between homosexual activity and the type of institution. She used questionnaires and interviews in two prisons, one labeled a treatment institution and the other a custody institution. Mitchell found that inmates in both prisons expressed negative views of one another (1975: 27). Homosexuality was more prevalent in the treatment institution (1975: 27). Mitchell suggested that this prevalence was due to more privacy and thus more opportunity in the treatment institution. Propper (1976, 1982) compared seven juvenile institutions, three of which were cocorrectional. She used questionnaires and interviews and collected information on features of the institution, characteristics of the inmates, and the extent of homosexuality and pseudofamily involvement. She found little variability in the amount of homosexuality across the different institutions.

Interestingly, the cocorrectional institutions did not show decreased levels of pseudofamily or homosexual involvement, although fewer females took on the male role in these institutions. In cocorrectional institutions, boys were sometimes recruited to fill the male roles in the pseudofamily systems. Homosexual marriages were rare, and the most common relationships were asexual mother-daughter or sister-sister ties (Propper, 1982: 133). Her findings showed less homosexuality than other studies did; 91 percent reported no homosexual activity. Staff estimates ranged from 7 percent to 14 percent. The background of the inmate, rather than the type of institution, was more predictive of homosexual involvement. Propper found that previous histories of foster care and previous homosexuality explained 29 percent of the variance in homosexual involvement.[7]

There have been several descriptions of the role types in the homosexual subculture of the women's prison. Ward and Kassebaum (1965) discussed the *jailhouse turnout*, which represented, according to the authors, 90 percent of the women involved in homosexual activity. This individual would return to heterosexuality upon release, unlike the "true homosexual," who engaged in such affairs before her incarceration (1965: 167). The individuals who took on masculine characteristics were called *butch, stud broad,* or *drag butch.* These women may have resorted to the masculine role because of the power and privileges it brings in a women's prison, especially if they were not visibly "feminine" to begin with, either because of physical features or size (Ward and Kassebaum, 1965; 168). The *butches* traded their femininity for power. They received goods and services from the *femmes* in a parody of a traditional sexual relationship. The women who took on the masculine role controlled the relationship in much the same way that women experienced male-female relationships outside of prison.

Toigo (1962) described the *hard daddy* role found in one women's institution, which contrasted with the *mom* or *soft mama* role (1962: 9). Characteristics of toughness, belligerence, dominance, dress, and short hair identified the girls who took on the masculine role. Use of nicknames also furthered the illusion, with *hard daddies* taking on masculine variations of their given name. The role of the butch in the women's prison is interesting in its illustration of how women see men. Women evidently pattern their male personalities after the men in their lives, and tend to be dominating, aggressive, and unfaithful.

Many officers believe that the adoption of the masculine role is often a protective device designed to insulate the woman from victimization. Her masculine characteristics are indications that she is not to be exploited or attacked.

> A lot of women when they come . . . they may be extremely feminine on the outside, but as a cover in order not to be picked on, they take on the masculine role, even though they have two or three kids on the outside, they have a husband and things like that. But in order not to be picked on once they come inside, they'll take on the masculine role in order to be left alone by other people. (Pollock, 1981)

Others see the adoption of the masculine role as an option after rejection.

> You either gonna be a femme or you gonna be a dyke, o.k.? If you come in here and nobody is attracted to you as a femme, you gotta belong so you do a complete turnaround, you become the masculine role, you got control, you go after who you want. (Pollock, 1981)

Giallombardo (1966, 1974) described pseudofamilies and homosexuality in an adult women's institution and several juvenile institutions. At Alderson, West Virginia, she described the social roles that are part of homosexuality, including *pinners, penitentiary turnouts, lesbians, femmes, stud broads, tricks, commissary hustlers, chippies, kick partners, cherries, punks,* and *turnabouts* (Giallombardo, 1966: 277–281). These roles describe the masculine or feminine orientation of the woman (*butch, femme,* or the *turnabout* who changes roles), the commitment to a homosexual lifestyle (*lesbian* or *turnouts*), and the motivation in entering a homosexual relationship (the *commissary hustler* for goods, and the *chippie* and *kick partner* for transitory excitement and sexual gratification rather than a lasting relationship). The extent or nature of the women's involvement illustrates the needs that are being met. For some, the prison relationship is no more than an attempt to combat the boredom of prison life. For others, the relationship may be more meaningful and real than any experienced on the outside. For some, an appearance of homosexuality may mask a simple friendship. For some, the relationships may be avenues to acquire desired goods or services.

Another study (Nelson, 1974) found that African-American women were more likely to be active in the homosexual subculture. The author suggested that the African-American woman's socialization to be independent and self-sufficient predisposes her to take up the *butch* role. She also found that African-American women were more likely to have had homosexual relationships before prison. It does seem to be true that African-American women are the dominant participants in the subculture of the prison. They emerge as the leaders and as the most active proponents of the homosexual adaptation. African-American women in prison may have a similar role to African-American men in prison, in that their background and experiences give them more coping skills for prison life. They may have more experience in the institutional environment, coming from foster homes, juvenile institutions, or other state facilities. They are used to being financially independent, even though their backgrounds often exhibit chronic dysfunctional dependent relationships with men. For these reasons, African-American women more often emerge as the dominant force in an institution and shape the subculture to a great degree.

Early explanations of prison homosexuality were psychological and viewed prison homosexuality as an abnormal effect of early developmental problems. Halleck and Herski (1962), for instance, found psychoanalytic reasons for the juvenile's involvement. The authors reported that none in their study had a "mature sexual adjustment," evidently assuming heterosexuality was the only "mature" sexual orientation. Juveniles' problems may have been attributed to sexual contacts with fathers or brothers (20 percent reported such contacts) or a lack of female identification—mothers were often inadequate, and the girls' image of females was that they are weak, helpless, and vulnerable (Halleck and Herski, 1962: 914). The "masculine" partner was reported to receive vicarious gratification of her own dependency needs through unconscious identification with the dependent "feminine" partner (Halleck and Herski, 1962: 914). The unfaithfulness and flighty character of these liaisons was reported to be a coping mechanism designed to protect the girls from their fears of being abandoned (Halleck and Herski, 1962: 918). These early theories ignored the possibility of homosexuality as a rational and free choice of sexual preference. Obviously, the mental health profession has changed its approach to homosexuality, which is no longer widely believed to be an abnormal orientation. However, some sociological aspects of prison homosexuality are still important to consider.

In the women's prison, the *femme* role has the advantage of status in being attached to a "male," some affection, and some sexual gratification; but the *femme* is also required to wait on her partner, to share commissary articles, and to not become jealous if her partner decides to take on another partner. The *butch* role holds the power in the relationship. The *butch* chooses whether or not to remain monogamous; "he" also receives services and goods from the *femme*. Thus, there are many advantages to the *butch* role, even though the disadvantage is that the woman may be suppressing her own personality because she must maintain a male front at all times. The corresponding roles in a prison for men are the *wolf* and *punk* roles. The *butch* role for women has a great many more advantages to it than the *punk* role for men, which involves losing one's sexual identity but receiving no status, power, or goods and services for the loss. It is not surprising that the *butch* role is usually a consensual one, whereas the *punk* is created only by force or coercion. However, even in prisons for men, there are examples of voluntary sex role switches. *Queens* may, by charisma or the protection of powerful friends, freely take on the female role and reap rewards from a courtesan lifestyle, picking and choosing multiple partners at will. These men who act as independent females, however, are rare and must always guard against being dominated by another inmate who would use violence to ensure subordination.

Current writers continue to note the importance of same-sex relationships in women's prisons. Rierden (1997: 59), in her observations and interviews at Niantic, Connecticut, discovered that *studs* and *femmes* were still the slang names for the roles of the woman acting as male aggressor and the feminine partner in the prison. Owen (1998) also discovered that a large percentage of women engaged in same-sex relationships. One inmate explained how it happens.

> The person I met was a friend first. But in a close environment like this, it is a woman's bond. Women are very emotional and we build little families and what have you. And one thing leads to another. You know, it is not force. There is no rapes and all that shit they have in the movies. . . . It was like the girl was irresistible. . . . (Owen, 1998: 138)

Owen's (1998) interviewees described same-sex relationships in a manner similar to that found in earlier studies. Women who take on the male role (*stud broad, husband, butch,* or *little boy*) receive goods and services and are in demand. They can be recognized by their masculine nickname and by the way they wear their clothes, cut their hair, and behave. Relationships are marked by mock marriages, but are also transitory and volatile. *Box whores, canteen whores,* or *hoovers* are those women who are exploited for their commissary goods. Women who are gay explain that they stay away from *the mix* because of the promiscuity and game-playing that goes on (Owen, 1998: 146–149).

Pseudofamilies (Make-Believe Families) A different phenomenon from homosexual relationships is the pseudofamilies that exist in some prisons. These relationships may or may not involve sex. Most of the relationships are familial, including parent-child, sibling-sibling, and even extended family relationships, such as grandparents, aunts, and uncles. Each relationship is a reflection of the stereotypical one in society. "Fathers" are authoritarian and guiding; "mothers" are nurturing and comforting. Siblings fight; parents control (Foster, 1975).

Adoption of role types has something to do with personal characteristics, but roles are not necessarily demographically accurate. For instance, an older woman may more often play the mother role, but some mature younger women who are respected also may collect "daughters." The mother-daughter relationship is the most common, and some mothers may have many daughters in the institution who look to her for comfort and support. She, in turn, listens to their problems and gives advice. In larger, more elaborate family systems, a mother might have a husband who becomes a father to her daughters (but not necessarily). In some institutions, the family systems are complex, and the intergenerational ties are very complicated. Most writers who describe these social relationships point out that women may form pseudofamilies because of their need for such roles; in effect, their identity is dependent on being "mother," "sister," or other familial role (Culbertson and Fortune, 1986: 33).

Toigo found that some pseudofamilies possessed more status than others in the juvenile institution he studied (1962: 10). Staff legitimated the presence of these family systems by rewarding family leaders for controlling their inmate family members. Indeed, it seems that if the staff use the informal subculture to control inmate behavior at all, most often it is the family diey utilize. For instance, a mother may be approached to keep her daughter from "cutting up," if staff guess the woman may be suicidal or depressed but do not have enough reason to put her under observation. The family leaders also may be approached and asked to calm down a consistently troublesome inmate if she is a member of a family. This parallels staff use of gang leaders to control the inmate population in a prison for men.

Commitments to such family systems differ. Whereas some women take the relationship very seriously, often the family relationships are more of a joke or a game than something influential or important in the woman's life. What may influence her commitment to the family are the other elements that make up the woman's prison life. When a women nears release or when she has maintained strong and continuing ties with her natural family, especially her children, the pull of the pseudofamily is weak. When a woman has come from a poor environment on the outside, when she is isolated from other ties, when the prison world is her only world, then often the relationships she develops there become more real than any she had on the outside. In a sense, she may be creating the type of family she wishes she had. A woman who has come from an abusive, tortured home may seek the mother she never had; the woman who is severed from her children, unable to mother, may displace her need to mother her own children by directing this maternal interest to other women in the prison.

One interesting observation about female inmates' involvement in pseudofamilies and dyadic relationships is the women's attempt to create ideal relationships that probably do not represent their own experiences in real life. The inmate "mother" may be a better mother to her inmate daughters than she was to her own children before imprisonment. The inmate couple may seek a romantic bond that neither woman ever before experienced, since many in prison have had only poor and exploitative relationships with men. Indeed, because of the limitations of the prison environment and the ever-present supervision, the inmate "couple" may be, for the first time in their lives, engaging in a relationship where the bond is one of affection and romance rather than sex.

Fox (1984) found that inmate participation in pseudofamilies changed between the 1970s and the 1980s. He stated that during the 1970s a large number of youthful offenders (ages 17 to 24) were sent to Bedford Hills, and they were more often a part of pseudofamily units than were older women. The administration used the kinship systems to control these "disruptive daughters," since more than half reported involvement. Close to half also reported close personal relationships, sometimes including sex, but often only mimicking the *butch-femme* relationship (Fox, 1984: 26; also see Fox, 1982). However, in the second half of the 1970s, visiting policies and programming became more liberalized. More women became active in social programs; also, men from a nearby facility came in for recreation and, for a short time, dances. Kinship systems, once strong, began to dissipate. By late 1978, only 27 percent of women reported active membership in a kinship unit; all families had fewer than four members; and involvement in close personal relationships also declined (Fox, 1984: 32).

Today, family programs and furloughs help strengthen real family ties. Women are more politicized in that they maintain and foster ties outside the community and enjoy some attention from community interest groups. This permeability decreases dependence on prison life and deprivation; consequently, the prison family system is less necessary. However, current writers still document its existence. Owen (1998) writes that the prison family still exists, at least in the California prison where she conducted interviews.

> The family is when you come to prison, and you get close to someone, if it is a stud-broad, that's your dad or your brother—I got a lot of them here. If it's a femme, then that is your sister. Some who is just a new commitment, you try to school them into doing things right, that is your pup. But if somebody is a three-termer, and doing a lot of time like I have, then that is your dog, road dog—prison dog. (Owen, 1998: 134)

> A kid is someone you take care of and then her friend would be your "kid-in-law." Now this is my mom, even though she is younger than me and this is my girlfriend. She is Mom because she always picks me up off the ground when everybody else knocks me down and walks all over me. . . . (Owen, 1998: 135)

Owen found little evidence of racial gangs, and her interviewees reported that almost everyone was involved in some type of family relationship (Owen, 1998: 136).

Girshick (1999) and Rierden (1997) also reported the existence of pseudofamilies. Although many women did not participate in this form of social relationship, the interviewees reported its prevalence:

> I see it like maybe the reason they do that is 'cause they don't know who they [sic] father is, maybe they don't have any sisters or brothers, maybe their mother's passed away, maybe they don't have any kids and want kids, want a mother, want a father, want a brother, want a sister. I don't want none of it. It's not real, for one thing. (Girshick, 1999: 91)

Dobash, Dobash, and Gutteridge (1986) provide a cross-cultural note. They found no evidence of pseudofamilies or homosexuality in Cornton Vale in Scotland or Holloway Prison in England. The women there were socially isolated, and when asked to name friends, few named other inmates and some even named staff members. It may be that the excessive maternality and strictness of the staff at these small prisons prevented the emergence of a homosexual subculture. An alternative hypothesis is that the women came from stronger families on the outside, although this hypothesis does not seem to be supported by the women's backgrounds, which were just as fragmented as American women's. Taylor (1968), on the other hand, did find romantic liaisons between girls in an Australian Borstal; thus, these social relationships may be a cross-cultural phenomenon after all.

"The Mix"

Many women in prison choose to isolate themselves and have minimal participation in the social world of the prison, moving between school or work and their cells, seldom venturing outside their created zones of security: "I pretty much deal with all positive people. . . . That's a lesson that I've learned here. I could be with this crew that gets into trouble, but you know, I shun them now" (DeGroot, 1998: 85).

In fact, in Owen and Bloom's (1995a) study, 60 percent of women reported spending the majority of their free time in their rooms. Girshick (1999: 83) also said that most of the women she interviewed reported that they spent most of their free time in their rooms where it was "safer and quieter." Others adapt to prison by full participation in the underworld of the prison. Owen's (1998: 3) recent study described the subcultural adaptation of *the mix,* as "a continuation of the behavior that led to imprisonment, a life revolving around drugs, intense, volatile, and often destructive relationships, and non—rule abiding behavior." She reported that some women "dip into" this world at the beginning of their prison terms but avoid it when they start to participate in programming. According to Owen, most women avoid *the mix* (1998: 8). One difference between Heffernan (1972) and Owen (1998: 8) is that Heffernan observed that homosexuality was a part of *the life* but Owen reported that pseudofamilies and homosexual dyads were not a part of *the mix* and, in fact, were sometimes the means to avoid its temptation.

It is clear that some women continue to "rip and roar" through their prison sentence, engaging in behaviors similar to those that led them to prison in the first place. Owen (1998) offered no demographic profile of the type of woman who chooses *the mix* versus those who prefer to stay away from it. One gets the impression from her interviewees, however, that the women who avoid it are those who have become tired of a criminal lifestyle, have realized the importance of children and family, and have engaged in a journey of self-discovery that helps them make more constructive choices in their lives. Some women remarked that they maintain their reputation for toughness, even though they no longer are tempted to fight: "But I still put out a reputation of hardness; that makes [the other women] not tempt me to fight or challenge me to prove anything" (Owen, 1998: 71).

"CUTTING UP," SUICIDE, AND SELF-ABUSE

Women may be more prone to expressions of despair that include self-injury. Women may attempt suicide or mutilate themselves because of emotional problems that existed prior to imprisonment, but there is no doubt that the deprivations of the prison also spur some women to such desperate acts. Women may experience the deprivation of family roles more severely than men do. They may find that the institutionalized lifestyle of the prison provides little comfort or succor. One study in England showed an average of 1.5 incidents of self-injury each week in Holloway prison (Cookson, 1977). The women involved tended to be younger with more previous incarcerations or psychiatric institutionalizations, and most had committed self-injury at least once before. They had higher hostility scores, indicating the close relationship between inwardly and outwardly directed aggression. Also, self-injury tended to occur in copycat epidemics at times (Cookson, 1977: 347).

Fox (1975, 1992) also studied self-mutilation among imprisoned women. His study at Bedford Hills indicated that women were more likely than men to attempt suicide or injure themselves; in other words, women tended to turn their aggression inward, whereas men turned their aggression outward. An officer described this tendency in the following way:

> I have seen it on a number of occasions. She won't harm anybody else but she will start to destruct her own body. I've seen them have cuts from here up to their shoulders. They've had stitches in: brand new stitches were put in and they got back here from the hospital and they would sit here and pull the stitches back out again. If you look at their arms, the men don't do it as much as the women, but if you look at the females' arms, they'll sit and they'll just cut and cut and cut. They don't want to hurt anybody else and the only person that they think of hurting is themselves. (Pollock, 1981)

Suicide risk increases with depression, low self-esteem, and social isolation (Scott et al., 1982). Female inmates also identify different reasons for "cutting up" than male inmates do. Women primarily feel the loss of relationships and support in prison; men suffer from other deprivations. Women are less able to retreat into a "manly stance" and consequently feel the loss of interpersonal support more than men do. Women also are prone to release their emotion in a catharsis: 64 percent of the females sampled had this self-release theme in their responses, whereas only 13 percent of the males sampled exhibited this theme (Fox, 1975: 194). This theme involves the need to express pent-up emotions, with a resulting feeling of relief when the person "explodes."

Another explanation for "cutting up" and suicide has to do with feelings of control and a need to feel something, even if it is pain. Women's life experiences have often been traumatic, and psychological defense mechanisms create a type of disconnection from one's self and emotions. "Cutting up" is often experienced by women as a way to reconnect with their emotions, a way to make sure they are still alive (Pollock, 1998: 29–31).

CHAPTER TWO
The Race Issue

THE WICKED WEB WE WEAVE

Kelley Christopher

"Part of the mechanics of oppressing people is to pervert them to the
extent that they become their own oppressors."

—Kumasi, 2009

Despite the low number of prisons and those incarcerated during the 1970's, the number of people incarcerated today is staggering. There are 2.4 million adults in prison today and another 5 million under some form of correctional supervision—on probation or parole (U.S. Department of Justice). In addition, no one group is overrepresented more than black Americans. One in three African-American men will serve time in prison if current trends continue and more black men are in prison or jail, on probation or parole than were enslaved in 1850. Not surprisingly, however, mass incarceration tends to be viewed—if examined at all—as a criminal justice issue as opposed to a civil rights or racial justice issue. Prisons, sadly, have become the new cotton field.

Beginning in the 1960's and through the 1970's, crime rates increased—particularly street crime and homicide which quadrupled and doubled, respectively. There are many theories about the sharp increase but it can actually be accounted for by the "baby boom" generation who, at that time, came into the peak crime-committing age—the number of young men in the 15 to 24 age group. At exactly the same time, unemployment rates for black men rose sharply, due in large part to a changing workforce they were ill-equipped to compete in. Instead of investigating the economic and demographic factors that contributed to the increase in crime rates, the media sensationalized it and speculated about a trend of lawlessness, lack of morality, and the absence of social stability that appeared on the heels of the Civil Rights Movement.

The racial imagery presented by the media following the assassination of Dr. Martin Luther King Jr. in 1968 only served to fuel the argument that civil rights for black Americans only led to rampant crime. Northern conservatives argued that, having spread out the welcome mat to blacks migrating from the south, cities like Rochester and Philadelphia were repaid with "black discontent and crime-ridden slums" (Weaver, 2007). In his 1964 presidential campaign, Barry Goldwater aggressively exploited the fear of black crime and the riots, laying the foundation for what became the "war on crime" that followed many years later under the Reagan administration.

On the heels of the Civil Rights movement came a steep decline in legitimate work opportunities for black Americans and a new enemy surfaced—crack cocaine. Crack became a convenient—and destructive—means of survival for an already-marginalized group of Americans. The drug was introduced into the fragile communities just three years after Regan's Drug War was launched. Some call this convenient, some call it an unfortunate coincidence, and some call it a conspiracy. Whatever the case, crack transformed these vulnerable communities into war zones.

In 1986, the media proclaimed that crack cocaine was the biggest story since the Vietnam War. Articles commonly reinforced ugly stereotypes already prevalent at the time— veiled innuendos of black women as crack whores and black males as predators or gang-bangers. During the same year, $2 billion was allocated to the drug war and new legislation authorized the death penalty for some drug-related crimes. It also allowed illegally obtained evidence to be admitted during drug trials. The final nail in the coffin came with the signing of the Anti-Drug Abuse Act of 1986. This new legislation included some of the harshest penalties to date for drug offenses including mandatory minimum sentences that were 100 to 1 for crack cocaine versus cocaine in its' powder form.

It is difficult for me to evaluate that legislation and find no racial bias in its' penning; crack cocaine is associated with blacks and powder cocaine with whites. Something else to consider; black males make up only 6% of Americas' population yet they make up 39% of our prison population. How does this happen in a "just" society? Better yet, how does this happen in a "just" criminal justice system? Are black males born with a higher propensity for drug use and/or criminal attributes? That concept is not only absurd but it borders with preposterous. Or could there be other social ills that perpetuate a cycle of disadvantage for some groups of Americans?

Despite its' suspicious penning, the Anti-Drug Abuse Act of 1986 passed through legislation without a critical voice being raised or anyone sounding the racism alarm. One senator, however, did proclaim that crack was merely a scapegoat used to distract the public attention from the *real* causes of Americas' social ills. He insisted that,

> If we blame crime on crack, our politicians are off the hook. Forgotten are the failed schools, the malign welfare programs, the desolate neighborhoods, the wasted years. Only crack is to blame. One is tempted to think that if crack did not exist, someone somewhere would have received a federal grant to develop it (Provine 2007).

The War on Drugs, however, proved to be very popular among white voters, particularly those opposed to affirmative action, civil right reinforcement, and black progress in general. The War was strategically cloaked in race-neutral language and it afforded whites opposed to racial reform a unique opportunity to stunt black progress without being openly exposed or charged with racism; and on to an unprecedented age of mass incarceration we forged.

In the United States, drug convictions are *the* single most prevalent cause for the explosion in incarceration rates. Drug offenses alone account for half of the increase in the state prison population and for two-thirds of the increase in federal inmate populations between 1985 and 2000 (Mauer 2006:33). To put that into perspective, in 1980, there were 41,100 people in prison for drug offenses; today that number exceeds a half million—an increase of 1,100%. Since the declaration of the drug war, 31 million people have been arrested for a drug offense (Mauer and King 2007). The fact is that there are more people in prison today on drug charges than there were in prison for *all* reasons in 1980 (Mauer 2009). The War on Drugs has contributed more to the systematic mass incarceration of people of color than anything we have ever experienced in our society.

Myth: The War on Drugs is aimed at the big-time drug dealers or drug "kingpins."

Fact: The vast majority of those arrested are for minor drug offenses. In 2005 alone, four out of five drug arrests were for possession and one out of five for sales. (U.S. Department of Justice).

Myth: The War on Drugs aimed its resources at *dangerous* drugs.

Fact: Marijuana is less dangerous than tobacco or alcohol but arrests for its possession accounted for almost 80% of the increase in drug arrests during the 1990's (Mauer 2005). Moreover, the vast majority of people in state prisons for drug offenses have no history of significant drug selling activity or violence.

In addition, the 1988 surgeon general's report lists tobacco as a more dangerous drug than marijuana. Supporting that claim, Francis Young, an administrative law judge for the Drug Enforcement Administration found that there are no credible medical reports that provide evidence that consuming marijuana, in any dose, has ever caused a single death. To put that in perspective, tobacco kills nearly 390,000 people annually and alcohol is responsible for roughly 150,000 deaths a year (Bandow 1991). Dress it up however you like, but the War on Drugs is the poster child for unprecedented and unrelenting punitiveness.

Ninety-five percent of all criminal cases are plea bargained out before they ever get to the trial phase (Fuller 2014). Yet the number of drug arrests that result in a prison sentence has quadrupled since 1980. The result has been a prison construction boom equal to nothing the world has ever witnessed. The number of people incarcerated soared from approximately 300,000 in 1980 to more than 2 million by the year 2000. By the end of 2007, more than 7 million people in the United States were in prison or under some form of correctional control (probation, parole, or jail) (Foster 2006).

There are practicing judges, however, that do not necessarily support mandatory sentencing laws attached to the Anti-Drug Abuse Act of 1986; it does, in fact, strips them of all discretionary authority to consider each defendant and each case on an individual basis. Nevertheless, harsh mandatory minimum sentencing has been upheld by the U.S. Supreme Court time and time again. For example, in *Harmelin v Michigan*, the Court upheld a *life sentence* for a defendant with no prior convictions who attempted to sell 23 ounces of crack cocaine (*Harmelin v Michigan*). The sentence in that case was found to be "reasonably proportionate" by the Supreme Court. Prior to 1986, the longest sentence Congress had ever imposed for possession of *any* drug in *any* amount was one year. It is remarkable that in the United States a life sentence is considered appropriate for a first-time drug offender—a sentence unheard of in any other developed country in the world. It is easy to justify tough mandatory minimum sentences for violent offenders—I can certainly get my head around that—but these sentences are most often imposed against non-violent drug offenders. That should, at the very least, cause us all to pause and maybe do some re-evaluation.

Many do not, in fact, agree with the lunacy of harsh mandatory minimums for drug offenders—even Supreme Court judges. At the 2003 American Bar Association's annual conference, Supreme Court Justice Anthony Kennedy condemned them stating that,

> Our {prison} resources are misspent, our punishments too severe, our sentences too loaded. I can accept neither the necessity nor the wisdom of federal mandatory minimum sentences. In all too many cases, mandatory minimum sentences are unjust (Jacobson 2005).

The story does not end once the offender has been convicted and served his/her time; nothing could be further from the truth. Once an individual is labeled a felon—whether they actually served time or not—they are relegated to a lifetime of discrimination and social and economic exclusion. Surprisingly, most individuals convicted of a felony do not, in fact, serve time at all. Yet they are ineligible for any public assistance, mandated to report the conviction on job applications, barred from public housing, and denied licenses for dozens of professions. These are, many times, the very things that will enable an individual to get back on stable ground and a decent shot at a pro-social and productive existence. For people guilty of merely possessing a small amount of recreational drugs or for experiencing drug addiction, being locked out of mainstream society becomes a new way of life—permanently.

Given these chronic conditions, it should not surprise us that a large percentage of people labeled felons enter the perpetual cycle of freedom/incarceration. According to the Bureau of Justice Statistics, nearly 68% of these individuals were re-arrested at least once within three years for a new offense—the vast majority for drug or property offenses or for offenses against pubic order (Bureau of Justice Statistics). If we continue to ignore a social structure that co-signs on this atrocity, this trend will most certainly continue. The criminal justice system today, like American society in general, simply reflects our nations' socioeconomic and racial boundaries.

The idea that most illegal drug sales and use occur only in the "hood" is not only ludicrous but it is also ignorant. Drug trafficking occurs there, of course, but it occurs *everywhere*; one does not need to make a special trip to the ghetto to purchase their drug of choice. Yet black men have been escorted into state and federal prisons on drug charges at a rate thirteen times higher than white men (Alexander 2012). The racial bias inherent in the drug war is the main reason why one in every four black men was incarcerated in 2006 compared to one in every 106 white men in the same year. The harsher truth is that one in every nine black men between the ages of 20 and 35 was behind bars in the same year (Alexander 2012). These are, for many Americans, the peak years for earning an education and embarking on their careers. These facts cannot be explained away by claiming that blacks simply have higher rates of drug use or drug activity. Even if that were the case, we as a society should be asking why. Yet we are silent. The hard truth is that there are curious—and abhorrent—racial and socioeconomic disparities inherent in the drug war; a war we are surely losing.

We claim to have embraced an age of color-blindness. To what, then, do we attribute extraordinary racial disparities within our criminal justice system? Could it be plain old-fashioned racism? Most law enforcement officials and politicians fiercely deny and publicly condemn racial discrimination of any kind and when accused of such an atrocity, outrage and horror is the typical response. Gone are the days when black men were being lynched but that by no means racism is a thing of the past. A dose of common sense is long overdue in public discussions about racial bias within our criminal justice system. What should be painfully obvious is that the American system of mass-incarceration operates with stunning efficiency to remove people of color from mainstream society, lock them in cages, and then release them back into society ill-equipped to serve the remainder of their lives as second-class citizens with any hope for a pro-social life. What in the world are we thinking?

How does this happen? It is surprisingly simple. First we grant law enforcement officials total discretion in regards to who to stop, search, arrest, and charge for drug offenses. This actually ensures that conscious and unconscious racial stereotypes and beliefs operate unchecked. Second, close the courthouse doors to any and all claims of racial discrimination proposed by any and all litigants or defendants. The courts require that anyone who attempts to challenge racial bias in the system show—in advance—clear proof of intentional racial discrimination. This simple two-step process has helped produce one of the most extraordinary systems of racialized social control the world has ever seen (Alexander 2012).

Warren McClesky was a black man facing the death penalty in 1987 after being convicted of killing a white police officer during an armed robbery in Georgia. McClesky, represented by the NAACP Legal Defense and Education Fund, challenged his death sentence on the grounds that Georgia's death penalty guidelines were saturated with racial bias and this violated the Eighth and Fourteenth Amendments. In his arsenal were the results of the Baldus study, authored by Professor David Baldus. The study found that defendants convicted of killing whites received the death penalty at a rate eleven times higher than for defendants convicted of killing blacks. Prosecutors are not blameless in this process; Georgia prosecutors sought the death penalty in 70% of cases that involved black defendants whose victims were white and in only 19% of the cases involving white defendants whose victims were black (*McClesky v Kemp* 1989).

Baldus and his colleagues were mindful of the fact that numerous factors may influence the decision-making process of prosecutors, juries, and judges other than race and because of this, Baldus subjected the raw data to rigorous and highly sophisticated statistical analysis to try and explain the disparities. Yet even when accounting for thirty-five non-racial variables, their team of researchers found that defendants charged with killing whites were 4.3 times more likely to receive the death penalty than defendants charged with killing blacks. I am sure I do not need to remind the reader that a death sentence, once carried out, is a permanent sanction; there is no going back and no room for mistakes. Yet they have been made more times than we like to acknowledge. (For more information see www.theinnocenceproject.org).

The Court accepted the results of the Baldus Study and its statistical validity yet they rejected McCleskys' claim of racial bias. The Court insisted that McClesky must prove that the prosecutor sought the death penalty because of race or that the jury in this case had imposed a death sentence on racial grounds. In addition, the Court decreed, the validity of the Baldus Study may show racial discrimination in Georgia's death penalty system but did not prove unequal treatment under the law in McClesky's particular case.

This presents two important considerations: how was it possible for McClesky's legal defense to prove that the prosecutor sought the death penalty because of racial bias? Second, how was it possible to prove that the jury in this case imposed the death penalty because of racial bias? Very few people will openly admit to racism even when the stakes are low much less when one has voted to terminate the life of a fellow human being. According to Michelle Alexander (2012), there is good reason to believe that the *McClesky* decision was ". . . not really about the death penalty at all; rather, the Court's opinion was driven by a desire to immunize the entire criminal justice system from claims of racial bias." (Alexander 2012).

Consider the statement made by Judge Clyde Cahill of the Federal District of Missouri in reference to another curious case. Judge Cahill was assigned to a case that also ended in an eyebrow-raising conclusion—the case of Edward Clary. Eighteen-year-old Clary had been caught in the St. Louis airport with 50 grams (less than two ounces) of crack cocaine. He had never been arrested, had never attempted to sell drugs, and had no prior contact with law enforcement. Keep in mind that a conviction for 500 grams of *powder* cocaine elicits a five-year sentence while only 5 grams of rock cocaine earns the same. Clary was convicted in Federal court and sentenced under Federal laws that sanction crack cocaine offenses one hundred times more severely than powder cocaine. The sentencing judge in Clary's case—an eighteen-year-old, first time offender—imposed a minimum of ten years in federal prison. On appeal, Judge Cahill conclude with,

The presumption of innocence is now a legal myth. The 100-to-1 ratio, coupled with mandatory minimum sentencing provided by federal statute, has created a situation that reeks with inhumanity and injustice... If young white males were being incarcerated at the same rate as young black males, the statute would have been amended long ago (*United States v Clary* 1994).

Judge Cahill sentenced Clary as if the drug he possessed was powder cocaine and not in its rock form. Clary served the four years imposed by Judge Cahill and was released.

There are many similarities between the days of Jim Crow and now. The Jim Crow era mandated and co-signed on residential segregation and relegated black citizens to the poorest sections of towns and cities across America. This was made possible—in part—by exclusive real estate covenants that barred racial and ethnic minorities of all kinds from renting or purchasing homes in white communities. Sometimes these restrictions targeted Hispanics, sometimes they targeted Jewish Americans—but they always targeted blacks. Mass incarceration operates in much the same way. Rather than confining black Americans in ghettos, mass incarceration practices lock them in cages, often hundreds of miles from home, and a viable support system. Most prisons today are located in very rural and hard-to-get-to locations and far from the sight of mainstream society. Interestingly, rural communities house only 20% of the U.S. population yet 60% of new prison construction (Wagner 2013). Out of sight, out of mind.

RESOURCES

Alexander, Michelle. (2012). *The new Jim Crow: Mass incarceration in the age of color-blindness.* New York, NY: The New Press.

Bandow, Doug. (1991). War on Drugs or War on America? *Stanford Law and Policy Review*, 3: 242, 245.

Beckett, Katherine. (1997). *Making crime pay: Law and order in contemporary politics.* New York: Oxford University Press.

Foster, Burk. 2006. Corrections: The Fundamentals. New Jersey. Pearson.

Fuller, John. 2013. Think Criminology. New Jersey. Pearson.

Harmelin v Michigan, 501 U.S. 967 (1991).

Jacobson, Michael. (2005). *Downsizing prisons: How to reduce crime and end mass incarceration.* New York: New York University Press.

Kumasi. (2009). Crips and Bloods: Made in America. Stacy Peralta.

Mauer, Marc. (2006). *Race to incarcerate*, rev. ed. New York: The New York Press.

Mauer, Marc and Ryan King. (2005). *The War on Marijuana: The Transformation of the War on Drugs in the 1990's.* Washington, D.C.: The Sentencing Project.

Mauer, Marc and Ryan King. (2007). A 25-year quagmire: The "war on drugs" and its impact on American society. Washington, D.C.: The Sentencing Project.

Mauer, Marc. (2009). Testimony of Marc Mauer for the House Judiciary Subcommittee on Crime, Terrorism, and Homeland Security, 111th Cong., *Hearing on Unfairness in Federal Cocaine Sentencing: Is it Time to Crack the 100 to 1 Disparity?*

McClesky v Kemp, 481 U.S. 279, 327, Brennan, J., dissenting.

Provine, Doris Marie. (2007). *Unequal under the law: Race in the War on Drugs.* Chicago: Chicago University Press. Citing the Congressional Record 132: September 24, 1986.

United States v Clary, 846 F.Supp. 768, 796–97 (E.D. Mo. 1994).

Wagner, Peter. Prisoners of the Census. 2013. www.prisonersofthecensus.org.

Weaver, Velsa M. (2007) Frontlash: Race and the development of punitive crime policy. *Studies in American Political Development*, 242.

THE SENTENCING PROJECT

FACT SHEET: TRENDS IN U.S. CORRECTIONS

Rate of Incarceration per 100,000, by Gender, Race, & Ethnicity, 2011

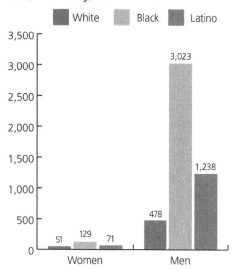

Source: Carson, E.A., Sabol, W.J. (2012). *Prisoners in 2011.* Washington, D.C.: Bureau of Justice Statistics.

RACIAL DISPARITIES

More than 60% of the people in prison today are people of color. For black men in their thirties, 1 in every 10 is in prison or jail on any given day. These trends have been intensified by the disproportionate impact of the War on Drugs.

People in State and Federal Prisons, by Race and Ethnicity, 2011

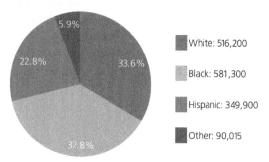

White: 516,200
Black: 581,300
Hispanic: 349,900
Other: 90,015

Source: Carson, E.A., Sabol, W.J. (2012). *Prisoners in 2011.* Washington, D.C.: Bureau of Justice Statistics.

Lifetime Likelihood of Imprisonment

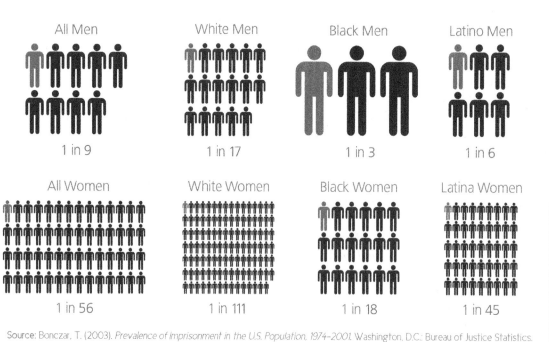

All Men	White Men	Black Men	Latino Men
1 in 9	1 in 17	1 in 3	1 in 6

All Women	White Women	Black Women	Latina Women
1 in 56	1 in 111	1 in 18	1 in 45

Source: Bonczar, T. (2003). *Prevalence of Imprisonment in the U.S. Population, 1974–2001.* Washington, D.C.: Bureau of Justice Statistics.

JUSTICE FOR ALL? CHALLENGING RACIAL DISPARITIES IN THE CRIMINAL JUSTICE SYSTEM

Marc Mauer

There are many indicators of the profound impact of disproportionate rates of incarceration in communities of color. Perhaps the most stark among these are the data generated by the U.S. Department of Justice that project that if current trends continue, one of every three black males born today will go to prison in his lifetime, as will one of every six Latino males. (Rates of incarceration for women overall are lower than for men, but similar racial/ethnic disparities pertain.) Regardless of what one views as the causes of this situation, it should be deeply disturbing to all Americans that these figures represent the future for a generation of children growing up today.

This article will first present an overview of the factors that contribute to racial disparity in the justice system, and then it will recommend changes in policy and practice that could reduce these disparities without compromising public safety.

In order to develop policies and practices to reduce unwarranted racial disparities in the criminal justice system, it is necessary to assess the factors that have produced the current record levels of incarceration and racial/ethnic disparity. These are clearly complicated issues, but four areas of analysis are key:

r Disproportionate crime rates

r Disparities in criminal justice processing

r Overlap of race and class effects

r Impact of "race neutral" policies

DISPROPORTIONATE CRIME RATES

A series of studies conducted during the past thirty years has examined the degree to which disproportionate rates of incarceration for African Americans are related to greater involvement in crime. Examining national data for 1979, criminologist Alfred Blumstein concluded that 80 percent of racial disparity could be explained by greater involvement in crime, although a subsequent study reduced this figure to 76 percent for the 1991 prison population. (Alfred Blumstein, *Racial Disproportionality of U. S. Prison Populations Revisited*, 64 U. COLO. L. REV. 743,751 (1993).) But a similar analysis of 2004 imprisonment data by sentencing scholar Michael Tonry now finds that only 61 percent of the black incarceration rate is explained by disproportionate engagement in criminal behavior. (Michael Tonry & Matthew Melewski, *The Malign Effects of Drug and Crime Control Policies on Black Americans,* 37 CRIME & JUSTICE 1 (2008).) Thus, nearly 40 percent of the racial disparity in incarceration today cannot be explained by differential offending patterns.

In addition, the national-level data may obscure variation among the states. A 1994 state-based assessment of these issues found broad variation in the extent to which higher crime rates among African Americans explained disproportionate imprisonment. (Robert D. Crutchfield, George S. Bridges & Susan R. Pitchford, *Analytical and Aggregation Biases in Analyses of Imprisonment: Reconciling Discrepancies in Studies of Racial Disparity,* 31 J. RES. CRIME & DELINQ. 166, 179 (1994).) Thus, while greater involvement in some crimes is related to higher rates of incarceration for African Americans, the weight of the evidence to date suggests that a significant proportion of the disparities is not a function of disproportionate criminal behavior.

DISPARITIES IN CRIMINAL JUSTICE PROCESSING

Despite changes in leadership and growing attention to issues of racial and ethnic disparity in recent years, these disparities in criminal justice decision making still persist at every level of the criminal justice system. This does not necessarily suggest that these outcomes represent conscious efforts to discriminate, but they nonetheless contribute to excessive rates of imprisonment for some groups.

Disparities in processing have been seen most prominently in the area of law enforcement, with documentation of widespread racial profiling in recent years. National surveys conducted by the U.S. Department of Justice find that while African Americans may be subject to traffic stops by police at similar rates to whites, they are three times as likely to be searched after being stopped.

Disparate practices of law enforcement related to the "war on drugs" have been well documented in many jurisdictions and, in combination with sentencing policies, represent the most significant contributor to disproportionate rates of incarceration. This effect has come about through two overlapping trends. First, the escalation of the drug war has produced a remarkable rise in the number of people in prisons and jails either awaiting trial or serving time for a drug offense—increasing from 40,000 in 1980 to 500,000 today. Second, a general law enforcement emphasis on drug-related policing in communities of color has resulted in African Americans being prosecuted for drug offenses far out of proportion to the degree that they use or sell drugs. In 2005, African Americans represented 14 percent of current drug users, yet they constituted 33.9 percent of persons arrested for a drug offense and 53 percent of persons sentenced to prison for a drug offense.

Evidence of racial profiling by law enforcement does not suggest by any means that all agencies or all officers engage in such behaviors. In fact, in recent years, many police agencies have initiated training and oversight measures designed to prevent and identify such practices. Nevertheless, such behaviors still persist to some degree and clearly thwart efforts to promote racial justice.

OVERLAP OF RACE AND CLASS EFFECTS

Disparities in the criminal justice system are in part a function of the interrelationship between race and class and reflect the disadvantages faced by low-income defendants. This can be seen most prominently in regard to the quality of defense counsel. While many public defenders and appointed counsel provide high-quality legal support, in far too many jurisdictions the defense bar is characterized by high caseloads, poor training, and inadequate resources. In an assessment of this situation, the American Bar Association concluded that "too often the lawyers who provide defense services are inexperienced, fail to maintain adequate client contact, and furnish services that are simply not competent." (ABA STANDING COMM. ON LEGAL AID & INDIGENT DEFENDANTS, GIDEON'S BROKEN PROMISE: AMERICA'S CONTINUING QUEST FOR RACIAL JUSTICE, (2004).)

The limited availability of private resources disadvantages low-income people in other ways as well. For example, in considering whether a defendant will be released from jail prior to trial, owning a telephone is one factor used in making a recommendation so that the court can stay in contact with the defendant. But for persons who do not own a phone, this seemingly innocuous requirement becomes an obstacle to pretrial release.

At the sentencing stage, low-income substance abusers are also disadvantaged compared to defendants with resources. Given the general shortage of treatment programs, a defendant who has private insurance to cover the cost of treatment is in a much better position to make an argument for a nonincarcerative sentence than one who depends on publicly funded treatment programs.

IMPACT OF "RACE NEUTRAL" POLICIES

Sentencing and related criminal justice policies that are ostensibly "race neutral" have in fact been seen over many years to have clear racial effects that could have been anticipated by legislators prior to enactment. Research on the development of punitive sentencing policies sheds light on the relationship between harsh sanctions and public perceptions of race. Criminologist Ted Chiricos and colleagues found that among whites, support for harsh sentencing policies was correlated with the degree to which a particular crime was perceived to be a "black" crime. (Ted Chiricos, Kelly Welch & Marc Gertz, *Racial Typification of Crime and Support for Punitive Measures,* 42 CRIMINOLOGY 359, 374 (2004).)

The federal crack cocaine sentencing laws of the 1980s have received significant attention due to their highly disproportionate racial outcomes, but other policies have produced similar effects. For example, a number of states and the federal government have adopted "school zone" drug laws that penalize drug offenses that take place within a certain distance of a school more harshly than other drug crimes.

The racial effect of these laws is an outgrowth of housing patterns. Because urban areas are more densely populated than suburban or rural areas, city residents are much more likely to be within a short distance of a school than are residents of suburban or rural areas. And because African Americans are more likely to live in urban neighborhoods than are whites, blacks convicted of a drug offense are subject to harsher penalties than whites committing a similar offense in a less-populated area. A state commission analysis of a school zone drug law in New Jersey, for example, documented that 96 percent of the persons serving prison time for such offenses were African American or Latino. (NEW JERSEY COMM'N TO REVIEW CRIMINAL SENTENCING, REPORT ON NEW JERSEY'S DRUG FREE ZONE CRIMES AND PROPOSALS FOR REFORM 23 (2005).)

RECOMMENDATIONS FOR POLICIES AND PRACTICES

As indicated above, racial and ethnic disparities in the criminal justice system result from a complex set of policies and practices that may vary among jurisdictions. If we are committed to reducing unwarranted disparities in the system, it will require coordinated efforts among criminal justice leaders, policymakers, and community groups. Following are recommendations for initiatives that can begin to address these issues.

Shift the Focus of Drug Policies and Practice

State and federal policymakers should shift the focus of drug policies in ways that would be more effective in addressing substance abuse and would also reduce racial and ethnic disparities in incarceration. In broad terms, this should incorporate a shift in resources and focus to produce a more appropriate balance between law enforcement strategies and demand reduction approaches emphasizing prevention and treatment. Specific policy initiatives that would support these goals include enhancing public health models of community-based treatment that do not rely on the criminal justice system to provide services; identifying models of drug offender diversion in the court system that effectively target prison-bound defendants; repealing mandatory sentencing laws at the federal and state level to permit judges to impose sentences based on the specifics of the offender and the offense; and expanding substance abuse treatment options in prisons and providing sentence-reduction incentives for successful participation.

Provide Equal Access to Justice

Federal and state policy initiatives can aid in "leveling the playing field" by promoting equal access to justice. Such measures should incorporate adequate support for indigent defense services and provide a broader range and availability of community-based sentencing options.

These and similar initiatives clearly involve an expansion of resources in the court system and community. While these will impose additional short-term costs, they can be offset through appropriate reductions in the number and duration of prison sentences, long-term benefits of treatment and job placement services, and positive outcomes achieved by enhancing family and community stability.

Adopt Racial Impact Statements to Project Unanticipated Consequences of Criminal Justice Policies

Just as fiscal and environmental impact statements have become standard processes in many areas of public policy, so too can racial impact statements be used to assess the projected impact of new initiatives prior to their enactment. In 2008, Iowa and Connecticut each enacted such legislation, which calls for policymakers to receive an analysis of the anticipated effect of proposed sentencing legislation on the racial/ethnic composition of the state's prison population. If a disproportionate effect is projected, this does not preclude the legislative body from enacting the law if it is believed to be necessary for public safety, but it does provide an opportunity for discussion of racial disparities in such a way that alternative policies can be considered when appropriate.

A similar policy is currently in use in Minnesota, where the Sentencing Guidelines Commission regularly produces such analyses. Policies designed to produce racial impact statements should be adopted by legislative action or through the internal operations of a sentencing commission in all state and federal jurisdictions.

Assess the Racial Impact of Current Criminal Justice Decision Making

The Justice Integrity Act, first introduced in Congress in 2008, is designed to establish a process whereby any unwarranted disparities in federal prosecution can be analyzed and responded to when appropriate. Under the proposed bill, the attorney general would designate ten U.S. attorney offices as sites in which to set up task forces composed of representatives of the criminal justice system and the community. The task forces would be charged with reviewing and analyzing data on prosecutorial practices and developing initiatives designed to promote the twin goals of maintaining public safety and reducing disparity. Such a process would clearly be applicable to state justice systems as well.

CONCLUSION

While reasonable people may disagree about the causes of racial disparities in the criminal justice system, all Americans should be troubled by the extent to which incarceration has become a fixture in the life cycle of so many racial and ethnic minorities. The impact of such dramatic rates of imprisonment has profound consequences for children growing up in these neighborhoods, mounting fiscal burdens, and reductions in public support for vital services.

These developments also contribute to eroding trust in the justice system in communities of color—an outcome that is clearly counterproductive to public safety goals. It is long past time for the nation to commit itself to a comprehensive assessment of the causes and remedies for addressing these issues.

Marc Mauer is the executive director of The Sentencing Project *and the author of* Race to Incarcerate. *He can be reached at mauer@ sentencingproject.org.*

ADDRESSING RACIAL DISPARITIES IN INCARCERATION

Marc Mauer

OVERVIEW OF RACIAL DISPARITY IN THE CRIMINAL JUSTICE SYSTEM

In 1954, the year of the historic *Brown v. Board of Education* decision, about 100,000 African Americans were incarcerated in America's prisons and jails. Following that decision, there has been a half century of enhanced opportunity for many people for whom it had previously been denied, and significant numbers of people of color have gained leadership positions in society. Yet, despite this sustained progress, within the criminal justice system, the figure of 100,000 incarcerated African Americans has now escalated to nearly 900,000.

The scale of these developments can be seen most vividly in research findings from the Department of Justice. If current trends continue, 1 of every 3 African American males born today can expect to go to prison in his lifetime, as can 1 of every 6 Latino males, compared to 1 in 17 White males. For women, the overall figures are considerably lower, but the racial/ethnic disparities are similar: 1 of every 18 African American females, 1 of every 45 Hispanic females, and 1 of every 111 White females can expect to spend time in prison (Bonczar, 2003). [Note: Criminal justice data on other racial groups, including Native Americans and Asians/Pacific Islanders, is generally very scarce and, therefore, this analysis generally focuses on trends regarding African Americans and Latinos. Available data, though, documents that Native Americans are incarcerated at more than twice the rate of Whites, while Asian Americans/Pacific Islanders have the lowest incarceration rate of any racial/ethnic group (Hartney & Vuong, 2009).]

High rates of criminal justice control can be documented not only by racial/ethnic group but even more so in combination with age, since younger people have higher rates of involvement in the justice system. Thus, 1 in 13 African American males in the age group 30 to 39 is incarcerated in a state or federal prison on any given day and additional numbers are in local jails (West & Sabol, 2010).

Communities of color are disproportionately affected not only by incarceration but also through higher rates of victimization as well. Data for 2009 (the most recent available) show that African Americans are considerably more likely than Whites to be victims of violent crime. This includes rates of victimization for robbery more than three times those of Whites as well as more than double the rate of aggravated assault. Hispanics are victimized at a rate about 15% higher than Whites but less than African Americans (Truman & Rand, 2010).

In theory, a variety of factors may be responsible for the high rates of incarceration of minority groups in the United States. These might include the relative degree of involvement in crime, disparate law enforcement practices, sentencing and parole policies and practices, and biased decision making.

CRIME AND ARREST RATES

Measuring relative rates of involvement in criminal activity is a complicated task. Since most crimes are either unreported or do not result in an arrest, there is no overall measurement of the number of crimes committed or the demographics of those engaged in criminal behavior. This is even more significant in "victimless" crimes such as a drug-selling transactions between consenting adults.

To develop a rough estimate of these dynamics, we can begin by examining arrest rates. The main drawback of this method is that arrests may reflect law enforcement behavior in addition to involvement in crime. Particularly in the case of drug offenses, this may not represent an accurate measure of the criminally involved population. Nevertheless, an examination of arrest data compiled by the FBI in its annual Uniform Crime Reports (categorized by race, but not ethnicity) reveals that African Americans constituted 30% of persons arrested for a property offense in 2009 and 39% of those arrested for a violent offense (Federal Bureau of Investigation, 2009), clearly disproportionate to the 12% Black share of the overall national population.

Examining rates of incarceration overall, a series of studies by leading criminologists have attempted to quantify the degree to which disparities in imprisonment reflect involvement in crime, as measured by arrest rates. An early study by Blumstein (1993) examined the prison population in 1979, in which he followed up with the same methodology for the 1991 inmate population. More recently, Michael Tonry and Matthew Melewslci analyzed these issues for the 2004 prison population (Tonry & Melewski, 2008). What we see over time from these studies is a steadily declining proportion of the prison population that can be explained by disproportionate arrests. Blumstein's study of the 1979 population concluded that 80% of the racial disparity was accounted for by greater involvement in crime, as measured by arrest rates. This figure was reduced to 76% for the 1991 population and then significantly declined to 61% in the Tonry and Melewski study. Much of the change noted in these studies appears to be an effect of the growing proportion of offenders incarcerated for a drug offense since the 1970s and, in turn, reflects disproportionate law enforcement and sentencing practices that adversely affect African Americans.

RACIAL DISPARITY AS A FUNCTION OF CRIMINAL JUSTICE DECISION MAKING

While differential involvement in crime (as measured by arrests) explains a significant portion of high rates of African American imprisonment, so, too, do policy and practice decisions contribute to these outcomes. This does not suggest that such decisions are necessarily a function of conscious racism by actors in the system, but they frequently may include unconscious bias in the use of discretion, allocation of resources, or public policy decision making.

Examinations of case processing over time also demonstrate that racial disparities in the justice system are cumulative. That is, disproportionate processing at one stage often contributes to widening disparities at succeeding points. For example, defendants who are detained in jail prior to trial are more likely to be convicted and receive lengthier prison terms than defendants released on bond (Schnake, Jones, & Brooker, 2010). The following is an overview of ways in which racial disparity has been documented at various stages of the criminal justice system.

Low Enforcement Practices

In recent years, considerable media and policy maker attention has been focused on law enforcement practices and their possible contributions to racial disparity. Beginning with high profile media accounts of racial profiling by state troopers on the New Jersey Turnpike in the 1990s, much public discussion has focused on the extent to which individual officers or agencies systematically detain or arrest persons of color on the basis of race. Litigation in a variety of jurisdictions has resulted in court orders for law enforcement agencies to engage in oversight and data collection of traffic stops and other police activity to ensure that police officers are not engaging in unwarranted profiling.

Data from the Bureau of Justice Statistics demonstrate that it is not necessarily traffic or pedestrian stops in themselves that are the focal point for disparate practices. As of 2005, national data indicate that White, Black, and Hispanic drivers were stopped by police at similar rates. But of those drivers who were stopped, African American motorists were more than 2.5 times as likely as Whites to be searched by police and Hispanics more than double the rate (Durose, Smith, & Langan, 2007).

Prosecution

There is no stage of the criminal justice system at which there are so little data on case processing outcomes as at the prosecutorial level. Because prosecutors operate at a city or county level and generally have no obligation to report data to a statewide agency, there is broad variation in the manner, comprehensiveness, and efficiency by which data are compiled. This is particularly critical to an examination of racial disparity for two reasons. First, since more than 90% of guilty verdicts are a result of a negotiated plea rather than a trial, the influence of the prosecutor on ultimate case outcomes is often far more significant than that of the judge. Second, because these negotiations essentially take place "behind closed doors," there is little means by which to evaluate the fairness or effectiveness of this decision making. To say this is not to suggest that most prosecutors engage in biased behavior, whether conscious or not, but it does mean that it is very difficult to assess the degree to which such practices exist or to make comparisons across prosecutors' offices regarding such issues. And as such notorious cases as the Tulia, Texas, drug prosecutions of the late 1990s illustrate, a case in which nearly a third of the African American male population in a small town was charged with drug selling, only to see many of the convictions later reversed, this discretion can have disastrous consequences.

While relatively few studies have been conducted on prosecutorial decision making, there is evidence that such practices may contribute to racial disparities within the justice system. A 1991 study of federal mandatory sentencing conducted by the U.S. Sentencing Commission, for example, found that for cases in which case factors suggested that a charge could be brought that carried a mandatory penalty, prosecutors were more likely to offer White defendants a negotiated plea below the mandatory minimum than African American or Latino defendants (United States Sentencing Commission, 1991).

Sentencing

In contrast to the prosecution function, a broad range of scholarship has examined the intersection of race and sentencing over several decades. In broad terms, the evidence indicates the following:

- There is strong evidence that race plays a role in the determination of which homicide cases result in a death sentence, whereby cases with White victims are considerably more likely to receive a death sentence (Baldus & Woodworth, 2004).
- In noncapital cases, race is often found to contribute to disparities in sentencing, but most often in combination with variables such as gender and employment (Spohn, 2000).
- Racial disparities at the sentencing stage are not necessarily a function of judicial bias but can often result from "race neutral" sentencing policies with skewed racial effects. This can be seen in the experience with many drug policies and habitual offender statutes (Crow & Johnson, 2008).

Research since the 1980s has demonstrated that offender/victim dynamics produce strong racially based outcomes in death penalty cases. Beginning with a study by David Baldus, the focus of the *McCleskey* case before the U.S. Supreme Court in 1987 (*McCleskey v. Kemp*, 1987), these studies have consistently shown that persons who kill Whites are about four times as likely to receive a death sentence as those who kill African Americans. These findings are not necessarily a function only of the sentencing decision but may also reflect prosecutorial discretion in how cases are charged. Notably, the Supreme Court has generally rejected claims of racial bias in such cases, ruling that while the data may show overall patterns of racial effects, such findings do not necessarily demonstrate racial bias in an individual case.

In noncapital cases, a comprehensive review of current research by sentencing scholar Cassia Spohn finds that

> . . . race and ethnicity do play an important role in contemporary sentencing decisions. Black and Hispanic offenders sentenced in State and Federal courts face significantly greater odds of incarceration than similarly situated white offenders. In some jurisdictions, they also may receive longer sentences or differential benefits from guideline departures than their white counterparts. (p. 458).

In recent decades, a significant contributor to racial disparities has been the set of policies adopted under the framework of the "war on drugs." Such sentencing policies as mandatory minimums and school zone drug enhancements, while theoretically race neutral, in practice have significant racial effects. This is a combined function of law enforcement and prosecutorial practices. Since the escalation of the war on drugs in the mid-1980s, there has been a trend of both increased drug arrests and prosecutions accompanied by significant racial and ethnic disparities. At the stage of law enforcement, the number of drug arrests nearly tripled from a level of 581,000 in 1980 to 1,663,000 by 2009. Along with that came a dramatic escalation in the number of incarcerated drug offenders, rising from about 41,000 persons in prison or jail in 1980 to nearly 500,000 by 2003 (Mauer & King, 2007).

Racial disparities in the prosecution of the drug war can be seen initially in arrest rates. African Americans constituted 21% of drug arrests in 1980, then rose to 36% in 1992 (Mauer, 2006), before declining to 34% by 2009 (Federal Bureau of Investigation, 2009), but still disproportionate to their share of the national population. While there are no comprehensive data on the number of people committing drug offenses, government surveys have consistently shown that African Americans use drugs at roughly the same proportions as Whites and Latinos. Therefore, all things being equal, one would expect that arrest rates for drug possession would reflect these trends. But since many drug arrests are for sales offenses, it is also necessary to investigate potential racial disparities in this area. There are little data on drug selling activity by race, but at least one study of drug selling behavior in six cities published by the National Institute of Justice indicates that "respondents were most likely to report using a main source who was of their own racial or ethnic background" (Riley, 1997, p. 1).

Racial disparities in drug arrests then translate into disparities in sentencing that are exacerbated by the proliferation of mandatory sentencing policies adopted since the 1980s, laws that are frequently applied to drug offenses. Overall, this has resulted in African Americans and Latinos constituting 65% of drug offenders in state prisons in 2008 (West and Sabol, 2010).

Among the sentencing policies that most dramatically reveal the dynamics of these developments are the federal policies adopted by Congress in 1986 and 1988 governing two forms of cocaine, powder and crack. Under these statutes, a 100:1 drug quantity disparity was established between offenses of powder cocaine and crack cocaine. Thus, selling 500 grams of powder cocaine triggered a mandatory 5-year prison term, while for crack cocaine, sale or possession of just 5 grams resulted in the same 5-year sentence. The racial impact of these laws was a function of the vast disparity in arrests, with African Americans constituting about 80% of persons charged with a crack cocaine offense, while powder cocaine offenders were much more likely to be White or Latino. The sentencing disparity was reduced by Congress in 2010, raising the threshold for crack cocaine to 28 grams, while leaving the powder cocaine quantity at 500 grams.

Other sentencing policies have been observed to produce unwarranted racial disparities as well. School zone drug laws adopted by many states have as their stated objective the goal of deterring drug selling to school children and aim to do so by applying enhanced penalties to offenses committed within a certain geographical range—often 500 or 1,000 feet—of a school. As written, though, many of these statutes apply much more broadly, such as including drug sales between two adults during nonschool hours.

The racial effects of these policies result from the implications of housing patterns. Since urban areas are much more densely populated than rural or suburban areas, it is more likely that any given drug offense will take place within a school zone district. And since persons of color disproportionately reside in urban areas, a drug offense committed by an African American or Latino person will be more likely to incur these enhanced penalties. In New Jersey, for example, 96% of all persons incarcerated under these laws in 2005 were African American or Latino (New Jersey Commission to Review Criminal Sentencing, 2007). Recognizing this disparity, the state legislature restored sentencing discretion to judges in such cases in 2010.

Sentencing policies that enhance penalties based on an offender's prior record likewise produce disproportionate racial effects even though they are race neutral on the surface. This is a result of minorities being more likely to have a prior record, whether due to greater involvement in criminal behavior or disparate processing by the justice system. While such enhancements have long been a consideration at sentencing, the recent proliferation of "three strikes" and habitual offender laws that greatly enhance such punishments has magnified the impact of such considerations.

In the case of Alexander Livener in 1998, (*U.S. v. Leviner*, 1998) Federal District Judge Nancy Gertner imposed a below-guideline sentence for an African American man convicted of being a felon in possession of a firearm. Under federal sentencing guidelines, Leviner's sentencing range was 4 to 6 years in prison, based on the offense conviction and his prior record. But Judge Gertner noted that most of his prior convictions were the result of traffic stops by Boston police. Given the history of racial profiling by law enforcement agencies, Judge Gertner reasoned that such practices essentially contributed to Leviner's prior record, and as a result she imposed a lesser sentence of 2.5 years.

IMPLICATIONS OF RACIAL DISPARITY IN INCARCERATION

One presumed goal of mass incarceration, to reduce crime, is increasingly subject to diminishing returns. With a surge of incarcerated drug offenders since the mid-1980s, there is now a growing population in prison for which there is little effect on public safety due to the fact that incarcerated low-level drug sellers are routinely replaced on the street.

Extreme racial disparities in the use of imprisonment result in communities of color being disproportionately affected by the collateral effects of incarceration. These include family stress and dissolution, neighborhoods experiencing high mobility of residents cycling in and out of prison, and growing numbers of people with limited employment prospects. Incarceration has been demonstrated to reduce African American male wage earnings by 44% by the age of 48 (The Pew Charitable Trusts, 2010).

PRISON POPULATION EXPANDS WITH CHANGES IN DRUG POLICY

Marc Mauer

For more than a quarter century the "war on drugs" has exerted a profound impact on the structure and scale of the criminal justice system. The changes in sentencing and enforcement for drug offenses have been a major contributing factor to the historic rise in the prison population. From a figure of about 40,000 people incarcerated in prison or jail for a drug offense in 1980, there has since been an 1100% increase to a total of 500,000 today. To place some perspective on that change, the number of people incarcerated for a drug offense is now greater than the number incarcerated for *all* offenses in 1980.

The increase in incarceration for drug offenses has been fueled by sharply escalated law enforcement targeting of drug law violations, often accompanied by enhanced penalties for such offenses. Many of the mandatory sentencing provisions adopted in both state and federal law have been focused on drug offenses. At the federal level, the most notorious of these are the penalties for crack cocaine violations, whereby low-level crack offenses are punished far more severely than powder cocaine offenses, even though the two substances are pharmacologically identical. Despite changes in federal sentencing guidelines, the mandatory provisions still in place require that anyone convicted of possessing as little as five grams of crack cocaine (the weight of two sugar packets) receive a five-year prison term for a first-time offense.

The dramatic escalation of incarceration for drug offenses has been accompanied by profound racial and ethnic disparities. African Americans comprise 13 percent of the United States' population and 14 percent of monthly illegal drug users, but represent 37 percent of persons arrested for a drug offense and 56 percent of persons in state prison for a drug conviction.

Despite the recent findings in The Sentencing Project's report, "The Changing Racial Dynamics of the War on Drugs," that between 1999 and 2005 state incarceration of African Americans for drug offenses declined 21.6 percent, perhaps due to a decline in the crack cocaine market, the same is not true for the federal system. Indeed, the number of federal prosecutions for crack offenses remains substantial, and the overall number of people in federal prison for a drug offense rose by 32.7% from 1999 to 2005. Racial disparities persist, with African Americans constituting more than 80% of the people convicted of a federal crack cocaine offense.

THE CASE OF CRACK COCAINE

In 1986 when Congress passed the Anti-Drug Abuse Act, the stated intent of the cocaine sentencing structure was to ensure mandatory sentences for major and serious traffickers – heads of drug organizations and those involved in preparing and packaging crack cocaine in "substantial street quantities." Congress calibrated the sentencing structure based on drug quantities that were believed to reflect the different roles in the drug trade, but in its effort to swiftly address rising concern over crack cocaine, the penalty structure became dramatically skewed. The rationale voiced at the time was that the smokable form of cocaine was more addictive, presented greater long-term consequences of use, and had a stronger association with violence in its distribution than the powder cocaine market. History has proven these concerns to be unfounded, yet Congress has remained silent.

Indeed, the actual differences between the two substances are far more subtle. Crack and powder cocaine share the same pharmacological roots, but crack cocaine is cooked with water and baking soda to create a smokable, rock-like substance. Crack cocaine is sold in small quantities and is a cheaper alternative to powder cocaine. However, crack and powder are both part of the same distribution continuum. Crack is, by definition, at the lower-level end of the distribution spectrum where small batches of powder cocaine are processed and sold in an inexpensive, smokable form.

The emergence of the crack cocaine market in the 1980s in a number of major urban areas was accompanied by massive media attention paid toward the drug's meteoric rise and its associated dangers. A core component of the media coverage was the thinly-veiled (and unfounded) link between the drug's use and low-income communities of color. In a matter of weeks, crack cocaine was widely believed by the American public to be a drug that was sold and used exclusively by poor African Americans. This framing of the drug in class and race-based terms provides important context when evaluating the legislative response.

The resulting federal legislation punished crack cocaine with historically punitive sanctions. Crack cocaine is the only drug in which simple possession can result in a mandatory sentence to prison. A defendant convicted with five grams of crack cocaine – between 10 and 50 doses – will receive a five-year mandatory minimum sentence. To receive the same sentence for a powder cocaine violation, a defendant would have to have been involved in an offense involving 500 grams – between 2,500 and 5,000 doses. This is commonly referred to as the "100-to-1 sentencing disparity." In order to trigger a 10-year mandatory sentence, a defendant would need to be charged with 50 grams of crack cocaine – between 100 and 500 doses – or 5,000 grams of powder cocaine – up to 50,000 doses. The quantity levels associated with the two drugs codify an equivalency of punishment for low-level crack cocaine sellers and high-level powder cocaine traffickers.

On average, crack cocaine defendants do not play a sophisticated role in the drug trade. Nearly two-thirds (61.5 percent) of crack cocaine defendants were identified as a street-level dealer, courier, lookout, or user. Among powder cocaine defendants, this proportion was 53.1 percent. Although the distribution of offender roles is similar between the two substances, the median quantity and applicable mandatory minimum are vastly different. The median quantity for a crack cocaine street-level dealer is 52 grams, which triggers a ten-year mandatory sentence. For a powder cocaine street-level dealer, the median quantity is 340 grams, which would not even expose a defendant to a five-year mandatory sentence. This disparity has led the Sentencing Commission to conclude that crack cocaine penalties "apply most often to offenders who perform low-level trafficking functions, wield little decision-making authority, and have limited responsibility." The Commission has further remarked that "[r]evising the crack cocaine thresholds would better reduce the [sentencing] gap than any other single policy change, and it would dramatically improve the fairness of the federal sentencing system."

Harsher penalties for crack cocaine offenses are sometimes supported because of the perception that crack is more likely to be associated with violence than powder cocaine. However, this is not supported by the evidence and subverts the goal of proportionality in sentencing. While there was a significant level of violence associated with crack after its introduction to urban areas in the 1980s, that violence was a function of the new drug markets and "turf battles," rather than any effect of the drug itself. Additionally, because of inappropriate assumptions about crack cocaine and violence being implicit in the statute, crack cocaine defendants are essentially sentenced for conduct in which they did not engage or face a penalty that takes into consideration the same conduct twice.

Data from the Sentencing Commission now document that a majority of both crack and powder cocaine offenders do not engage in any associated violence, such as bodily injury or threats, and any distinction between the two drugs is not sufficient to warrant additional penalties. An analysis of federal cocaine cases for 2005 demonstrates that 73% of powder cocaine offenses and 57.3% of crack cocaine offenses did not involve a weapon, and that only in a small number of cases (0.8% for powder and 2.9% for crack) were weapons used by the offender.

Violent behavior by drug offenders should be treated seriously, but the sentencing guidelines already provide sufficient opportunity for judges to penalize such conduct. By making the inappropriate assumption that a crack cocaine offense is categorically linked with violent behavior, the statutory penalty leads to one of two key errors. First, individuals who have not engaged in any associated violent conduct are subjected to a penalty structure that presumes uncommitted conduct. Second, for persons who have been charged with a concurrent violent offense, the 100:1 ratio is tantamount to a "double counting" of the charged conduct, thereby exposing defendants to disproportionately severe punishments. The federal criminal code already has a wide range of penalties and enhancements for violent conduct at the disposal of prosecutors and the circumstances of the individual case should govern their applicability.

CRACK COCAINE AND THE AFRICAN AMERICAN COMMUNITY

The impact of crack cocaine policy on the African American community has been devastating. While two-thirds of regular crack cocaine users in the United States are either white or Latino, 80 percent of persons sentenced in federal court for a crack cocaine offense are African American. Thus, African Americans disproportionately face the most severe drug penalties in the federal system.

These racial inequities have come as the result of deliberate decisions by policymakers and practitioners. When crafting mandatory minimum sentences, Congress had sought to establish generalized equivalencies in punishment across drug types by controlling for the perceived severity of the drug via the adjustment of quantity thresholds. However, in practice, sentences are frequently disproportionately severe relative to the conduct for which a person has been convicted because mandatory minimum sentences rely upon the quantity of the charged substance as a proxy for the degree of involvement of a defendant in the drug offense. Thus, the sentencing statutes function as blunt instruments of punishment that are ineffective at appropriately assessing and calibrating sentences based on the specific circumstances of the charged crime.

Since their introduction, mandatory minimum sentences have consistently been shown to have a disproportionately severe impact on African Americans. A study by the Sentencing Commission found that African Americans were 21 percent more likely to receive a mandatory minimum sentence than white defendants facing an eligible charge. A separate study by the Federal Judicial Center also concluded that African Americans faced an elevated likelihood of receiving a mandatory minimum sentence relative to whites. More recently, the Commission, in a 15-year overview of the federal sentencing system, concluded that "mandatory penalty statutes are used inconsistently" and disproportionately affect African American defendants. As a result, African American drug defendants are 20 percent more likely to be sentenced to prison than white drug defendants.

The Commission observed that federal sentencing changes in the 1980s, notably in the guise of mandatory minimum sentencing and sentencing guidelines, have had "a greater adverse impact on Black offenders than did the factors taken into account by judges in the discretionary system immediately prior to guidelines implementation" and that there is some question as to "whether these new policies are necessary to achieve any legitimate purpose of sentencing." In other words, the cure has proven to be worse than the disease.

CHAPTER THREE
Corrections

LIFE SENTENCES TODAY

The Sentencing Project

Life sentences in America today stand at an unprecedented level: as of 2012, 159,520 people in prison were serving a life sentence and 49,081 (30.8%) of them have no possibility for parole. Nationally, one in every nine people in prison today is serving a life sentence.[1] Though LWOP is available in nearly every state,[2] such prisoners are disproportionately represented in Florida, Pennsylvania, Louisiana, California, and Michigan. Combined, these five states account for over half (57.7%) of all LWOP sentences nationwide. In seven states—Alabama, California, Massachusetts, Nevada, New York, Utah, and Washington—more than 15% of the prison population is sentenced to life.[3] Additionally, in 22 states and the federal government, at least 35% of the lifer population is ineligible for parole.[4]

Despite a shift toward determinate sentencing in recent decades, many states maintain some form of indeterminate sentencing framework that is applied to parole-eligible lifers. Offenders who fall within this structure can potentially earn parole within a range of years; in some states, these ranges include an upper limit of natural life. For example, in Colorado trial judges can sentence people convicted of a sex offense to an indeterminate sentence that ranges from a minimum of one day to a maximum of life imprisonment.[5] In Vermont, failure to register as a sex offender can, in some instances, trigger a sentence of five years to life and prisoners are considered lifers until they are released.[6] Some empirical evidence suggests that prisoners serve longer terms in states with indeterminate sentencing schemes that have discretionary parole, especially for those convicted of violent offenses.[7] The large number of parole-eligible lifers in some of these states may partially be explained by indeterminate sentencing structures that allow for a maximum term of life and a minimum term as short as five years.

Regardless of whether a state has an indeterminate or determinate sentencing structure, excessively long sentences are available and used with increasing regularity. However, the alternative is also true: sentencing reforms that reflect fairness, proportionality, and a realistic opportunity for release can be incorporated into either a determinate sentencing structure or one that relies on a range of years to allow for individual tailoring.

---

1 The continued rise in lifers presents one aspect of the issues associated with the expansion of lengthy sentences. Lengthy sentences other than those identified as lifelong sentences are also a common feature of the American criminal justice system. An example would be a sentence of 120 years. Data on the extensive use of these "virtual life" sentences has not yet been systematically collected but would likely show that sentences spanning many decades, easily exceeding an average lifespan, are increasingly common.

2 Alaska is the exception.

3 Utah's indeterminate sentencing system allows a range of up to life for all first degree felony convictions. Though most people are eventually released, there remains the potential for lifelong incarceration. During any year, about 5 to 6% of the total releases in Utah are offenders serving 5-to-life sentences.

4 The states are Arkansas, Delaware, Florida, Illinois, Indiana, Louisiana, Maine, Massachusetts, Michigan, Mississippi, Missouri, Montana, Nebraska, New Hampshire, North Carolina, North Dakota, Oklahoma, Pennsylvania, South Carolina, South Dakota, Virginia, and West Virginia.

5 C.R.S.A. 18-1.3-904. This law went into effect in 1968.

6 13 V.S.A. 5411d, enacted 2003.

7 Petersilia, J. (2003). *When Prisoners Come Home: Parole and Prisoner Reentry*. Oxford: Oxford University Press.

CRIME OF CONVICTION

Life sentences were originally limited to those convicted of only the most serious crimes, such as homicide, particularly as an alternative to the death penalty, but their use has expanded considerably over time to include a greater range of offenses.[8] While homicide remains the offense for which a majority of lifers are sentenced, life sentences are today authorized for assault, robbery, sex-related crimes, drug offenses, and even some property offenses.

In our survey of state corrections agencies, we requested information about the crime of commitment for each person serving a life sentence.[9] Overall, 64.3% (87,933) of those serving a life sentence had been convicted of a homicide. However, it is notable that more than 10,000 people serving life sentences have been convicted of a nonviolent crime, including more than 2,500 for a drug offense and 5,400 for a property crime.

Consider the case of 63-year-old Oklahoma lifer Larry Yarbrough, a married restaurant owner with five children and 13 grandchildren. Oklahoma's tough drug law resulted in sentencing Mr. Yarbrough to life without

Table 3.1   National Distribution of Crime of Conviction among Lifers

Crime	% Life-Sentenced
Homicide	64.3%
Sexual Assault/Rape	13.7%
Aggravated Assault/Robbery/Kidnapping	14.1%
Drug Offense	2.0%
Property Offense	4.0%
Other	2.0%

Figure 3.1   Crime of Conviction for Life-Sentenced Population

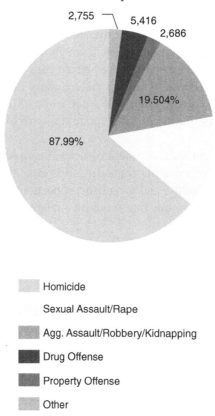

8   Capers, B. (2012). Defending Life. In Ogletree, C. J., and A. Sarat. *Life Without Parole: America's New Death Penalty?* New York: New York University Press, Pp.167–189.

9   Offense data was not provided for approximately 23,000 prisoners, or 14.3% of the total number of people serving life sentences.

parole for selling an ounce of cocaine and three marijuana cigarettes. He has been in prison for 18 years. The Oklahoma Board of Pardons and Parole has repeatedly recommended his release, pointing to his successful rehabilitation in prison and service to the community's blind and disabled, a clean disciplinary record throughout his sentence, and the unnecessary cost of continuing to incarcerate him. The Parole Board most recently recommended a sentence commutation in 2011, which was again denied by the Governor.

RACE AND ETHNICITY OF LIFE-SENTENCED INDIVIDUALS

It is widely established that racial and ethnic minorities are more likely to enter the criminal justice system and that racial and ethnic differences become more pronounced at the deeper stages of the system. In 2009, African Americans and Latinos comprised over 60% of people in prison, and black males were incarcerated in state and federal prisons at 6.4 times the rate of white non-Hispanic males.[10]

Racial disparities are evident among those serving life as well. Nationally, almost half (47.2%) of life-sentenced inmates are African American, though the black population of lifers reaches much higher in states such as Maryland (77.4%), Georgia (72.0%), and Mississippi (71.5%). In the federal system, 62.3% of the life-sentenced population is African American. Non-whites constitute nearly two-thirds of the total population serving life sentences.

Sixteen percent of the people serving life sentences nationwide are Latino, with the highest concentrations in New Mexico (44.1%), California (35.7%), Arizona (30.9%), and Colorado (26.4%).

Table 3.2　Racial Distribution of Life Sentenced Population

State	Life Population	Percent Black	Percent White	Percent Other
Alabama	5,318	65.8%	34.0%	0.2%
Arizona	1,494	19.5%	43.7%	36.8%
Arkansas	1,400	53.1%	45.2%	1.7%
California	40,362	34.2%	22.1%	8.0%
Colorado	2,621	19.6%	50.5%	3.4%
Connecticut	359	52.9%	27.0%	0.6%
Delaware	528	64.8%	35.0%	0.2%
Florida	12,149	54.1%	42.0%	3.9%
Georgia	7,938	72.0%	24.8%	0.6%
Hawaii	412	6.1%	23.1%	66.7%
Idaho	524	2.9%	76.9%	6.1%
Illinois	2,741	52.0%	32.8%	0.6%
Indiana	242	35.5%	59.5%	0.8%
Iowa	680	26.6%	70.9%	2.5%
Kansas	1,061	39.0%	58.2%	2.8%
Kentucky	908	27.3%	70.4%	2.3%
Louisiana	4,657	73.4%	26.2%	0.4%
Maine	59	1.7%	96.6%	1.7%
Maryland	2,470	77.4%	21.7%	0.6%

(Continued)

10　Mauer, M. (2013). The Changing Racial Dynamics of Women's Incarceration. Washington, D.C. The Sentencing Project.

Table 3.2   Racial Distribution of Life Sentenced Population (*Continued*)

State	Life Population	Percent Black	Percent White	Percent Other
Massachusetts	1,975	35.6%	55.8%	8.6%
Michigan	5,137	64.8%	34.0%	1.0%
Minnesota	528	37.5%	52.5%	10.0%
Mississippi	2,073	71.5%	27.8%	0.7%
Missouri	2,807	52.3%	46.9%	0.8%
Montana	97	0.0%	73.4%	26.6%
Nebraska	531	32.6%	60.4%	6.9%
Nevada	2,719	25.5%	57.9%	16.6%
New Hampshire	213	5.2%	91.1%	3.8%
New Jersey	1,166	61.7%	25.0%	13.2%
New Mexico	408	10.3%	38.2%	7.4%
New York	10,245	60.5%	24.5%	15.1%
North Carolina	3,110	56.8%	34.9%	5.1%
North Dakota	65	7.7%	72.3%	20.0%
Ohio	6,075	52.0%	44.7%	3.2%
Oklahoma	2,515	32.2%	53.6%	8.9%
Oregon	807	12.1%	72.9%	5.2%
Pennsylvania	5,104	64.5%	25.7%	1.2%
Rhode Island	207	29.0%	45.9%	1.9%
South Carolina	2,219	64.9%	34.2%	0.9%
South Dakota	181	7.2%	69.6%	23.2%
Tennessee	2,225	49.8%	49.7%	0.6%
Texas	9,031	40.5%	34.3%	2.8%
Utah	2,048	6.7%	64.5%	28.9%
Vermont	121	8.3%	86.8%	4.1%
Virginia	2,145	41.9%	36.6%	0.5%
Washington	2,623	16.4%	74.6%	9.1%
West Virginia	635	14.8%	81.1%	3.5%
Wisconsin	1,185	45.1%	52.2%	2.6%
Wyoming	182	6.6%	74.2%	6.6%
FEDERAL	5,420	62.3%	33.6%	4.0%
TOTAL	159,520	47.2%	34.7%	6.0%

Note: Most states provided the ethnicity of "Hispanic" separately from race categories. In cases where "Hispanic" was provided as a mutually exclusive category, we divided the number of Hispanics by their representation in the general population, 2.5% Black, 53% White, and 44.5% Other, as reported in the 2010 U.S. Census (Humes, K. R., Jones, N. A., and Ramirez, R. R. (2011). *Overview of Race and Hispanic Origin: 2010*. Washington, DC: .S. Census Bureau. See page 6. Tennessee did not provide data in 2012 other than life and LWOP totals. We used the proportions of information obtained in 2008 to arrive at current estimates for race, gender, ethnicity, and age. Alaska does not have life or LWOP sentences so it is excluded from this table.

Concerns about racial disparity become even more significant when examining the racial groups of those serving life without parole. While 47.2% of the lifer population is African American, 58% of LWOP prisoners are African American and reaching at least two-thirds of the LWOP population in seven states.

These figures mirror the broader pattern in the criminal justice system in which blacks are represented at an increasingly disproportionate rate across the continuum from arrest to incarceration. African Americans comprise 12% of the general population but 28% of total arrests, and 38% of those convicted of a felony in state court and in state prison.

FEMALE POPULATION OF LIFE-SENTENCED PRISONERS

There are now 5,361 women serving life sentences in the U.S., representing an increase of 14.2% since the most recent review of national data in 2008.[11] Among these, nearly 300 have no opportunity for parole. Women serving life sentences often have particularly tragic histories. Among the females serving LWOP for offenses committed in their teenage years, the vast majority experienced sexual abuse in their childhood.[12]

An example is the story of Sara Kruzan, a sex trafficking victim sentenced to life without parole for a crime committed as a teenager. Ms. Kruzan had been forced into prostitution at the age of 13 by a man 20 years her senior. At 16, after years of rape and abuse by him and others, she snapped and killed her pimp. Despite a recommendation by the California Youth Authority to handle Ms. Kruzan in juvenile court because of her amenability to treatment, the prosecutor and judge agreed she was competent to stand trial in adult court, where life sentences without the possibility of parole are the default sentence for homicide convictions. Ms. Kruzan served nearly 15 years in an adult prison while her legal team worked tirelessly for a review of her sentence and an opportunity for release. After gathering 60,000 signatures for a national petition and mounting a media and public education campaign, California Governor Schwarzenegger commuted her sentence in 2012 and in June 2013, Ms. Kruzan was released.

Far too many women have similar stories as Ms. Kruzan and are still in prison. Among women convicted of intimate partner violence-related homicides, the majority have been battered.[13] This is even more evident among women serving life sentences.[14] Statistics from nationally representative inmate survey data show that 83.8% of life-sentenced women were sexually or physically abused and that abuse is significantly more common among female lifers than male lifers or female prisoners not serving life sentences.[15]

Figure 3.2   Racial Distribution of Prisoners Serving LWOP in Seven States

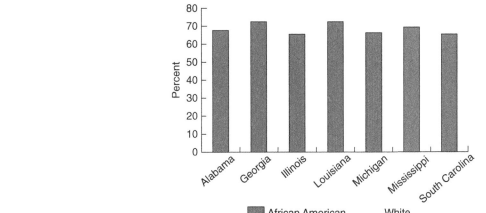

11 Nellis, A. & King, R. 2009. *No Exit: The Expanding Use of Life Sentences in America*. Washington, D.C.: The Sentencing Project.
12 Nellis, A. (2012). *The Lives of Juvenile Lifers: Findings from a National Survey*. Washington, D.C.: The Sentencing Project.
13 Campbell, J. C. (1995). Prediction of Homicide of and by Battered Women. In Jacquelyn C. Campbell (ed.) *Assessing Dangerousness: Violence by Sexual Offenders, Batterers, and Child Abusers*. Thousand Oaks, CA: Sage; O'Keefe, M. (1997). Incarcerated Battered Women: A Comparison of Battered Women Who Killed Their Abusers and Those Incarcerated for Other Reasons. *Journal of Family Violence, 12*(1): 1–19.
14 Dermody-Leonard, E. (2002). Convicted Survivors: The Imprisonment of Battered Women Who Kill. New York: State University of New York Press; Dye, M. H. & Aday, R. H. (2013). 'I just wanted to die': Preprison and Current Suicide Ideation Among Women Serving Life Sentences. *Criminal Justice and Behavior, 40*(8): 832–849.
15 Leigey, M. E. & Reed, J.K.L. (2010). A Woman's Life before Serving Life: Examining the Negative Pre-Incarceration Life Events of Female Life-Sentenced Inmates. *Women and Criminal Justice, 20*: 302–322.

Understanding the Expansion of Life Sentences in American Prisons

The persistent growth in life sentences even during a period of declining rates of crime is likely to reflect two trends. First, more people are being admitted to prison with life and LWOP sentences. Second, those with parole-eligible life sentences are increasingly less likely to be released or, if they are, their release comes much later than similarly situated individuals in earlier decades. Early research by The Sentencing Project found that lifers admitted to prison in 1991 could expect to serve an average of 21.2 years, but that lifers admitted in 1997 served an average of 29 years, reflecting a 37% increase in time served.[16] Thus, in contrast to the public misperception that lifers serve short prison terms, the average life sentence today results in nearly three decades of incarceration.

Figure 3.3 Expansion of Life Sentences, 1984–2012

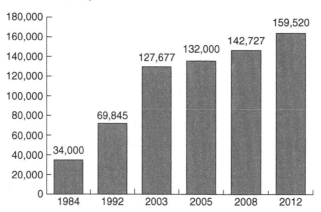

Sources: Figures for 1984 obtained from: American Correctional Association (1984). Corrections Compendium. Vol. 3 (9). Figures for 1992 obtained from: Maguire, K., Pastore, A. L., & Flanagan, T. J. (Eds.) (1993). *Sourcebook of Criminal Justice Statistics 1992.* Washington, D.C.: Bureau of Justice Statistics. Figures for 2003 obtained from: Mauer, M., King, R., & Young, M. (2004). The *Meaning of 'Life': Long Prison Sentences in Context.* Washington, D.C.: The Sentencing Project. Figures for 2005 obtained from: Liptak, A. (2005, October 5). *Serving Life with No Chance at Redemption.* The New York Times. Figures for 2008 obtained from Nellis, A., & King, R. S. (2009). *No Exit: The Expanding Use of Life Sentences in America.* Washington, D.C.: The Sentencing Project. Data for 2012 collected from each state's department of corrections by The Sentencing Project.

Figure 3.4 The Rise in Life without Parole Sentences

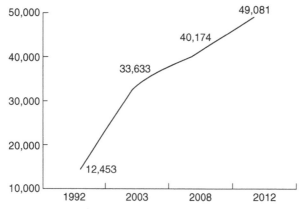

Sources: Figures for 1992 obtained from: Maguire, K., Pastore, A. L., & Flanagan, T. J. (Eds.) (1993). *Sourcebook of Criminal Justice Statistics 1992.* Washington, D.C.: Bureau of Justice Statistics. Figures for 2003 obtained from: Mauer, M., King, R., & Young, M. (2004). *The Meaning of 'Life': Long Prison Sentences in Context.* Washington, D.C.: The Sentencing Project. Figures for 2005 obtained from: Liptak, A. (2005, October 5). *Serving Life with No Chance at Redemption.* The New York Times. Figures for 2008 obtained from Nellis, A., & King, R. S. (2009). *No Exit: The Expanding Use of Life Sentences in America.* Washington, D.C.: The Sentencing Project. Data for 2012 collected from each state's department of corrections by The Sentencing Project.

---

16   Mauer, M., King, R., & Young M. (2004). *The Meaning of 'Life': Long Prison Sentences in Context.* Washington, DC: The Sentencing Project.

The extent to which parole denials can lead to excessive incarceration can be seen in the case of Frank Soffen, a 74-year-old lifer who has been incarcerated for more than half his life. Mr. Soffen was convicted of second degree murder and sentenced to a Massachusetts prison for a double homicide in 1972. Massachusetts does not have a medical release program for elderly or chronically ill prisoners, so his release depends entirely on a favorable review by the parole board and approval of the Governor. He has been eligible for parole since 1987 but despite an exemplary prison record that includes saving a correctional officer's life during an attempted stabbing by another inmate, has been repeatedly denied release. Today, Mr. Soffen is confined to a wheelchair and has suffered numerous medical problems including liver disease, kidney disease, and four heart attacks while incarcerated.

The second factor driving the rise in the lifer population is that more people are entering prison with life sentences without a chance for parole. For example, in 1994 Georgia passed a "two-strike" law which requires that upon conviction of a first strike, individuals convicted of kidnapping, armed robbery, rape, aggravated sodomy, aggravated sexual battery, and aggravated child molestation be sentenced to at least 10 years without parole. A second strike results in life without parole. The mandatory sentence for all homicide convictions is LWOP. Within the first few years, 57 people had been sentenced to LWOP under the new law. By mid-2012, 737 Georgia prisoners were serving LWOP, a 270% increase over its population of 199 LWOP prisoners in August 2000. And, despite the intended purpose of its law, LWOP sentences have not been reserved for the worst of the worst: only a slight majority (56.5%) of life-sentenced Georgia inmates with no chance for parole have been convicted of a homicide.

THE IMPACT OF "THREE-STRIKES" LAWS

In certain states the adoption of "three strikes and you're out" laws has significantly expanded the number of individuals sentenced to life. California maintains a quarter (25.2%) of the nation's life-sentenced population. Twenty-two percent (8,914 of the 40,362 lifers) are serving life sentences because of the state's notoriously tough Three-Strikes law.[17] This law, enacted in 1994, mandated a life sentence with the possibility of parole upon a third conviction but unlike other states, the third offense could be any felony, not necessarily a serious or violent one.

While the law was passed with the promise that it would take persons convicted of serious and violent offenses off the streets, in reality fewer than half of the individuals sentenced under the law had been convicted of a violent offense as their third strike. Fifty-five percent were convicted of a nonviolent offense, including 16% for a drug offense and 30% for a property crime.[18]

Although the three-strikes structure in California receives attention for its severity, the state is not alone in adopting habitual offender laws that result in life or LWOP upon a second or third conviction. Life without parole is a mandatory sentence upon conviction under three strikes laws in 13 states and the federal government.[19] In some states, the impact of these laws on the life-sentenced population is profound. In Washington, for instance, two-thirds of the people serving parole-ineligible life sentences have been sentenced under the state's three strikes law which went into effect in 1994.

THE FALSE PROMISE OF PUBLIC SAFETY

Support for life and LWOP sentences is in part premised on the assumption that the recipients of these sentences will reoffend if released. Recidivism among life-sentenced prisoners who are granted parole is low, however, calling into question the accuracy of public safety arguments in support of lengthy terms of imprisonment.

---

17   California Department of Correction and Rehabilitation (2013). Second and Third Striker Felons in the Adult Institution Population. Sacramento: CDCR.

18   Nellis, A.& King, R. (2009). *No Exit: The Expanding Use of Life Sentences in America.* Washington, DC: The Sentencing Project.

19   Ogletree, C., & Sarat, A. (2012). Introduction: Lives on the Line: From Capital Punishment to Life without Parole. In C. Ogletree & A. Sarat (Eds.), *Life without Parole: America's New Death Penalty?* (pp. 1–24). New York: New York University Press.

Table 3.3   Impact of Three Strikes Law on LWOP in Washington

Year	LWOP Population	% LWOP Prisoners Sentenced Under Three-Strikes
1999	358	6.7%
2000	412	18.2%
2001	429	24.9%
2002	448	33.9%
2003	470	38.7%
2004	500	42.8%
2005	510	47.1%
2006	537	50.8%
2007	554	54.5%
2008	557	58.7%
2009	559	64.4%
2010	554	69.7%
2011	665	61.4%
2012	637	68.1%

Sources: Washington Department of Corrections; Washington Sentencing Guidelines Commission (2012). Third Strike Offenses Triggering Mandatory LWOP in Washington 1999–2012. *Statistical Survey of Adult Felony Sentencing. Washington Sentencing Commission*. Available online: www.cfc.wa.gov/Publications.html.

A 2004 analysis by The Sentencing Project found that individuals released from life sentences were less than one-third as likely to be rearrested within three years as all released persons.[20] More recently, a 2011 California-based study tracked 860 people convicted of homicide and sentenced to life, all of whom were paroled beginning in 1995. Longitudinal analysis of their outcomes finds that in the years since their release, only five individuals (less than 1%) have been returned to prison or jail because of new felonies.[21]

To measure the potential for public safety implications of life-sentences, it is valuable to examine the behavior of life-sentenced prisoners who are still incarcerated; the behavior of people in prison is likely to be predictive of their behavior on release. Research literature is replete with support for the perspective that persons serving life sentences are some of the easiest prisoners to manage because of their compliance with prison rules and their interest in mentoring newer prisoners in positive ways.

For lifers, prison becomes their social universe for the long-term and maintaining order is a priority. Lifers are frequently lauded by correctional workers and called upon to be models for younger inmates.[22] Despite their ability to cope with prison life, the consequences of long-term imprisonment are still apparent. Those sentenced to lengthy terms of incarceration are more likely to become institutionalized, lose pro-social contacts in the community, and become removed from legitimate opportunities for success upon release.[23]

20   Mauer, M., King, R.S., & Young, M. (2004). *The Meaning of 'Life': Long Prison Sentences in Context.* Washington, DC: The Sentencing Project.
21   Weisberg, R. Mukamal, D., & Segall, J.D. (2011). *Life in Limbo: An Examination of Parole Releases for Prisoners Serving Life Sentences with the Possibility of Parole in California.* Stanford University: Stanford Criminal Justice Center.
22   Johnson, R., & Dobranska, A. (2005). Mature Coping among Life Sentenced Inmates: An Exploratory Study of Adjusted Dynamics. *Corrections Compendium*: 8–28.
23   Orsagh, T & Chen, J.R., (1988). The Effect of Time Served on Recidivism: An Interdisciplinary Theory. *Journal of Quantitative Criminology*, 4(2):155–171.

Recommendations for Reform

ELIMINATE SENTENCES OF LIFE WITHOUT PAROLE

Life without parole sentences are costly, shortsighted, and ignore the potential for transformative growth. States with life and LWOP sentences should amend their statutes to make all life sentences parole-eligible. The six states and the federal system with LWOP-only sentences should replace this structure with parole eligible terms. An example may come from Canada, where all persons serving life are considered for parole after serving 10 to 25 years.

Such a change would not necessarily mean that all parole eligible persons would be released; individualized calculations of public safety risk would determine this. However, each person in prison should have a meaningful opportunity for release that serves as a goal to work toward. The decision for release could be made by a professional parole board or the original sentencing judge and would take into account the individual's prospects for a successful transition to the community.

INCREASE THE USE OF EXECUTIVE CLEMENCY

One might think that clemency is an option for relief from an LWOP sentence, but governors nationwide have denied virtually all clemency requests over the past three decades.[24] Petitioners must depend on a shift in the political landscape in order to hope for relief through clemency. One's readiness for release should be a decision that is determined by a panel equipped to review the prisoner's original sentence and his or her rehabilitation since then, rather than being subject to the political atmosphere.

Some states have eased the ways in which inmates can be released from long sentences, And, in June 2009, a federal judge in Pennsylvania reaffirmed a lower-court ruling that eases the clemency request process for Pennsylvania inmates serving life sentences which began before 1997. Before this time, pardon recommendations required a simple majority vote by the state Pardons Board before being passed to the governor for review, but the law changed in late 1997 to require a unanimous vote instead. The present ruling allows inmates sentenced before 1997, perhaps as many as 3,000, to apply for a pardon under these earlier rules.

Pennsylvania is not alone in modifying its clemency application procedures; other states have made changes too. Unfortunately, these early release valves are rarely used. In Wisconsin, for instance, the Governor expanded a policy in 2009 that permits LWOP inmates to petition for release on the basis of age and infirmity but so far there have not been any inmates released under this policy. Virginia and several other states have a mechanism in place for geriatric release, but this, too, is rarely utilized.

PREPARE PERSONS SENTENCED TO LIFE FOR RELEASE FROM PRISON

The emergence of reentry as a criminal justice policy issue in the last decade has largely ignored persons serving a life sentence. Typically, reentry programs are provided to persons within six months of their release date and offer transition services in the community upon release. However, for persons serving a life sentence, their release date is not fixed and they are often overlooked as policymakers and correctional administrators consider reentry strategies. Additionally, persons serving a life sentence have unique reentry needs based upon the long duration of their prison term. The failure to design reentry strategies for persons serving a life sentence neglects one in nine persons in prison by denying them the opportunity to participate in valuable programming.

Reentry and reintegration principles must be extended to persons serving a life sentence. Correctional programs can contribute to a successful release and persons serving life should be encouraged to access the types of services that will help them transform their lives and improve their presentation before the parole board. One model is the *Life-Line* program, first enacted in Canada and now in its early stages in Colorado. In *Life-Line*, persons who have successfully reintegrated into society after serving a life sentence serve as mentors to those about to be released. So-called "in-reach workers" prepare individuals while they are still in prison for the challenges they will face and also assist those who have been released to the community.

---

24 Gill, M. M. (2010). Clemency for Lifers: The Only Road Out Is the Road Not Taken. Federal Sentencing Reporter, 23(1), 21–26.

RESTORE THE ROLE OF PAROLE

In 1967, the President's Crime Commission recommended that parole boards be staffed by correctional professionals rather than political appointees. However, more than 40 years later, parole boards remain the domain of political appointees and two-thirds of states lack any standardized qualifications for service. This has resulted in a highly politicized process that too often discounts evidence and expert testimony. Parole boards should be staffed with members who have a background in corrections or relevant social services in order to best assess suitability for release. They should also use risk-based release polices that consider a range of static and dynamic factors including criminal history, offense severity, prison disciplinary record, and program participation while incarcerated.

State Trends in the Use of Life Sentences

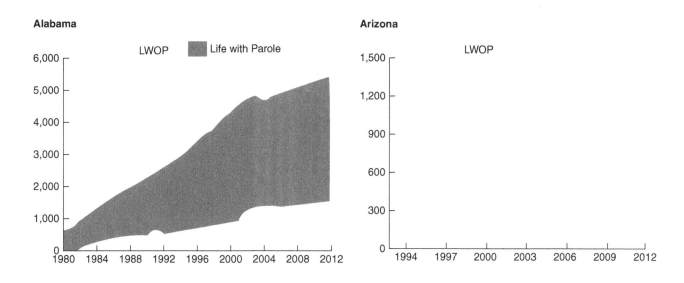

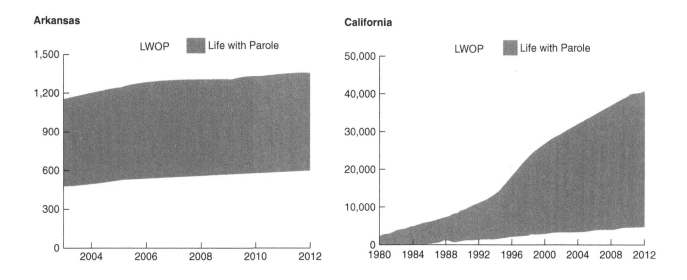

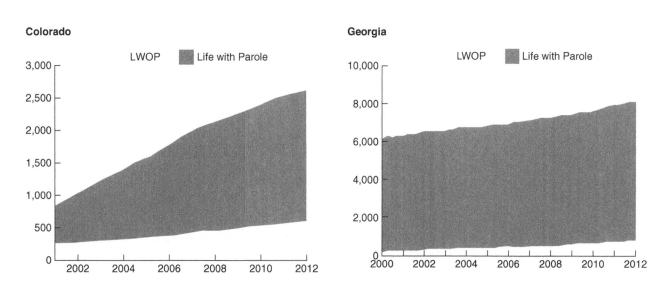

Indiana

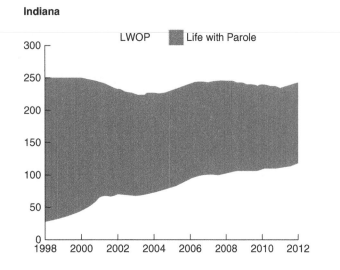

Iowa

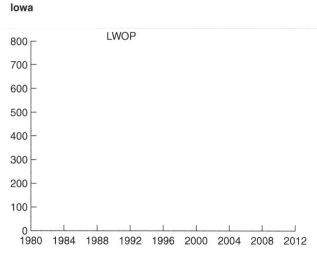

Kansas

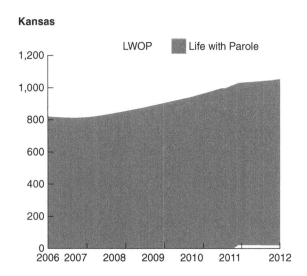

Kentucky

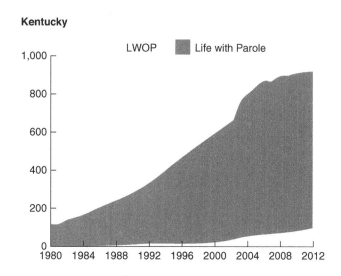

Louisiana

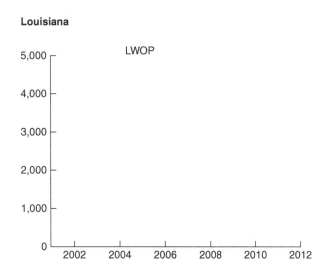

Massachusetts

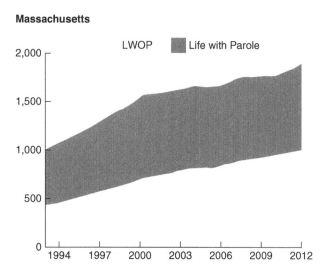

Michigan

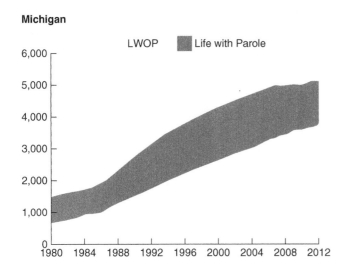

Minnesota

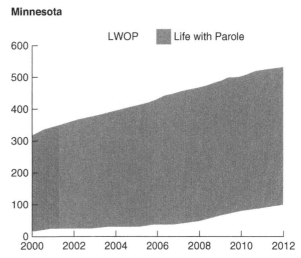

Mississippi

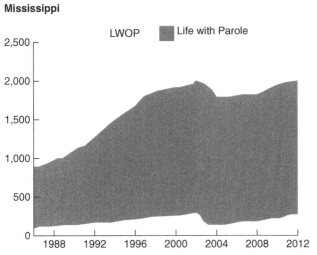

Missouri

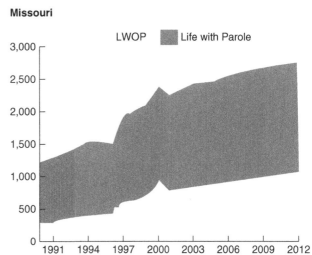

Nebraska

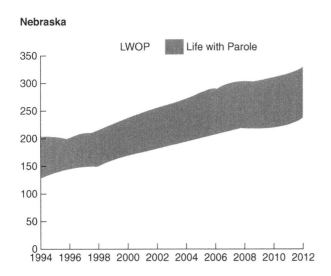

New Jersey

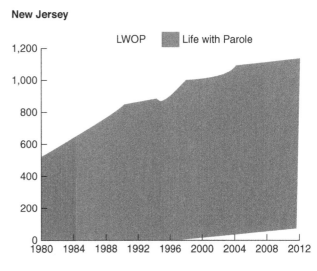

New York

North Carolina

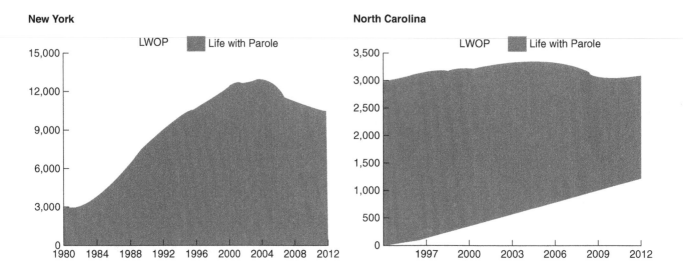

North Dakota

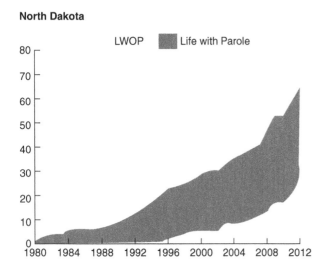

Oklahoma

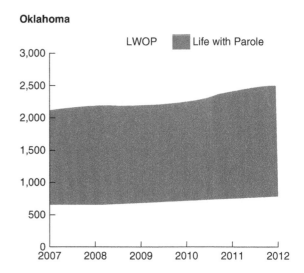

Pennsylvania

Rhode Island

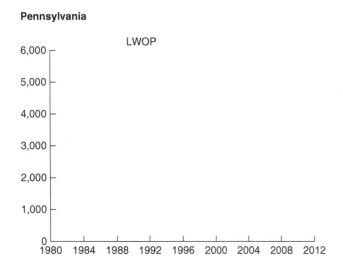

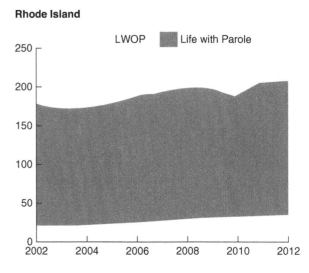

South Carolina

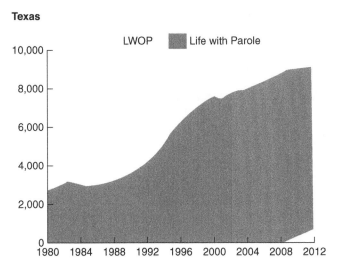

South Dakota

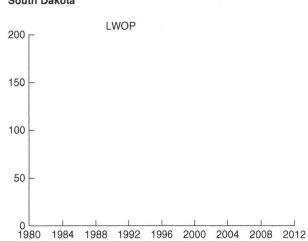

Texas

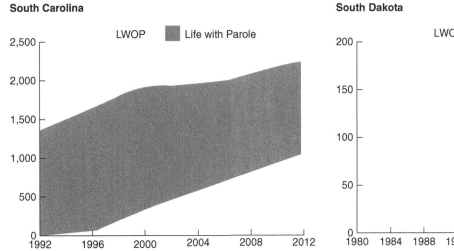

Washington

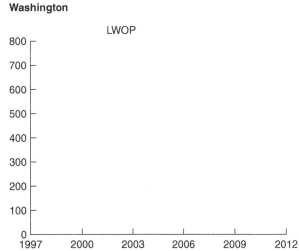

West Virginia

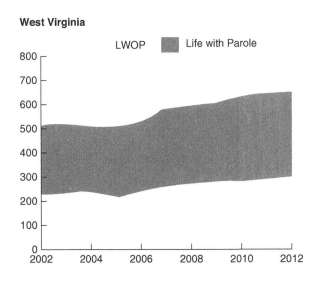

Wyoming

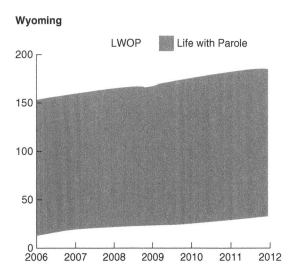

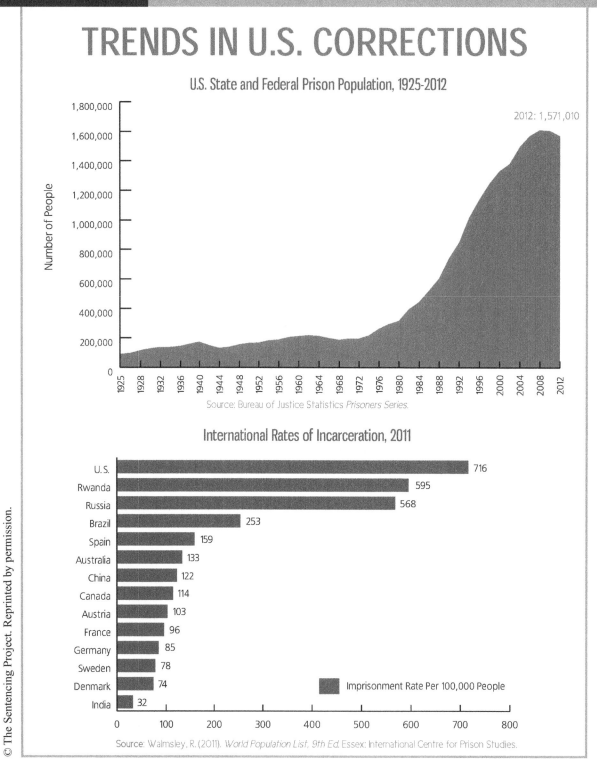

TRENDS IN U.S. CORRECTIONS

U.S. State and Federal Prison Population, 1925-2012

2012: 1,571,010

Source: Bureau of Justice Statistics *Prisoners Series.*

International Rates of Incarceration, 2011

Country	Imprisonment Rate Per 100,000 People
U.S.	716
Rwanda	595
Russia	568
Brazil	253
Spain	159
Australia	133
China	122
Canada	114
Austria	103
France	96
Germany	85
Sweden	78
Denmark	74
India	32

Source: Walmsley, R. (2011). *World Population List, 9th Ed.* Essex: International Centre for Prison Studies.

The Sentencing Project • 1705 DeSales Street NW, 8th Floor • Washington, D.C. 20036 • sentencingproject.org

MASS INCARCERATION

The United States is the world's leader in incarceration with 2.2 million people currently in the nation's prisons or jails — a 500% increase over the last forty years. Changes in sentencing law and policy, not changes in crime rates, explain most of this increase. These trends have resulted in prison overcrowding and fiscal burdens on states to accommodate a rapidly expanding penal system, despite increasing evidence that large-scale incarceration is not an effective means of achieving public safety.

State & Federal Prison Population by Offense, 2011

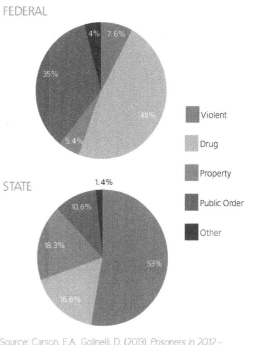

FEDERAL

- Violent
- Drug
- Property
- Public Order
- Other

STATE

State Expenditures on Corrections, 1985-2012

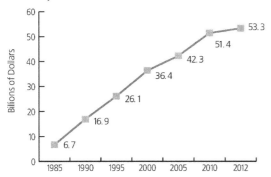

Source: National Association of State Budget Officers (1985–2012). *State Expenditure Report Series.* Washington, DC: National Association of State Budget Officers.

Source: Carson, E.A., Golinelli, D. (2013). *Prisoners in 2012 – Advance Counts.* Washington, D.C.: Bureau of Justice Statistics; Carson, E.A., Sabol, W.J. (2012). *Prisoners in 2011.* Washington, D.C.: Bureau of Justice Statistics.

Population Under Control of the U.S. Corrections System, 1980 & 2010

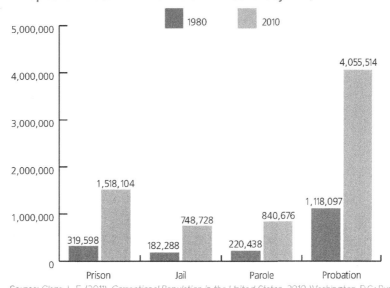

Source: Glaze, L. E. (2011). *Correctional Population in the United States, 2010.* Washington, D.C.: Bureau of Justice Statistics; *Corrections: Key Facts at a Glance.* Washington, DC: Bureau of Justice Statistics.

The Sentencing Project • 1705 DeSales Street NW, 8th Floor • Washington, D.C. 20036 • sentencingproject.org

Number of People in Prisons and Jails for Drug Offenses, 1980 and 2011

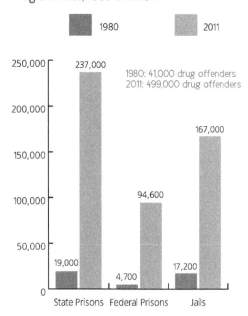

1980: 41,000 drug offenders
2011: 499,000 drug offenders

Sources: Carson, E.A., Sabol, W.J. (2012). *Prisoners in 2011.* Washington, D.C.: Bureau of Justice Statistics; Mauer, M. and King, R. (2007). *A 25-Year Quagmire: The War on Drugs and its Impact on American Society.* Washington, D.C.: The Sentencing Project.

DRUG POLICY

Sentencing policies of the War on Drug era resulted in dramatic growth in incarceration for drug offenses. Since its official beginning in 1982, the number of Americans incarcerated for drug offenses has skyrocketed from 41,000 in 1980 to half a million in 2010. Furthermore, harsh sentencing laws such as mandatory minimums keep drug offenders in prison for longer periods of time: in 1986, released drug offenders had spent an average of 22 months in federal prison. By 2004, federal drug offenders were expected to serve almost three times that length: 62 months in prison.

At the federal level, prisoners incarcerated on a drug conviction make up half the prison population, while the number of drug offenders in state prisons has increased eleven-fold since 1980. Most of these people are not high-level actors in the drug trade, and most have no prior criminal record for a violent offense.

Number of People in Federal Prisons for Drug Offenses, 1980-2010

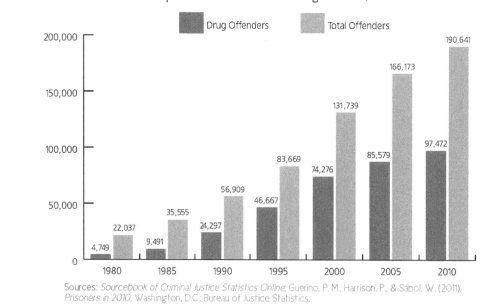

Sources: *Sourcebook of Criminal Justice Statistics Online;* Guerino, P. M., Harrison, P., & Sabol, W. (2011). *Prisoners in 2010.* Washington, D.C.: Bureau of Justice Statistics.

LIFE SENTENCES

The number of prisoners serving life sentences continues to grow even while serious, violent crime has been declining for the past 20 years and little public safety benefit has been demonstrated to correlate with increasingly lengthy sentences. The life population has more than quadrupled since 1984. One in nine people in prison is now serving a life sentence and nearly a third of lifers have been sentenced to life without parole.

Number of People Serving Life Without Parole Sentences, 1992-2012

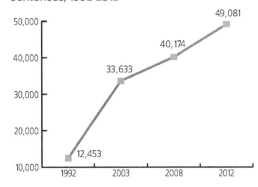

Number of People Serving Life Sentences, 1984-2012

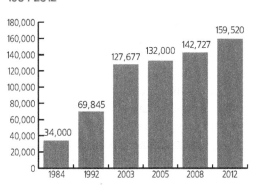

Source: Nellis, A. (2013). *Life Goes On: The Historic Rise in Life Sentences in America.* Washington, D.C.: The Sentencing Project.

YOUTH

There has been a troubling shift in the nation's responses to at-risk youth over the past 25 years. The creators of the juvenile justice system originally viewed it as a system for providing prevention, protection, and redirection to youth, but it is more common for youth today to experience tough sanctions and adult-type punishments instead. While reforms are underway in many jurisdictions, there remains an urgent need to reframe our responses to youth delinquency.

Number of Youth Held in Adult Prisons and Jails, 1985-2011

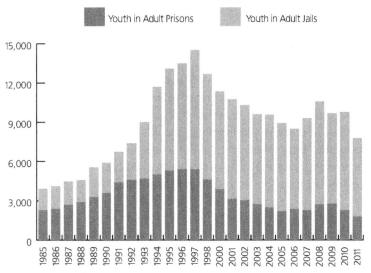

Sources: Austin, J., Johnson, K. D., & Gregoriou, M. (2000). *Juveniles in Adult Prisons and Jails: A National Assessment.* Washington, DC: Bureau of Justice Assistance; Bureau of Justice Statistics *Prison and Jail Inmates at Midyear Series.* Bureau of Justice Statistics *Prisoner Series.* Strom, K. J. (2000). *Profile of State Prisoners under Age 18: 1985-1997.* Washington, DC: Bureau of Justice Statistics.

REPORT OF THE SENTENCING PROJECT TO THE UNITED NATIONS HUMAN RIGHTS COMMITTEE
Regarding Racial Disparities in the United States Criminal Justice System
August 2013
The Sentencing Project

The United States criminal justice system is the largest in the world. At yearend 2011, approximately 7 million individuals were under some form of correctional control in the United States, including 2.2 million incarcerated in federal, state, or local prisons and jails.[25] The U.S. has the highest incarceration rate in the world, dwarfing the rate of nearly every other nation.[26]

Such broad statistics mask the racial disparity that pervades the U.S. criminal justice system. Racial minorities are more likely than white Americans to be arrested; once arrested, they are more likely to be convicted; and once convicted, they are more likely to face stiff sentences. African-American males are six times more likely to be incarcerated than white males and 2.5 times more likely than Hispanic males.[27] If current trends continue, one of every three black American males born today can expect to go to prison in his lifetime, as can one of every six Latino males—compared to one of every seventeen white males.[28] Racial and ethnic disparities among women are less substantial than among men but remain prevalent.[29]

The source of such disparities is deeper and more systemic than explicit racial discrimination. The United States in effect operates two distinct criminal justice systems: one for wealthy people and another for poor people and minorities. The former is the system the United States describes in its report: a vigorous adversary system replete with constitutional protections for defendants. Yet the experiences of poor and minority defendants within the criminal justice system often differ substantially from that model due to a number of factors, each of which contributes to the overrepresentation of such individuals in the system. As Georgetown Law Professor David Cole states in his book *No Equal Justice*,

> These double standards are not, of course, explicit; on the face of it, the criminal law is color-blind and class-blind. But in a sense, this only makes the problem worse. The rhetoric of the criminal justice system sends the message that our society carefully protects everyone's constitutional rights, but in practice the rules assure that law enforcement prerogatives will generally prevail over the rights of minorities and the poor. By affording criminal suspects substantial constitutional rights in theory, the Supreme Court validates the results of the criminal justice system as fair. That formal fairness obscures the systemic concerns that ought to be raised by the fact that the prison population is overwhelmingly poor and disproportionately black.[30]

By creating and perpetuating policies that allow such racial disparities to exist in its criminal justice system, the United States is in violation of its obligations under Article 2 and Article 26 of the International Covenant on Civil and Political Rights to ensure that all its citizens—regardless of race—are treated equally under the law. The Sentencing Project notes that the Committee has specifically asked the U.S. government to address the racial disparities in its criminal justice system in paragraph 4 of its List of Issues. We welcome this opportunity to provide the Committee with an accurate portrait of the current racial disparity in the U.S. criminal justice system.

---

25 U.S. Bureau of Justice Statistics, *Correctional Populations in the United States, 2011*, 1, 3 tbl.2 (Nov. 2012).
26 *See* International Centre for Prison Studies, *World Prison Brief* (2013).
27 U.S. Bureau of Justice Statistics, *Prisoners in 2011*, 8 tbl.8 (Dec. 2012).
28 Marc Mauer, *Addressing Racial Disparities in Incarceration*, 91 supp. 3 The Prison Journal 87S, 88S (Sept. 2011) (hereinafter Mauer).
29 Id.
30 David Cole, *No Equal Justice: Race and Class in the American Criminal Justice System*, 8–9 (1999) (hereinafter Cole).

Established in 1986, The Sentencing Project works for a fair and effective U.S. criminal justice system by promoting reforms in sentencing policy, addressing unjust racial disparities and practices, and advocating for alternatives to incarceration. Staff of The Sentencing Project have testified before the U.S. Congress and state legislative bodies and have submitted amicus curiae briefs to the Supreme Court of the United States on various issues related to incarceration and criminal justice policy. The organization's research findings are regularly relied upon by policymakers and covered by major news outlets.

This report chronicles the racial disparity that permeates every stage of the United States criminal justice system, from arrest to trial to sentencing. In particular, the report highlights the influence of implicit racial bias and recounts the findings of the burgeoning scholarship on the role of such bias in the criminal justice system. The report then details the ways in which the Supreme Court of the United States has curtailed potential remedies by discounting the importance of implicit bias and requiring that intentional discrimination be proven in constitutional challenges. Finally, the report offers recommendations on ways that federal, state, and local officials in the United States can work to eliminate racial disparity in the criminal justice system and uphold its obligations under the Covenant.

RACIAL DISPARITY IN POLICE ACTIVITY

Roughly 12% of the United States population is black. Yet in 2011, black Americans constituted 30% of persons arrested for a property offense and 38% of persons arrested for a violent offense.[31] Black youths account for 16% of all children in America yet make up 28% of juvenile arrests.[32]

One contributing factor to the disparity in arrest rates is that racial minorities commit certain crimes at higher rates. Specifically, data suggests that black Americans—particularly males—tend to commit violent and property crimes at higher rates than other racial groups.[33] Other studies, however, demonstrate that higher crime rates are better explained by socioeconomic factors than race: extremely disadvantaged neighborhoods experience higher rates of crime regardless of racial composition.[34] Because African Americans constitute a disproportionate share of those living in poverty in the United States,[35] they are more likely to reside in low-income communities in which socioeconomic factors contribute to higher crime rates. As such, Ohio State University researchers Lauren Krivo and Ruth Peterson found that "it is these differences in disadvantage that explain the overwhelming portion of the difference in crime, especially violent crime, between white and African American communities."[36]

A close examination of some other areas of the law demonstrates that higher crime rates cannot fully account for the racial disparity in arrest rates. A growing body of scholarship suggests that a significant portion of such disparity may be attributed to implicit racial bias, the unconscious associations humans make about racial groups. Implicit biases (commonly referred to as stereotypes) are activated when individuals must make fast decisions with imperfect information; biases—regardless of their accuracy—"fill in" missing information and allow individuals to make decisions in the limited time allowed.[37] Extensive research has shown that in such situations the vast majority of Americans of all races implicitly associate black Americans with adjectives such as "dangerous," "aggressive," "violent," and "criminal."[38] Since the nature of law enforcement frequently requires police officers to make snap judgments about the danger posed by suspects and the criminal nature of their activity, subconscious racial associations influence the way officers perform their jobs.

31　FBI Criminal Justice Information Services Division, *Crime in the United States, 2011*, tbl.43A, *available at* http://www.fbi.gov/about-us/cjis/ucr/crime-in-the-u.s/2011/crime-in-the-u.s.-2011/tables/table-43 (Sept. 2012).

32　National Council on Crime and Delinquency, *And Justice for Some: Differential Treatment of Youth of Color in the Justice System*, 3 (2007).

33　*See* Cole at 41–42.

34　*See* Lauren Krivo & Ruth Peterson, *Extremely Disadvantaged Neighborhoods and Urban Crime*, 75 Soc. F. 619 (1996) (hereinafter Krivo & Peterson).

35　See Human Rights Committee, *Concluding Observations of the Human Rights Committee on the United States of America*, ¶ 21, U.N. Doc. CCPR/C/USA/CO/3/Rev.1 (Dec. 18, 2006).

36　Krivo & Peterson at 642.

37　*See, e.g.,* Sandra Graham & Brian S. Lowery, *Priming Unconscious Racial Stereotypes About Adolescent Offenders*, 28 Law & Hum. Behav. 483, 485 (2004).

38　*See, e.g.,* Jennifer L. Eberhardt et al., *Seeing Black: Race, Crime, and Visual Processing*, 87 J. Personality & Soc. Psychol. 876, 876 (2004).

The effects of racial bias are particularly well demonstrated in the areas of traffic stops and drug law enforcement. Between 1980 and 2000, the U.S. black drug arrest rate rose from 6.5 to 29.1 per 1,000 persons; during the same period, the white drug arrest rate increased from 3.5 to 4.6 per 1,000 persons.[39] Yet the disparity between the increase in black and white drug arrests does not correspond to any significant disparity in black drug activity. In 2012, for instance, the National Institute on Drug Abuse published a study surveying drug usage among secondary school students in the United States from 1975–2011. The study found that white students were slightly more likely to have abused an illegal substance within the past month than black students.[40] Yet from 1980–2010, black youth were arrested for drug crimes at rates more than double those of white youth.[41] Disparity between black drug activity and black arrest rates is also present in adult populations: in Seattle in 2002, for instance, African Americans constituted 16% of observed drug dealers for the five most dangerous drugs but 64% of drug dealing arrests for those drugs.[42] While these arrests were for trafficking rather than possession, the modest evidence available suggests that most drug users purchase drugs from a dealer of their own race.[43]

Data on traffic stops also demonstrates the influence of racial bias on law enforcement practices and arrest rates. In the U.S. Department of Justice's report on *Contacts Between Police and the Public* released in 2011, the Bureau of Justice Statistics found that while white, black, and Hispanic drivers were stopped at similar rates nationwide, black drivers were three times as likely to be searched during a stop as white drivers and twice as likely as Hispanic drivers.[44] Furthermore, black drivers were twice as likely to experience the use or threat of violent force at the hands of police officers than both white and Hispanic drivers.[45] Such statistics are consistent with research indicating that the implicit racial association of black Americans with dangerous or aggressive behavior significantly increases police officers' willingness to employ violent or even deadly force against them.[46]

The national statistics mask greater disparities in some locales. In one New Jersey study, racial minorities made up 15% of drivers on the New Jersey Turnpike, yet 42% of stops and 73% of arrests made by police were of black drivers—even though white drivers and racial minorities violated traffic laws at almost identical rates. Other data from New Jersey showed that whites were less likely to be viewed as suspicious by police—even though stopped white drivers were twice as likely to be carrying illegal drugs as stopped black drivers and five times as likely to be carrying contraband as stopped Hispanic drivers.[47] In Volusia County, Florida, 148 hours of video footage documenting more than 1,000 highway stops by state troopers showed that only five percent of drivers on the roads were racial minorities but minorities constituted more than eighty percent of the people stopped and searched by police.[48] The police practice of targeting minority drivers has become so widespread that many black communities have begun referring to the phenomenon as "DWB" or "driving while black."[49]

The most widely publicized example of racial profiling in recent times is the "stop and frisk" tactic employed by the New York Police Department (NYPD). African Americans constitute 25% and Hispanic Americans constitute 29% of New York City's population.[50] Yet between 2010 and 2012, 52% of those stopped by the NYPD during "stop and frisk" were black and 32% were Hispanic.[51] White New Yorkers are 44% of the city's

39   Katherine Beckett et al., *Race, Drugs, and Policing: Understanding Disparities in Drug Delivery Arrests*, 44 Criminology 105, 106 (2006).

40   National Institute on Drug Abuse, *Monitoring the Future: National Survey Results on Drug Use*, 1975–2011, 130 tbl.4–7 (2012).

41   Office of Juvenile Justice and Delinquency Prevention, *Law Enforcement and Juvenile Crime, available at* http://www.ojjdp.gov/ojstatbb/crime/JAR_Display.asp?ID=qa05274 (Dec. 2012).

42   Beckett, 44 Criminology at 117 tbl.2. The five drugs observed were methamphetamine, heroin, powder cocaine, crack cocaine, and ecstasy.

43   K. Jack Riley, National Institute of Justice, *Crack, Powder Cocaine, and Heroin: Drug Purchase and Use Patterns in Six Major U.S. Cities*, 1 (Dec. 1997).

44   Christine Eith & Matthew R. Durose, Bureau of Justice Statistics, *Contacts Between Police and Public, 2008*, 1 (Oct. 2011).

45   *Id.* at 12 tbl.18.

46   See Joshua Correll et al., *The influence of stereotypes on decisions to shoot*, 37 Eur. J. of Soc. Psy. 1102, 1115 (2007); Joshua Correll et al., *The Police Officer's Dilemma: Using Ethnicity to Disambiguate Potentially Threatening Individuals*, 83 J. Personality and Soc. Psy. 1314, 1328 (2002).

47   Alexander at 133.

48   David A. Harris, *"Driving While Black" and All Other Traffic Offenses: The Supreme Court and Pretextual Traffic Stops*, 87 J. Crim. L. & Criminology 544, 561 (1997).

49   Cole at 36.

50   U.S. Census Bureau, *Census 2010* (2010).

51   Second Supplemental Report of Jeffrey Fagan, Ph.D. at 11 tbl.3, Floyd v. City of New York, 2013 U.S. Dist. LEXIS 68790 (S.D.N.Y. 2013) (08 Civ. 01034 (SAS)) (hereinafter Fagan).

population,[52] but only 9% of those stopped were white.[53] Nevertheless, among those stopped, arrest rates were virtually the same across races,[54] and blacks and Hispanics were slightly less likely than whites to be caught with weapons or contraband such as drugs.[55]

NYPD often cites the fact that racial minorities tend to be clustered in neighborhoods designated as "high crime areas" to justify racial disparity in stop rates. Yet data compiled by Dr. Jeffrey Fagan shows that when New York's neighborhoods are divided into quintiles based on crime rates, NYPD officers cite "high crime area" as the justification for stops at nearly identical rates in every quintile.[56] In other words, police consider neighborhoods with the lowest crime rates to be "high crime areas" just as much as neighborhoods with the highest crime rates. The racial disparity in the implementation of "stop and frisk" has led to ongoing class action litigation against the NYPD led by the Center for Constitutional Rights. In August 2013, U.S. District Court Judge Shira Scheindlin ruled that the policy violated the Fourteenth Amendment's promise of equal protection and mandated that the police department implement a variety of specific remedies.

RACIAL DISPARITIES IN TRIALS

Contact with law enforcement officials and arrests are merely the first step in minority defendants' journey through the criminal justice system. Once racial minorities enter the system, they continue to confront racial bias at every stage of litigation. This section highlights the influence of racial bias on all the major actors in a criminal trial: defense counsel, prosecutors, judges, and juries. It is important to note that the portions of following section that address indigent defense counsel and prosecution are not sweeping indictments of all public defenders and prosecutors in the United States. Thousands of public defenders and prosecutors work diligently and effectively each day to represent their clients and ensure that justice is done in a racially fair manner. Nevertheless, data demonstrates that implicit racial bias—in combination with challenges caused by inadequate resources and training—influences both indigent defense and prosecutorial decisionmaking and contributes to racial disparity in the criminal justice system in significant ways. Where current policies allow implicit racial bias to go unmonitored and unchecked, they warrant closer scrutiny and present opportunities for reform.

Indigent Defense Counsel

Fifty years after the celebrated Supreme Court decision *Gideon v. Wainwright* held that indigent defendants have a right to publicly appointed defense counsel in all criminal trials,[57] U.S. Attorney General Eric Holder declared that "America's indigent defense counsel systems exist in a state of crisis."[58] Most indigent defense agencies are grossly understaffed and underfunded. In 2012, more than 70% of public defender offices reported that obtaining adequate funding and providing adequate compensation for their attorneys were extremely or very challenging to the ability of their office to provide indigent defense services.[59]

An analysis of funding at both the state and federal levels indicates that effective indigent defense is not a priority in many jurisdictions in the United States. At the state and local level, 15,026 public defenders in 957 indigent defense offices handled 5,572,450 cases in 2007.[60] On average, each office handled 5,823 new cases and each public defender handled 371 cases—more than one new case for each day of the year. The states

---

52   U.S. Census Bureau, *Census 2010* (2010).

53   Fagan at 11 tbl.3.

54   *Id.* at 34 tbl.14. Arrest rates were 6.73% for whites, 6.19% for blacks, and 6.36% for Hispanics.

55   *Id.* at 35 tbl.15. Weapons or contraband were seized in 2.16% of white stops, 1.43% of black stops, and 1.49% of Hispanic stops.

56   *Id* at 33 fig.13.

57   372 U.S. 335 (1963).

58   Eric Holder, Remarks at the Justice Department's 50th Anniversary Celebration of the U.S. Supreme Court Decision in *Gideon v. Wainwright* (Mar. 15, 2013), http://www.justice.gov/iso/opa/ag/speeches/2013/ag-speech-1303151.html.

59   U.S. Gov't Accountability Office, GAO-12-569, *Indigent Defense: DOJ Could Increase Awareness of Eligible Funding and Better Determine the Extent to Which Funds Help Support This Purpose*, 10 (May 2012) (hereinafter GAO-12-569).

60   Bureau of Justice Statistics, *Census of Public Defender Officers, 2007*, 3 tbl.1 (Sept. 2010).

spent a total of $2.3 billion on indigent defense in 2007, or $414.55 per case.[61] Furthermore, of the $5.9 billion in federal grants that agencies could have used for indigent defense, fully two thirds of agencies reported that they did not allocate any funding for that purpose.[62] Indeed, only 54% of agencies reported that they were even aware that discretionary funds *could* be used for indigent defense.[63] Of the agencies that did allocate grant money to indigent defense, the amount allocated for that purpose constituted only 4.7% of their total grant money allocations.[64]

The crippled state of indigent defense in the United States disproportionately affects racial minorities because black and Hispanic defendants are far more likely to need the services of a public defender than their white counterparts. The median income for black and Hispanic Americans is roughly $20,000 less than the median income for white Americans.[65] The poverty rate is roughly 25% for both black and Hispanic Americans, compared to 9% for white Americans.[66] In the criminal justice context, such statistics mean that black and Hispanic defendants are often more likely than white defendants to rely on an indigent defense system of overworked, underpaid attorneys—therefore increasing their chances of being convicted.

The chronic overburdening of public defenders also creates an opportunity for implicit racial bias to influence the decisions they make. Because public defenders are responsible for many more cases than they can effectively manage, they must decide which of their cases will receive the bulk of their limited resources and attention—a process called "triage" because of its similarity to that of emergency room doctors in deciding which of their patients to treat first. As professors Song Richardson and Phillip Goff write, "for most [public defenders], the question is not 'how do I engage in zealous and effective advocacy,' but rather 'given that all my clients deserve aggressive advocacy, how do I choose among them?'"[67]

As the law enforcement context demonstrates, implicit racial bias thrives in situations in which individuals must make snap judgments with imperfect information, particularly when they are cognitively depleted, anxious, or distracted—precisely the type of environment in which most public defenders in the United States work on a daily basis. Racial bias may affect public defenders' initial appraisal of which cases are worth their time and energy as well as how they interact with their clients.[68] While specific research has yet to be done on the extent to which implicit racial bias influences the indigent defense system, extensive documentation on the impact of implicit racial bias in similar fields strongly suggests that such bias has some impact on public defenders and further contributes to racial disparity in the criminal justice system.[69]

Prosecution

The office of prosecutor is regarded by many as the most powerful position in the U.S. criminal justice system.[70] Prosecutors decide which cases to investigate, which suspects to charge, which charges to bring, and which penalties to pursue upon conviction. As the U.S. criminal justice system has been flooded with an unprecedented number of defendants over the past three decades, prosecutors have become increasingly subject to the mounting pressures of "triage" similar to public defenders. While the exercise of discretion in such circumstances is not unreasonable, it also creates the opportunity for biased decisionmaking that may contribute further to racial disparity.

The racial disparity revealed by several studies of prosecutorial decisions suggests that implicit racial bias does in fact influence prosecutors' decisionmaking. A study conducted shortly after the Supreme Court

61   *Id.*
62   *Id.*
63   *Id.* at 29 tbl.8.
64   *Id.* at 32–33 figs.9 & 10. The majority of discretionary grant funding was used for law enforcement purposes. See *id.* at 2–25 figs.5&6.
65   U.S. Census Bureau, *Income, Poverty, and Health Insurance Coverage in the United States: 2010*, 6 tbl.1 (Sept. 2011).
66   *Id.* at 15 tbl.14.
67   L Song Richardson & Phillip Atiba Goff, *Implicit Racial Bias in Public Defender Triage*, 122 Yale L.J. 2626, 2632 (2013).
68   For an extensive discussion of the ways implicit racial bias may affect each of these areas, see *id.* at 2635–38.
69   *See, e.g.,* Chet D. Schrader & Lawrence M. Lewis, *Racial Disparity in Emergency Department Triage*, 49 J. Emergency Med. 511 (2013); Dan-Olof Rooth, *Implicit Discrimination in Hiring: Real World Evidence* (Inst. for the Study of Labor, Discussion Paper No. 2764, 2007); Joshua Correll et al., *The Influence of Stereotypes on Decisions to Shoot*, 37 Eur. J. Soc. Psychol. 1102 (2007).
70   *See* Angela J. Davis, *Arbitrary Justice: The Power of the American Prosecutor,* 5 (2008) (hereinafter Davis).

reauthorized the use of capital punishment in 1976 found that the probability of a black defendant being indicted for killing a white person was more than twice as high as that of a white defendant killing a black person. Furthermore, prosecutors were significantly more likely to upgrade cases to felony murder status in cases in which defendants were black rather than white.[71] Similarly, a study conducted in 1993 in Los Angeles found that 95% of the 4,632 crack cocaine defendants prosecuted in California state court were black and 100% of the 42 crack cocaine defendants prosecuted in federal court were either black or other racial minorities.[72]

One of the most well-studied interactions between racial bias and prosecutorial decisionmaking involves substantial assistance departures. Federal law allows prosecutors to request that a judge "depart" from the mandatory minimum sentence for a crime in a particular case when the defendant has provided "substantial assistance" to law enforcement. Research shows that prosecutors request substantial assistance departures at higher rates for "salvageable" and "sympathetic" defendants—those who are white, female, and have children.[73] A 2001 analysis of more than 77,000 cases in the federal system from 1991 to 1994 revealed that black and Hispanic male defendants were significantly less likely to receive substantial assistance departures than white male defendants. This disparity remained even when the data was controlled for the severity of the offense, prior criminal history, and the specific district court's sentencing tendencies.[74] When prosecutors did request substantial assistance departures for nonwhite male defendants, the average downward adjustment such defendants received was roughly six months less than that for white male defendants.[75] Accordingly, departures from standard sentencing guidelines accounted for 56% of the total racial disparity in sentence lengths in the federal system from 1991–1994.[76]

Juries, Trial Judges, and Presumptions of Innocence

Prosecutors and defense attorneys fulfill important roles in American trials by presenting evidence, questioning witnesses, and framing legal issues, but they do not make the final determination of guilt or innocence for defendants. In the American system, that role falls to the jury or—in some cases in certain jurisdictions—the trial judge. One of the most celebrated hallmarks of the United States criminal justice system is the presumption of innocence, the concept that defendants are innocent and must be treated as such until they are proven guilty in a court of law. Yet a growing body of research suggests that implicit racial bias affects trial judges and jury members' ability to evaluate guilt and innocence objectively, skewing their judgment of black defendants' cases toward guilty verdicts regardless of the evidence presented at trial.

In 1986, the Supreme Court held in *Batson v. Kentucky* that it is unconstitutional for prosecutors to strike jurors from a jury in a criminal trial on the basis of race.[77] Nevertheless, the all-white jury remains far too common a phenomenon in the U.S. An analysis of juries in death penalty cases in 2001, for instance, found that 25% of the examined juries had no black members and roughly 70% had two or fewer.[78] The authors' analysis revealed both a strong "white male dominance effect" and a "black male presence effect" in cases involving black defendants and white victims: the presence of five or more white male jurors dramatically increased the likelihood of conviction and subsequent imposition of a death sentence in such cases, while the presence of one or more black male jurors substantially reduced the probability of the same.[79] Furthermore, jury members' conception of appropriate punishment polarized along racial lines in black defendant/white victim cases, with

---

71   William Bowers & Glenn Pierce, *Arbitrariness and Discrimination under Post-Furman Capital Statutes*, 26 Crime & Delinq. 563, 611–14 (1980).

72   Richard Berk & Alec Campbell, *Preliminary Data on Race Crack Charging Practices in Los Angeles*, 6 Fed. Sentencing Rep. 37 (1993).

73   The "salvageable" and "sympathetic" descriptors were coined by I.H. Nagel & S.J Schulhoefer, *A tale of three cities: An empirical study of charging and bargaining practices under the federal sentencing guidelines*, 66 So. Cal. L. Rev. 501 (1992).

74   David Mustard, *Racial, Ethnic, and Gender Disparities in Sentencing: Evidence from the Federal Courts*, 44 J. L. & Econ. 285, 308–09 tbl.10 (2001).

75   *Id.* at 311.

76   *Id.* at 303.

77   476 U.S. 79 (2012).

78   William Bowers et al., *Death Sentencing in Black and White: An Empirical Analysis of the Role of Jurors' Race and Jury Racial Composition*, 3 U. Pa. J. Const. L. 171, 191 n.99 (2001).

79   *Id.* at 193.

white jurors strongly favoring death and black jurors strongly favoring life imprisonment.[80] Such racial effects were notably absent in capital cases in which the defendant and the victim were members of the same race.[81]

As with other areas of the criminal justice system, research indicates that such racial effects are likely more attributable to implicit racial bias and subconscious activation of racial stereotypes than to explicit racial discrimination. Because American social norms have evolved considerably over the past fifty years, most white American jurors are no longer comfortable expressing overt racial prejudice in their decisionmaking. Nevertheless, research consistently demonstrates that white jurors are substantially more likely to convict black defendants than white defendants based on similar evidence.[82] Interestingly, University of Michigan researchers Samuel Sommers and Phoebe Ellsworth found that white juror racial bias essentially vanishes in cases in which race is a salient factor of the trial.[83] Sommers and Ellsworth theorize that the prominence of racial issues in a trial may serve as a subtle reminder to white jurors to be on guard against prejudice in their decisionmaking; when race is non-salient in a trial, the same white jurors may let their guard down and allow their decisions to be subconsciously affected by racial stereotyping.[84]

A verdict is not immune from the effects of implicit racial bias when it is rendered by a trial judge rather than a jury. A 2009 study led by Cornell Law Professors Jeffrey Rachlinski and Sheri Johnson found the same—or perhaps even higher—levels of implicit racial bias in trial judges as in the general population.[85] The authors' analysis further showed that judges' bias influences their decisions in determining both whether to convict defendants and the sentence to impose in each case.[86]

RACIAL DISPARITY IN SENTENCING

Once minority defendants are convicted, they are likely to be sentenced more harshly than white defendants convicted for similar crimes. As in other areas of the criminal justice system, much overt racial discrimination in the sentencing process has been eliminated over the past decades—yet race remains a significant factor in sentencing decisions. In 2000, Professor Cassia Spohn concluded after her comprehensive survey of 40 studies covering 30 years of sentencing outcomes at both the state and federal levels:

> Although it is irrefutable that the primary determinants of sentencing decisions are the seriousness of the offense and the offender's prior criminal record, race/ethnicity and other legally irrelevant offender characteristics also play a role. Black and Hispanic offenders—and particularly those who are young, male, or unemployed—are more likely than their white counterparts to be sentenced to prison; they also may receive longer sentences than similarly situated white offenders. Other categories of racial minorities—those convicted of drug offenses, those who victimize whites, those who accumulate more serious prior criminal records, or those who refuse to plead guilty or are unable to secure pretrial release—also may be singled out for more punitive treatment.[87]

Professor Spohn's conclusion has been further verified by research conducted over the past decade. In his 2001 analysis of 77,236 federal cases from 1991 to 1994, for instance, Professor David Mustard found that even when cases were controlled for the severity of the offense, the defendant's prior criminal history, and the specific district court's sentencing tendencies, blacks received sentences 5.5 months longer than whites and

---

80   *Id.* at 200.

81   *Id.* at 201.

82   *See, e.g.,* Samuel R. Sommers & Phoebe C. Ellsworth, *White Juror Bias: An Investigation of Prejudice Against Black Defendants in the American Courtroom,* 7 Psy. Pub. Pol'y & L. 201, 217 (2001); *see also* Justin Levinson et al., *Guilty by Implicit Racial Bias: The Guilty/Not Guilty Implicit Association Test,* 8 Ohio St. J. Crim. L. 187 (2010) (finding that mock jurors possessed an implicit association between "black" and "guilty").

83   Sommers & Ellsworth at 219.

84   *Id.* at 209.

85   Jeffrey J. Rachlinski et al., *Does Unconscious Bias Affect Trial Judges?,* 84 Notre Dame L. Rev. 1195, 1210 (2009).

86   *Id.* at 1220–23.

87   Cassia Spohn, *Thirty Years of Sentencing Reform: The Quest for a Racially Neutral Sentencing Process,* 55–56, available at http://www.justicestudies.com/pubs/livelink3–1.pdf (2000).

Hispanics received sentences 4.5 months longer than whites.[88] When income was considered as a variable, the disparity became even greater: blacks with incomes of less than $5,000 were sentenced most harshly of all, receiving sentences that were on average 6.2 months longer than other defendants.[89] Because the average sentence length was 46 months, this data means that poor black defendants received sentences on average 13% longer than other defendants.

Capital Punishment

Racial disparity is particularly pronounced in cases involving the most severe penalty imposed by the U.S. criminal justice system: the death penalty. The United States has executed 1,335 individuals[90] since the Supreme Court reinstated capital punishment in its 1976 decision *Gregg v. Georgia*.[91] As of January 1, 2013, more than 3,100 prisoners awaited execution on death row in the U.S.[92] Of those, 42% were black.[93]

Numerous studies have shown that two racial variables affect capital punishment sentencing: the race of the perpetrator and the race of the victim. First, defendants convicted of the homicide of a white victim are substantially more likely to face the death penalty than those convicted of killing nonwhite victims. White people constitute half of murder victims in the United States each year,[94] but 77% of persons executed since 1976 were convicted of killing white victims.[95] Comparatively, black people also constitute half of murder victims,[96] but only 13% of persons executed since 1976 were convicted of killing black victims.[97] A 1990 Government Accountability Office survey of 28 separate studies found that in 82% of the studies, the race of the victim was shown to influence the likelihood of a defendant receiving the death penalty, with those convicted of murdering white victims more likely to be sentenced to death than those convicted of murdering black victims even when the cases were controlled for crime- specific variables.[98]

Second, black defendants are more likely to be sentenced to death regardless of the race of their victims. An extensive 1998 study of Philadelphia death penalty cases found that black defendants were 38% more likely to be sentenced to death, even when the researches controlled for the severity of the homicide.[99] The GAO confirmed that 75% of the 28 studies it surveyed in 1990 found that black defendants were more likely to receive the death penalty than white defendants.[100]

When these two factors are taken together, the impact of race on capital sentencing is staggering. Since 1976, the United States has executed *thirteen times* more black defendants with white victims than white defendants with black victims.[101] Such statistical disparities have led many of the most respected American jurists to call for the abolition of the death penalty altogether because of its racially disparate impact, among other factors.[102]

---

88   Mustard, *supra* note 50, at 300. Significantly, females of all races received sentences 5.5 months shorter than males of all races.

89   *Id.* at 301.

90   Death Penalty Information Center, http://www.deathpenaltyinfo.org/number-executions-state-and-region-1976 (last visited June 13, 2013).

91   428 U.S. 153 (1976).

92   Deborah Fins, NAACP Legal Defense Fund, *Death Row USA: Winter 2013*, 1 (2013) (hereinafter *Death Row USA*). The exact number was 3,125.

93   *Id.*

94   Bureau of Justice Statistics, *Homicide Trends in the United States, 1980–2008*, 3 tbl.1 (November 2011).

95   *Death Row USA at 5.*

96   Bureau of Justice Statistics, *Homicide Trends in the United States, 1980–2008*, 3 tbl.1 (November 2011).

97   *Death Row USA* at 5.

98   U.S. Gov't Accountability Office, GAO GGD-90–557, *Death Penalty Sentencing: Research Indicates Pattern of Racial Disparities*, 5 (Feb. 1990) (hereinafter GAO GGD-90–557).

99   David Baldus et al., *Racial Discrimination and the Death Penalty in the Post-*Furman *Era: An Empirical and Legal Overview, with Recent Findings from Philadelphia*, 83 Cornell L. Rev. 1638 (1998).

100   GAO GGD-90–557 at 6.

101   Death Penalty Information Center, http://www.deathpenaltyinfo.org/race-death-row-inmates-executed-1976#deathrowpop (last visited June 13, 2013).

102   *See, e.g.,* William Brennan, Jr., *Neither Victims Nor Executioners*, 8 Notre Dame J.L. Ethics & Pub. Pol'y 1, 4 (1994).

The "War on Drugs"

The United States government's War on Drugs has perhaps contributed more than any other single factor to the racial disparities in the criminal justice system. Since its official beginning in 1982, the number of Americans incarcerated for drug offenses has skyrocketed from 41,000 in 1980 to nearly a half-million in 2007.[103] Furthermore, harsher sentencing laws such as mandatory minimums keep drug offenders in prison for longer periods of time: in 1986, released drug offenders had spent an average of 22 months in federal prison. By 2004, federal drug offenders were expected to serve almost three times that length: 62 months in prison.[104]

Data demonstrates that the War on Drugs has been waged in racially disparate ways. From 1999–2005, African American constituted roughly 13% of drug users on average[105] but 36% of those arrested for drug offenses[106] and 46% of those convicted for drug offenses.[107] While the War on Drugs creates racial disparity at every phase of the criminal justice process, disparities in sentencing laws for various types of drugs and harsh mandatory minimum sentences disproportionately contribute to disparity.

One of the most frequently decried aspects of the War on Drugs is the chronic disparity between federal sentencing laws for crack and powder cocaine offenses. For more than two decades, the ratio of the amount of powder cocaine needed to trigger the same sentence as an amount of crack cocaine was 100:1—even though crack and powder are pharmacologically identical.[108] Because black Americans constitute 80% of those sentenced under federal crack cocaine laws each year,[109] the disparity in sentencing laws leads to harsher sentences for black defendants for committing similar offenses to those of their white or Latino counterparts convicted of possessing powder cocaine. While the Fair Sentencing Act of 2010 reduced the crack/cocaine sentencing quantity disparity to 18:1, thousands continue to languish in prison serving sentences applied under the old laws because the act has not been applied retroactively.[110]

Furthermore, the Fair Sentencing Act did nothing to alter the harsh federal mandatory minimum sentences imposed for virtually all drug offenses. Mandatory minimums are most often triggered by sale of a certain quantity of a given drug; federal law prescribes a five-year mandatory minimum sentence for sale of one gram of LSD, for example.[111] Once the mandatory minimum is triggered, judges must impose the mandatory sentence regardless of mitigating factors such as the defendant's role in the offense or the likelihood of committing a future offense. In 2010, the number of black male offenders convicted of a federal offense subject to a mandatory minimum sentence was twice that of convicted white males.[112] Mandatory minimum provisions doubled the average length of sentences received by black defendants, from 76 months for all federal offenses to 152 months when the federal offense was subject to a mandatory minimum provision.[113]

The blind application of mandatory minimums often leads to travesties of justice like the case of Tonya Drake, a twenty-five year old mother of four on welfare. A stranger on the street approached her, gave her a $100 bill and a package, and told her that if she mailed the package for him she could keep the change—which amounted to $47.40. Unbeknownst to Tonya Drake, the package contained crack cocaine. She is now serving ten years in federal prison. At her sentencing hearing, Judge Richard Gadbois, Jr., said, "This woman doesn't belong in prison for ten years for what I understand she did. That's just crazy, but there's nothing I can do about it."[114]

---

103   Marc Mauer & Ryan King, *A 25-Year Quagmire: The War on Drugs and Its Impact on American Society*, 2 (2007).

104   *Id.* at 7–8.

105   Marc Mauer, *The Changing Racial Dynamics of the War on Drugs*, 8 tbl.3 (2009).

106   *Id.* at 10 tbl.5.

107   *Id.* at 11 tbl.6.

108   Alexander at 51.

109   U.S. Sentencing Commission, *2012 Sourcebook of Federal Sentencing Statistics*, tbl.34 (2012).

110   Kara Gotsch, *Breakthrough in U.S. Drug Sentencing Reform: The Fair Sentencing Act and the Unfinished Reform Agenda*, 9 (2011).

111   21 U.S.C. § 841.

112   United States Sentencing Commission, *Report to the Congress: Mandatory Minimum Penalties in the Federal Criminal Justice System*, 142 fig.7–15 (Oct. 2011).

113   *Id.* at 139 tbl.7–3.

114   Cole at 142.

Unfortunately, Tonya Drake's story is far from an anomaly in the War on Drugs. Literally hundreds of thousands of Americans—disproportionately Americans of color—have seen their lives ravaged by the U.S.'s policies regarding drug activity. The War on Drugs is a perfect illustration of the way the effects of racial bias become amplified as defendants move through the criminal justice system: bias causes law enforcement officers to stop, search, and arrest racial minorities at disproportionate rates; minority defendants bear a disproportionate risk of facing stiff charges but have smaller chances of receiving a substantial assistance departure or being represented by effective defense counsel; they are more likely to be convicted by juries and trial judges on similar evidence; and they are likely to receive harsher penalties for similar crimes. Each step in the process further widens the racial gap in the criminal justice system.

CLOSING THE COURTHOUSE DOOR: DISCRETION, RACIAL BIAS, AND THE SUPREME COURT

Even as the effects of racial bias on every aspect of the criminal justice system have become increasingly well documented and understood, opportunities for meaningful reform have been increasingly foreclosed. Over the past half-century, various Supreme Court decisions have refused to acknowledge the importance of implicit racial bias and have therefore allowed its effects on the criminal justice system to flourish. This process occurs in two phases: first, the Court grants law enforcement officials and prosecutors wide discretion in determining whom to stop, search, arrest, and charge, thereby increasing the opportunity for racial bias to influence decisionmaking. Second, the Court shuts down challenges to such policies rooted in evidence of their racially disparate impact, requiring instead that plaintiffs show explicit and intentional discrimination on the part of criminal justice personnel. The colorblindness of the Constitution—once a hallmark of the protections of minority rights in the United States—has instead become a mechanism whereby racial minorities are frequently locked out of the courthouse and into prison cells.

Increasing Discretion of Law Enforcement Personnel

Two lines of precedent over the past forty years have drastically expanded the discretion of law enforcement personnel under the Fourth Amendment, which protects citizens against "unreasonable searches and seizures." The first began with *Terry v. Ohio* in 1968, in which the Supreme Court held that a brief investigatory stop did not require police to meet the full probable cause standard of the Fourth Amendment.[115] Rather, such a stop is constitutional so long as police possess "reasonable suspicion that crime is afoot."[116] Furthermore, if there is reason to believe that a suspect might be armed or carrying contraband, police may conduct a brief "frisk" of a suspect's person. In the 45 years since *Terry* was decided police forces across the United States have used the language in *Terry* to justify employing "stop and frisk" tactics for an ever-expanding list of reasons. In New York City, for example, the justification for officers' reasonable suspicion in more than fifty percent of stops was "furtive movements"—a nebulous term that has escaped precise definition by even the most seasoned police veterans.[117]

The second line of precedent involves "consent searches," which allow police officers to circumvent the probable cause requirement when suspects voluntarily consent to be searched. While consent searches have always been a standard law enforcement practice in the U.S., the Court significantly diluted the meaning of "voluntary" in the 1991 case *Florida v. Bostick*.[118] The Court ruled that the appropriate test for whether consent is voluntary is whether a reasonable person would have felt free to terminate the encounter with the police. Applying the test to Bostick's case, the Court determined a reasonable person on a crowded bus with police standing over him, displaying badges and guns and blocking his exit, should have felt free to terminate the encounter.[119]

---

115   392 U.S. 1 (1968).
116   *Id.* at 30.
117   Fagan at 22 tbl.11.
118   501 U.S. 429 (1991).
119   *Id.* at 439.

In so ruling, the Supreme Court ignored the coercion inherent in every citizen interaction with the police. As Judge Prentice Marshall observed in a different case, "implicit in the introduction of the officer and the initial questioning is a show of authority to which the average person encountered will feel obliged to stop and respond. Few will feel that they can walk away or refuse an answer."[120] It is not surprising, therefore, that one officer testified that he had searched more than 3,000 bags without once being refused consent.[121]

Lowering the Standard for Indigent Defense Counsel

While the Court's decision in *Gideon v. Wainwright* guarantees defendants the right to counsel in all criminal trials, two cases decided together in 1984, *Strickland v. Washington*[122] and *United States v. Cronic*,[123] have allowed the quality of indigent defense to diminish by lowering the standard of what is considered competent performance by defense attorneys in criminal trials. In the words of Georgetown Law Professor David Cole, "too often, assistance of counsel for the poor can be like getting brain surgery from a podiatrist."[124]

In *Strickland* and *Cronic*, the Court established "a strong presumption that counsel's conduct falls within the wide range of reasonable professional assistance."[125] In order to overcome such a "highly deferential" standard, defendants must prove that their attorneys' performance was "outside the wide range of professionally competent assistance."[126] Defendants must then prove that their attorneys' incompetence prejudiced the outcome of their trials—in other words, that there is a "reasonable probability that the result would have been different" if the defendants had received effective counsel.[127]

Application of the *Strickland* standard by the U.S. federal judiciary has exacerbated the "state of crisis" in indigent defense. Very few defendants have been able to meet the *Strickland* standard to have their convictions invalidated due to ineffective indigent defense counsel; consequently, federal, state, and local governments have been permitted to underfund and understaff their public defense agencies. Courts have found that defendants failed to meet the *Strickland* standard when their defense counsel slept during portions of the trial, when counsel abused cocaine and heroin throughout the course of the trial, and when counsel admitted that he was not prepared on the law or the facts of the case.[128] In one case, an attorney in a capital murder trial was found competent even though he "consumed large amounts of alcohol each day of the trial, drank in the morning, during court recess, and throughout the evening, and was arrested during jury selection for driving to the courthouse with a .27 blood-alcohol content."[129] The attorney's alcoholism was so severe that he died of the disease between the end of the trial and the date the California Supreme Court handed down its decision in the case.[130]

Closing the Door to Challenges Based on Racially Disparate Impact

As the Court has expanded discretion in some areas of the criminal justice system, it has refused to hear challenges based on the racially disparate impact of such discretion in two others: prosecution and capital punishment.

In the 1896 decision of *Yick Wo v. Hopkins*, the Court established that selective prosecution—the practice of only charging defendants of a certain race of certain crimes—was unconstitutional under the Fourteenth Amendment to the Constitution. Yet in the 127 years since *Yick Wo*, the Court has not invalidated a single federal or state criminal case because prosecutors exercised their discretion in a racially disparate manner.

120   *Illinois Migrant Council v. Pilliod*, 398 F.Supp. 882, 889 (N.D. Ill. 1975).
121   Cole at 16.
122   466 U.S. 668 (1984).
123   466 U.S. 668 (1984).
124   Cole at 76–77.
125   *Id.* at 689.
126   *Id.* at 690.
127   *Id.* at 694.
128   *Id.*
129   *People v. Garrison*, 765 P.2d 419, 440 (Cal. 1989).
130   *Id.*

Rather, the Court has made claims of selective prosecution—like claims of ineffective defense counsel—practically impossible to prove.

In 1992, the Supreme Court ruled in *United States v. Armstrong* that defendants must prove a "colorable showing" of selective prosecution before proceeding even to the discovery phase of trial.[131] Because the vast majority of the evidence that would prove claims of selective prosecution is in prosecutors' offices, defendants cannot access it without the authority of court orders that arise from discovery motions. By refusing to allow claims of selective prosecution to advance to discovery unless the defendant proves a "colorable showing," the Court essentially requires defendants to prove a claim in order to get access to the evidence they need to prove it.

In an attempt to meet the "colorable showing" standard, Armstrong's lawyers submitted evidence demonstrating that no white individuals had been prosecuted for crack cocaine offenses in a three-year period. Additionally, the defense submitted two sworn statements. The first recounted the observation of a halfway house intake coordinator that in his experience treating crack addicts, whites and blacks dealt and used the drug equally. In the second, a defense attorney stated that many white defendants were prosecuted for crack offenses in state court. The government also submitted a list of 2,400 individuals charged with crack offenses over a three-year period; all but eleven were black and none were white. Yet the Court overturned the trial court's finding that such evidence was enough to meet the colorable showing standard, finding that Armstrong's evidence was insufficient even to warrant further investigation in the discovery phase.

In 1987, the Supreme Court faced the most conclusive evidence demonstrating the link between race and the criminal justice system it had ever seen in *McCleskey v. Kemp*.[132] McCleskey, a black man sentenced to death in Georgia, argued that the implementation of the death penalty in Georgia violated the Eighth and Fourteenth Amendments to the Constitution because of its racially disparate impact. To support his claims, McCleskey relied on an exhaustive study conducted by Professor David Baldus and his colleagues who studied more than 2,000 murder cases in Georgia in the 1970s. As in Baldus's later study in Philadelphia, the Georgia study revealed that black defendants with white victims were significantly more likely to be sentenced to death than white defendants with black victims.[133]

In its 5–4 majority opinion, the Court called into question the reliability of the Baldus study, but ultimately ruled that the study's validity did not matter. Even if the Baldus study were accurate and vast racial disparities existed in Georgia's implementation of capital punishment, the Court decided, it was not cruel and unusual punishment unless McCleskey and similarly situated black defendants could show that the prosecutor, judge, or jury acted with *intentional* racial animus in their specific cases. Since traditional rules in both the federal and state criminal justice systems bar defendants from probing into prosecutors' and juries' motivations, such a showing is practically impossible to make. Unless a jury member or prosecutor voluntarily admits to acting for racially biased reasons—taboo in the United States' colorblind society—minority defendants cannot challenge the racially disparate impact of capital punishment under the Constitution. Not surprisingly, the *McCleskey* standard has never been met.[134]

RECOMMENDATIONS TO THE COMMITTEE

As the evidence presented in this report indicates, the causes of the racial disparities in the U.S. criminal justice system are complex and deeply rooted. While the laws of the United States may be facially colorblind, a growing body of evidence shows that the individuals who apply such laws do not make cognitively colorblind decisions. As studies repeatedly demonstrate, the belief that the United States of the present is unaffected by the centuries of its explicitly racist past—while perhaps well- intentioned—is at best wishful thinking and potentially blinds decision makers to the implicit racial bias that lingers in the American consciousness.

---

131   517 U.S. 456 (1992).

132   481 U.S. 279 (1987).

133   In the Georgia study, black defendants with white victims were sentenced to death 22% of the time while white defendants with black victims received the death penalty 3% of the time. The disparity held true even when the study factored in thirty nonracial factors such as multiple murders, long criminal records, or strong eyewitness testimony. See Cole at 133.

134   *Id.* at 136.

There are concrete measures, however, that the United States can adopt to reduce both the existence and the effects of racial bias in its criminal justice system. Eliminating racial disparity in its criminal justice system will not be easy for the United States, but it can and must take steps to do so in order to uphold its obligations under its own constitution and international law. As such, The Sentencing Project respectfully urges the Committee to recommend that the United States adopt the following ten measures.

1. Establish a National Criminal Justice Commission

The United States should establish a National Criminal Justice Commission to examine incarceration and racial disparities. The commission should develop recommendations for systemic reform of the criminal justice system at the federal, state, and local levels.

2. Scale back the War on Drugs

The United States should substantially scale back its War on Drugs. Specifically, the Department of Justice should reconsider and reduce the volume of low-level drug offenders prosecuted in federal court. The resources saved by decreasing the number of prosecutions should be invested in evidence-based drug prevention and treatment measures.

3. Eliminate mandatory minimum sentences

The United States should eliminate mandatory minimum sentences. Judges should be allowed to consider individual case characteristics when sentencing a defendant in every case.

4. Abolish capital punishment

The United States should abolish capital punishment. Regardless of its other moral implications, history has repeatedly demonstrated that the capital punishment system of the United States cannot operate in a racially neutral manner. At the very least, the United States should pay particular attention to increasing the quality of defense representation in capital cases and increase oversight of such cases to ensure that they are administered as fairly and race-neutrally as possible.

5. Fully fund indigent defense agencies

The United States should fully fund and staff indigent defense agencies. The federal government should increase the number and value of grants specifically allocated for indigent defense and establish oversight and accountability systems to ensure such funds are used as intended. The government should also ensure that state and local governments know which discretionary grants can be used to fund indigent defense agencies and encourage them to use an appropriate portion of discretionary grant funding for that purpose. The United States should provide funding and resources sufficient for the defense bar to operate at the same level of effectiveness at trial as prosecutors.

6. Adopt a policy requiring the use of racial impact statements

The United States should adopt a policy requiring the use of racial impact statements for proposed sentencing policies. Such a policy would require legislators to prepare an analysis assessing the possible racial consequences of any proposed legislation before enacting it in order to avoid any unintended disparate racial effects.[135] Three states—Iowa, Connecticut, and Oregon—have adopted racial impact statements since 2008.

---

135   Marc Mauer, *Racial Impact Statements: Changing Policies to Address Disparities*, 23 vol. 4 Criminal Justice 16 (Winter 2009).

7. Allow social framework evidence and structural reform litigation in trials

The United States should modify its racial discrimination jurisprudence in two ways: permit social framework evidence and structural reform litigation. The admission of social framework evidence in discrimination trials would permit juries and judges to consider expert testimony regarding the general existence and effects of implicit bias against racial minorities in reaching verdicts in discrimination cases against specific entities.[136] Structural reform litigation would allow racial minorities to challenge specific government policies as discriminatory on the basis of their demonstrated racially disparate impact without being required to prove intentional racial discrimination.[137] Under a structural reform litigation model, the plaintiff in *McCleskey v. Kemp* would have been allowed to proceed with his case by relying on the evidence that black men were significantly more likely than white men to receive the death penalty in Georgia without needing to show that any individual actor in his specific case had acted in an intentionally discriminatory manner. Though some limited precedent already exists for both social framework evidence and structural reform litigation in American jurisprudence,[138] the U.S. Congress should solidify their existence and importance by codifying them in Titles VI, VII, and XI of the Civil Rights Act of 1964.[139]

One state has provided a model for how social framework evidence could be incorporated into existing law. In 2009, North Carolina enacted the Racial Justice Act, which prohibited prosecutors or courts from seeking or imposing the death penalty on the basis of race. The act allowed death row inmates to challenge their sentences using social framework evidence, including statistics that demonstrated the racially disparate application of the death penalty in their districts. If defendants proved that race was a significant factor in the imposition of the death penalty in their cases, their sentences were automatically commuted to life in prison without the possibility of parole. Unfortunately, North Carolina repealed the Racial Justice Act in 2013 after Gov. Pat McCrory stated that the law effectively shut down capital punishment in the state.[140]

8. Enact the Racial Profiling Act of 2013

The United States should enact the End Racial Profiling Act of 2013. Indeed, the act serves as a model of what effective racial bias legislation could look like in every area of the criminal justice system. The act, reintroduced into the United States Senate by Senator Ben Cardin in May 2013, would prohibit racial profiling, mandate training on racial profiling for federal law enforcement officials, and require that federal officials collect data on the racial impact of all routine or spontaneous investigatory activities. The act would also make federal funds to state and local law enforcement agencies contingent on their adoption of effective policies that prohibit racial profiling. Finally, the act would authorize the Department of Justice to provide grants for the development of effective, non-discriminatory policing practices and require the attorney general to provide periodic reports to assess the ongoing effects of any practices that have been shown to be racially discriminatory.

9. Develop and implement training to reduce racial bias

The United States should develop and implement training designed to mitigate the influence of implicit racial bias for every actor at every level of the criminal justice system: police officers, public defenders, prosecutors, judges, and jury members. While it is difficult to eliminate completely racial bias at the individual level, studies have repeatedly shown that it is possible to control for the effects of implicit racial bias on individual

---

136   *Id.* at 493–94.

137   *Id.* at 494–98.

138   *See, e.g.,* Price Waterhouse v. Hopkins, 490 U.S. 228 (1989), *superseded by statute,* Civil Rights Act of 1991, Pub. L. No. 102–166, 105 Stat. 1074, *as recognized in Univ. of S.W. Tex. Med. Ctr. v. Nassar,* 133 S.Ct. 2517, 2520 (permitting social framework evidence in a sex discrimination case); Farrakhan v. Gregoire, No. CV-96-076-RHW, 2006 U.S. Dist. LEXIS 45987 at *3 (E.D. Wash. July 7, 2006) (finding for plaintiffs in a challenge to Washington's felony disenfranchisement law based on racially disparate impact), *aff'd* 590 F.3d 989 (9th Cir. 2008), *rev'd en banc* 623 F.3d 990 (9th Cir. 2010).

139   42 U.S.C. § 2000.

140   CNN, *"Racial Justice Act" repealed in North Carolina,* http://www.cnn.com/2013/06/20/justice/north-carolina-death-penalty (June 21, 2013).

decisionmaking.[141] In other words, while it may be impossible in the current culture of the United States to ensure that individuals are cognitively colorblind, it is possible to train individuals to be *behaviorally* color-blind.[142] The United States should work with leading scholars on implicit bias to develop the most effective training programs to reduce the influence of implicit racial bias.

10. Adopt racial disparity-conscious policies

Finally, as a general measure, the United States should adopt policies that reflect a basic understanding that while laws that are racially neutral on their face represent admirable progress in the struggle against racism in the U.S., such facial neutrality has proven insufficient to eliminate racial bias and consequently racial disparity in the criminal justice system. Policies should be guided instead by an awareness that facially colorblind laws may be applied in a racially disparate manner due to *both* implicit racial bias and explicit racial discrimination. The United States should affirmatively adopt a commitment to behavioral realism—the idea that the law should be based on the most accurate model of human thought, decisionmaking, and action provided by the sciences—called for by Professors Jerry Kang and Kristen Lane.[143] Such a concept is not unprecedented in American jurisprudence: one of the most celebrated Supreme Court decisions in U.S. history, *Brown v. Board of Education*, relied on behavioral realism in overturning the "separate but equal" doctrine; the Supreme Court's reasoning in that case was based on advancing research in the study of psychology and the effects of segregation on schoolchildren.[144]

The foregoing suggestions by no means constitute an exhaustive list of steps the United States could and should take to begin to address the racial disparities in its criminal justice system. Nevertheless, The Sentencing Project earnestly believes that these steps are firmly within the purview of the United States government and would substantially reduce existing racial disparity while dramatically improving the quality and integrity of the criminal justice system. While many of these steps are admittedly difficult, each one is vital if the United States is to fulfill its obligations to its citizens and the international community.

CONCLUSION

For decades, the United States of America has employed mass incarceration as a convenient answer to inconvenient questions. In doing so, the U.S. government has glossed over the glaring racial inequalities that permeate every aspect of its criminal justice system. The government has both fostered and perpetuated those inequalities in clear violation of its obligations under the International Covenant on Civil and Political Rights as well as other international agreements.

More importantly, however, the proliferation of racial disparities in the U.S. criminal justice system has a real impact on the lives of people of color living in the United States. Behind each statistic lies the face of a young black man whose potential has been cut short by a harsh prison sentence mandated by draconian drug laws. Behind each percentage point lies the face of a Latina child who will only know her parents through hurried, awkward visits in a prison visitation room. Behind each dataset lies a community of color bereft of hope because its young people have been locked away.

It is the human face—a face of color—of the racial injustice of the United States criminal justice system that is the most compelling reason for reform. It is time for the United States to take affirmative steps to eliminate the racial disparities in its criminal justice system.

---

141   *See, e.g.*, Ashby Plant & Michelle Peruche, *The Consequences of Race for Police Officers' Response to Criminal Suspects*, 16 Psy. Sci. 180, 183 (2005) (finding that repeated training of police officers on computer simulations eliminated racial shooter bias and that the effects were still present 24 hours later); Rachilinski et al., *supra* note 61, at 1221 (finding that implicit racial bias in trial judges is substantially mitigated when judges become aware of the need to monitor themselves for it); Mark Bennett, *Unraveling the Gordian Knot of Implicit Bias in Jury Selection: The Problems of Judge-Dominated Voir Dire, the Failed Promise of Batson, and Proposed Solutions*, 4 Harv. L. & Pol'y Rev. 149, 169 (describing the efforts of one federal district judge to mitigate implicit racial bias in jurors by training them on it before trial); *cf.* Sommers & Ellsworth, *supra* note 58 (finding that white juror bias was essentially eliminated in trials in which race was a salient factor, likely because jurors were reminded to be on guard against racially motivated decisions).
142   *See* Kang & Lane, *supra* note 118, at 487.
143   *See* Jerry Kang & Kristen Lane, *Seeing Through Colorblindness: Implicit Bias and the Law*, 58 UCLA L. Rev. 465, 466 (2010).
144   347 U.S. 483, 489 n.4 (1954).

CHAPTER FOUR
Capital Punishment

DEATH ROW

Mark Costanzo

People sentenced to death are sent to death row. Located in the maximum-security units of state penitentiaries, death rows are nonetheless a world apart Because the men (and the few women) on the row have been judged to be beyond redemption not even halfhearted attempts at rehabilitation are made. In most states, the inhabitants of death row spend from twenty to twenty-two hours per day in their cells. For a couple of hours each day, they are free to play games and roam a concrete yard bounded by fences and razor wire.

The one commodity death-row inmates have in abundance is time, Their constant enemies are crushing boredom and loss of, all hope. There is too much time to think. One observer put it this way: "The inhabitants of the row live lives that don't bear much thinking about. There's the ugly past that got them to this place, the miserable present, and the future they don't want to come."[66]

After the trial, after the appeals have been exhausted, and after long years of confinement on the row, the execution date finally arrives. The nature of life on death row, the rituals and procedures used to kill condemned prisoners, and the effects of living on death row are the subject of the next section.

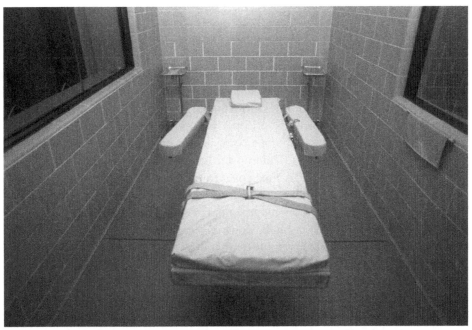

age fotostock / SuperStock.

BETWEEN SENTENCING AND EXECUTION: LIFE ON DEATH ROW

Death row is a prison within a prison. It is a special area of the prison designed to hold inmates who are waiting to be killed. It is little more than a warehouse, a massive holding tank, a storage facility for people awaiting their appointment with the executioner. Death rows are usually housed in the maximum-security sections of major state penitentiaries, in an area segregated from the general prison population. Because very few inmates will get out of death row alive (some will be executed, many will have their sentences overturned, many will die natural deaths), there is no attempt to educate, rehabilitate, or in any way improve the residents of the row. The conditions of confinement are far more restrictive than those of the general prison population. With a few notable exceptions, there is no access to training programs or prison work.

Most death-row inmates spend about twenty-one hours a day in a six-by-nine foot cell. In the cell are usually a toilet, a sink, a narrow bed, and a small metal locker. If you tore out the bathtub in your family bathroom and replaced it with a bed, you would have something a bit nicer than an average cell on death row. Imagine spending the next ten years of your life in your reconstructed bathroom. Each day you have 24 hours to fill; each week you have 168 hours. Even if you eat your meals very slowly and sleep 10 hours per day, there are still hundreds of days and thousands of hours to fill each year. The idleness, monotony, and relentless boredom are enough to unravel the sanity of most men.

Three times a day, the occupants of death row receive a meal through a slot in their cell door. Twice a week they are locked into a metal cage with a shower head for a ten-minute shower. Perhaps two or three hours a day they are permitted to go outdoors to a fenced-in concrete area known as "the yard." At night the lights in the cells are dimmed, but the lights in the corridor still burn brightly. Ventilation is poor, and the air is stagnant and full of the smells of men who seldom shower as well as the smells from scores of toilets. It is too hot in summer, too cold in winter, and it is almost always noisy. Men yell to one another through the bars, radios and televisions play, rolling carts clatter through the corridors, steel doors slam shut.

Television is the primary diversion on many death rows, and the presence of TV serves the interests of the prison staff. A journalist who has written extensively about death row puts it this way:

> God, it drives the hard-liners in the legislature and the firebrands of talk radio crazy to think that prisoners on death row have TV sets in their cells. Coddling the criminals! Indulging them with luxuries! It would be hard to find a prison guard, though, who opposed the sets. Television is the only thing that makes death row manageable. The prison staff has a special nickname for those TV sets . . . "electronic tranquilizers."[82]

THE PRICE TAG

To be sure, the cost of life imprisonment without parole (LWOP)—the alternative to a death sentence—is very high. A full accounting of the cost of LWOP must include the construction, financing, and operation costs of a maximum-security cell. The annualized costs of building and operating such a cell are approximately $5,000, and the cost of maintaining a maximum-security prisoner is approximately $20,000 per year.[104] Taking into account the average age of incarceration for someone convicted of homicide (30.8 years) and the average life expectancy for males in U.S. prisons, Raymond Paternoster has estimated that the total cost of LWOP ranges from $750,000 to $1.1 million per prisoner.[105] Actual costs could be substantially reduced if prisoners serving life sentences worked while in prison. That is, murderers could work to reduce the cost of their own confinement. This is already done in a limited way—many prisoners perform custodial work and some even produce products for prison-based industries—but it could be done more extensively.

Given the high price of imprisonment, it is possible to imagine a hypothetical case where an execution might be less expensive than life imprisonment. For example, if a healthy twenty-year-old was sentenced to prison and died of natural causes sixty years later, it *might* be more expensive than if he had been sentenced to death and refused to appeal his sentence. But such hypothetical cases miss the point: Cost estimates must include the cost of financing our system of capital punishment. It is not the cost of a particular case that is relevant, it is the full cost of sustaining an elaborate death-penalty system that consumes substantial time and resources and hangs like a weight on our criminal courts.

Although the cost of LWOP is high, the cost of capital punishment is far higher. In California, our most populous state, it is estimated that taxpayers could save $90 million annually by abolishing the death penalty.[106] Between 1977 and 1996, California spent more than $1 billion on its death penalty but managed to execute only five men. One of the men asked to be killed. In New York, the Department of Correctional Services calculated that reinstatement of the death penalty would cost the state $118 million each year.[107]

Even the per-execution cost is enormous. In Florida, the average cost is $3.2 million.[108] In Wisconsin, the Legislative Fiscal Bureau has estimated that reinstating the death penalty would cost the state between $1.6 million and $3.2 million per execution.[109] In California, capital trials are six times more expensive than other murder trials.[110] Texas kills more condemned prisoners than any other state and it is also the state that has done the most to minimize the time between trial and execution. Yet even in Texas each capital case costs taxpayers an average of $2.3 million, nearly three times the cost of imprisonment: in a maximum-security cell for forty years.[111] Texas spent more than $183 million on the death penalty during a six-year period.[112] Harris County (which includes the city of Houston) has the dubious distinction of leading the country in the number of capital trials. In 1994, Harris County commissioners attempted to raise taxes to cover the staggering costs of capital trials. Angry voters rejected the tax hike, so fire and ambulance services had to be cut instead. Harris County is not alone. Capital trials create a crushing financial burden for many counties because counties bear a disproportionate share of the cost.

In the most thorough investigation of cost to date, Phillip Cook and Donna Slawson collected data on cost for each phase of the legal process in North Carolina. Their conclusion: Compared to first-degree murder cases in which the death penalty is not sought, the *extra* cost of adjudicating a capital case through to execution is $2.16 million.[114] But this figure underestimates the true cost because it includes only costs to state and local government (excluding all private and federal costs).

Of course, we spend time as well as money. Both the California and Florida supreme courts spend roughly half their time reviewing death-penalty cases.[115] This means that state supreme courts don't have enough time to resolve important issues affecting civil and criminal law. Personnel from state attorney generals' offices also spend considerable time responding to appeals, and governors must spend time reviewing requests to commute death sentences.

While supporters of the death penalty may quibble with the cost estimates from a particular study, the bottom line is clear: Maintaining a system of capital punishment is far more expensive than sending murderers to prison until they die of natural causes. No systematic study has reached a contrary conclusion. Even if the debilitating cost of the death penalty could be cut by half—a very unlikely event—it would still be the more expensive option. Clearly, whatever benefits Americans receive from maintaining a system of capital punishment come at a very high price. The punishment of death punishes taxpayers and drains away precious resources from the criminal justice system.

WHY THE DEATH PENALTY IS SO COSTLY

One reason that maintaining the death penalty is so expensive is that capital trials are more complex and time-consuming than other criminal trials at every stage in the legal process: crime investigation, pretrial preparation, jury selection, guilt trial, penalty trial, and appeals. Most of the money is spent early in the process—on preparing for and conducting the capital murder trial.

Trial preparation begins when the district attorney's office decides to seek the death penalty. A competently conducted capital trial requires a thorough investigation of both the crime and the offender. Because of the penalty phase, pretrial investigators will attempt to locate and interview anyone who may be able to offer testimony that can serve as mitigating evidence (e.g., members of the defendant's family, friends, co-workers, neighbors, and teachers). The personal history of the defendant is painstakingly reconstructed in an effort to explain the defendant's crime. Investigations in capital cases take three to five times longer than noncapital murder investigations and carefully conducted investigations frequently take as long as two years to complete. The use of various experts—mental health professionals, polygraphers, medical experts, forensic scientists, and jury-selection consultants—also adds to the costs. Finally, pretrial motions (i.e., requests for a ruling from the judge on various legal issues) are numerous and complex. Capital cases typically involve the filing of two to six times as many motions as noncapital cases.[116]

The process of selecting jurors also takes longer in capital trials. Few prospective jurors are able or willing to commit themselves to participating in a trial that may last for weeks or months. Attorneys in capital cases are permitted to excuse more jurors than usual for no stated reason and are given greater latitude in questioning potential jurors. Thus, jury pools must be larger. In many states, jurors are questioned individually so that their answers will not influence other potential jurors. As noted in Chapter 2, capital trials include the added complication of death qualification. Finally, attorneys take more time during *voir dire* because jurors are being selected for two trials—a guilt trial and a separate penalty trial. For these reasons, jury selection takes about five times longer in capital trials than in noncapital murder trials.[117]

Attorneys in capital cases must investigate and prepare for a charge of first-degree murder *and* other felony charges that qualify the offense as capital (e.g., rape or robbery). Because of the enormous workload, both defense and prosecution teams usually include two attorneys and many investigators. The need to formulate a guilt-phase strategy that complements the penalty-phase strategy further complicates the job of prosecutors and defenders. Capital guilt phases consume ten to twenty times as many attorney labor-hours as noncapital cases, and capital trials generally last three times longer than comparable noncapital trials.[118] Most important, the extra costs associated with capital trials are incurred not only when a defendant is sentenced to death, but also when a defendant is acquitted or sentenced to life imprisonment. Since only a minority of capital offenders are sentenced to death—estimates range from less than 30 percent to only 10 percent[119]—most of the money that is spent to maintain our system of capital punishment is spent on the lengthy, expensive trials of defendants who end up being sentenced to life imprisonment. Thus, the cost per death sentence is astronomical.

Although most of the money spent on capital punishment is spent before appeals even begin, the labyrinthine appeals process for capital cases is also expensive. Estimates of the cost of appealing a single capital case range from $170,000 to $219,000.[120] Capital appeals generally cost more than noncapital appeals be cause of the complexity of the legal issues involved, the number of different issues that can be raised, and the availability of multiple avenues for appeal. Because a high proportion of appeals in capital cases are successful, and because the defendant's life is at stake, there is ample incentive for pursuing every avenue of appeal. When an appeal is successful, the state must bear the cost of fighting the death sentence *as well as* the cost of imprisoning the convict for life. This is the key to understanding the true cost of the death penalty: We pay the high price of a capital trial *not only* when a defendant is sentenced to death, but *also* when a defendant is acquitted or sentenced to life imprisonment. And only about three out of every ten capital cases culminate in a sentence of death. For the minority of defendants who do receive a death sentence, we pay for an expensive capital trial *and* an expensive appeals process. When an appeal is successful, the state bears the cost of fighting the death sentence *in addition to* the cost of life imprisonment.

Finally, the price tag for capital punishment includes the considerable expense of operating death rows. Death row is an expensive maximum-security unit within a large penitentiary. As many analysts have noted, the demands of running a death row create problems for prison officials. "Without the sentence of death, the condemned would not necessarily be the most dangerous prison inmates demanding the limited single cells available for strict security. In consequence, the prison system is severely restricted in its ability to find secure space for its own troublemakers."[121] The mere existence of death row has an unsettling effect on the entire prison population, and during the days preceding and following a scheduled execution, disruptive behavior by inmates peaks.

Compared to the massive costs of capital trials, appeals, and incarceration on death row, the cost of building, maintaining, and operating an execution chamber is only a tiny drop in a large bucket. But it is worth mentioning. The chamber and the additional personnel time needed to run the execution machinery and to prepare the condemned prisoner for death also add to the cost.

The majority of defendants accused of capital crimes do not the in the execution chamber. Some aren't convicted, many are convicted but not sentenced to death, many have their sentence reversed on appeal, a few have their death sentences commuted, and others the before being marched to the execution chamber.

Still, the vast and intricate procedural machinery of capital punishment must continue to be financed. Massive resources are squandered, courts and prisons are strained, just so that, eventually, a few condemned prisoners can be killed. Whatever satisfaction we receive from executions must be weighed against the time and money spent to sustain our system of capital punishment.

The true price of the death penalty looms even larger when one considers what economists call "opportunity costs"—in this case, the value of what could have been purchased if the death penalty had not been purchased. Put differently, the tremendous sums of money expended each year to maintain a system of capital punishment could be spent more productively elsewhere, for example, on programs designed to prevent or suppress crime. In recent years, many states have been forced to take extraordinary steps to deal with shrinking budgets. Early intervention and education programs have been cut, and violent offenders have been released early from prisons. Yet capital punishment has been spared by budget cutters. By focusing on killing a handful of individual offenders, we divert precious attention and millions of dollars away from reforms that address the causes of violent crime.

Is the Death Penalty fairly Applied?

Till the infallibility of human judgment shall have been proved to me, I shall demand the abolition of the death penalty.

—Marquis de Lafayette

In 1995 Orenthal James Simpson went on trial for the savage murder of his former wife, Nicole Brown Simpson, and her friend Ronald Goldman. Mr. Simpson was handsome and charming, a record-setting football hero, a persuasive pitchman for several products, and a sometime movie actor. Most important, he was a multimillionaire.

One of the first decisions faced by the L.A. district attorney's office was whether to seek the death penalty. They decided not to. That decision was certainly reasonable. Mr. Simpson had no prior felony convictions and, because one of the victims was the mother of his two young children, executing him would have made the children orphans. He was also a beloved celebrity, a hero to many Americans. It would have been difficult to persuade a jury to sentence O.J. to die by execution. Also, political pressures may have been decisive. The DA had been elected with strong support from the black community and leaders in that community made it clear that they would prefer that the death penalty not be at stake. Finally, seeking the death penalty is rare; the Los Angeles District Attorney's Office decides to seek the ultimate penalty in only 16 percent of eligible cases.[130]

But, as many critics of the decision pointed out at the time, prosecutors could also have found reasons for pursuing an execution. There were, after all, two victims, and both of their throats had been brutally slashed, leaving them nearly decapitated. One of the victims had no personal relationship with the defendant. There was also a history of violence: Simpson had been arrested as a teenager, he had pleaded no contest to a charge of spousal abuse five years earlier, and there was clear evidence of recurrent wife beating. The history of violence, the vicious nature of the crime, and the number of victims might have been used to justify a decision to seek the death penalty. My point is not that prosecutors should have tried to have Mr. Simpson killed. This book argues against the death penalty. The point is that wealth and position tipped the scales of justice in Mr. Simpson's favor from the very earliest stages in the process.

A decision not to seek an execution changes the dynamics of the case. Jurors in capital cases must be "death qualified"; prospective jurors who claim that they are incapable of voting for a sentence of death are automatically excused from service (see Chapter 2). Because death-qualified jurors tend to be more conviction prone than those not death qualified, the probability of an acquittal is increased when prosecutors decide not to seek the death penalty.

Perhaps the decision not to seek the death penalty for O. J. Simpson had nothing to do with the wealth of the defendant. But other decisions surely did. Simpson's preliminary hearing began just three weeks after the murder. The hearing was much lengthier than most, with defense attorneys vigorously asserting the rights of their client. Within four months, the trial had commenced. Eleven defense lawyers appeared in court on behalf of O. J. Simpson, and more worked behind the scenes. The full defense team also included private investigators, jury-selection consultants, and several highly paid expert witnesses who challenged every claim made by the prosecution and presented alternative interpretations of the evidence. Huge amounts of time and money were poured into the trial—it lasted nearly nine months and produced over 45,000 pages of testimony. The total cost for the defense was estimated to be somewhere between $6 million and $8 million. The final verdict was "not guilty."

All the Justice Money Can Buy

In an appearance on *Larry King Live,* one of Simpson's attorneys was asked whether O.J. bought a not-guilty verdict. His response: "O. J. didn't buy justice; every defendant deserves the kind of defense O.J. was able to afford." Perhaps he was right. If you or someone you cared about was accused of murder, you would surely want a defense team as skillful and thorough as O. J.'s. Of course, the critical point is that almost no other person charged with murder can afford the kind of defense Mr. Simpson was able to buy. Although in principle every defendant has broad constitutional rights, in practice, full use of those rights costs money—lots of it. And money is something defendants in murder trials have very little of. As Justice William O. Douglas observed, "One searches our chronicles in vain for the execution of any member of the affluent strata of this society."

As a contrast, consider the case of Ernest Dwayne Jones. His trial took place down the hall from Simpson's. Mr. Jones stood accused of raping and viciously stabbing to death Julia Miller, his girlfriend's mother. Her body was found with two kitchen knives sticking out of her neck. "There were no eyewitnesses. Jones was mentally disturbed, had a history of being sexually abused, and had grown up with two alcoholic parents. He also had a previous history of violence. Ten years prior, he had been convicted of rape and he had served six years in prison.

In Jones's trial there was one public defender and one prosecutor. The prosecution's DNA evidence, which was analyzed by the same company used in the Simpson case, was presented in a day. Unlike the Simpson trial, there were no renowned defense experts to raise suspicions about contamination or bias in the laboratory analysis. There was no defense attorney with special expertise in DNA evidence to grill the prosecution expert. In fact, in the Jones trial, the DNA expert was not even cross-examined by the defender. The trial lasted twelve days and Jones was found guilty. It took another four days to complete the penalty phase and sentence Mr. Jones to death. When asked to compare the two trials, the foreman of the Jones jury said, "If they brought in other experts and overwhelmed us with clever data and impressive people, they might at least have got the jury to hang." He added that "if [Jones] had gotten Johnnie Cochran and his resources, he wouldn't be sentenced to death."[131] But Jones couldn't afford the team of lawyers that might have saved his life.

Or consider the case of Demetrie Mayfield, who was tried not in Los Angeles County but in neighboring San Bernadino County. His case was even more similar to Simpson's. Mayfield was accused of murdering a woman friend and a man who (like Ronald Goldman) was apparently in the wrong place at the wrong time. Mayfield's attorney spent a total of forty hours preparing for the trial. His only real interview with the defendant took place the morning before the trial began. Mayfield now lives on death row.[132]

Imagine that you have been charged with capital murder. Perhaps it was a case of mistaken identity, perhaps you had to kill in self-defense, maybe someone you were with pulled the trigger. You would want a swift, thorough investigation of the crime, you would want all potential witnesses interviewed, you would want experts to sift painstakingly through the physical evidence, you would want to hire a jury-selection expert, you would want to hire your own experts to contradict the prosecution's experts. Most of all, you would want the best, most experienced defense attorney you could find. The lawyer is crucial. Your lawyer will prepare the case, prepare the witnesses, file motions, cross-examine witnesses, explain slippery concepts (like premeditation, aggravation, and mitigation) to the jury, object to improper questions by the prosecution, fight to get favorable evidence admitted and to get unfavorable evidence excluded. All of these services are available to every American—for a price. If the price is more than you can afford, you are entitled to a court-appointed attorney. But not necessarily a good or experienced attorney. Maybe you'll get lucky and wind up with a good attorney. But would you be willing to bet your life on it?

The sad, shameful fact is that money makes the difference between life and death for many defendants. Far too often, it is not those who commit the most despicable crimes who are sent to death row, but those who lack the money to mount an adequate defense. Money can buy a thorough investigation of the crime, expert analysis and testimony, a careful search for mitigating factors that may need to be presented during a penalty phase. Most important, money can buy a skillful, experienced lawyer. Rich people can afford to select their lawyers, but poor people are at the mercy of the attorney assigned to them.

Because very few capital defendants can afford to hire their own lawyer, they are represented by either a public defender or a court-appointed private attorney. Public defenders work for state-funded offices that specialize in representing indigent clients. Fortunately, there are many dedicated public defenders who are both capable and experienced in defending people accused of capital crimes, and these defenders manage to provide effective representation despite relatively low pay and heavy workloads. But there are not nearly enough to go around. Most public defenders' offices are located in large cities and many states have no such office. In these states, capital defendants are represented by court-appointed lawyers: private attorneys assigned by trial judges.

The effectiveness of defense attorneys in capital cases varies wildly. Most states have a cap on spending for each capital trial. For example, Alabama pays attorneys at the rate of $20 per hour, and Mississippi pays only

$11.75 per hour.[133] Stephen Bright, a lawyer who has defended many capital defendants, reports that his pay for representing a capital defendant in Mississippi amounted to less than $2 per hour. He notes that in many capital cases, "the court reporter is paid more than the lawyer appointed to defend the accused."[134] Because of unrealistic limits on the total amount of money the state allocates for the defense of a capital client, the available funds are often exhausted before the trial even begins. Appallingly, capital defendants with court-appointed lawyers are more than twice as likely to be sentenced to death than defendants with privately retained attorneys.[135]

In most cases the balance of resources between defense and prosecution is not equal. Like public defenders, prosecutors tend to carry a heavy caseload. But they tend to be better paid and they have considerably more resources at their disposal. Typically, defenders must file motions to fund investigations, to obtain laboratory analysis of physical evidence, to hire psychologists or jury experts or expert witnesses. In contrast, prosecutors are able to use the local police forces as their investigative teams, and they have access to crime labs and pathologists from the coroner's office. While court-appointed lawyers are often inexperienced and unfamiliar with relevant law, prosecutors' offices are staffed with experienced attorneys, and even novice prosecutors have ready access to the expertise of more seasoned colleagues. Outside of public defenders' offices, there is no comparable network for defenders in capital trials.

In Alabama, Judy Haney was charged with killing her husband. Midway through the trial, her court-appointed attorney was held in contempt for coming to court drunk. The attorney spent the night in jail but proceeded to act as her lawyer when the trial resumed the next morning. A few days later, Haney was convicted and sentenced to death. Her careless lawyer had neglected to present crucial mitigating evidence that the dead husband had abused Haney and her children for nearly fifteen years. Despite the considerable failings of her attorney, the conviction and the death sentence were upheld by the Alabama Supreme Court.

In Texas, Jesus Romero was executed in 1992. His sentence had been upheld even though he had received a woefully inadequate defense. Here is the entire penalty-phase argument of his court-appointed lawyer: "You are an extremely intelligent jury. You've got that man's life in your hands. You can take it or not. That's all I have to say."[136] This is hardly the impassioned, eloquent appeal we would hope for when a defendant's life is at stake. It appears that other attorneys are nearly as terse. For example, in Louisiana, capital trials last an average of three days and penalty phases last an average of 2.9 hours.[137]

John Young was executed in 1985 in Georgia. Not long after Young's trial, his defense lawyer was sent to prison for state and federal narcotics convictions. The attorney later submitted an affidavit to the appeals court confessing that he had spent "hardly any time preparing for the case" and had been unable to concentrate on the case because of "a myriad of personal problems.'[138] The repentant attorney went on to say that he had failed to investigate the life of the defendant in search of mitigating evidence. This was unfortunate, because an investigation would have revealed a tragic story. At the age of three, the defendant had witnessed the murder of his mother while he was lying in bed with her. He was raised by an alcoholic relative who allowed him to become involved in child prostitution and drug abuse. Such information would not have affected the guilt phase of the trial, but it might have moved a jury to sentence Young to life in prison. As Justice Thurgood Marshall observed, many defense attorneys

> are handling their first criminal cases, or their first murder cases, when confronted with the prospect of a death penalty. Though acting in good faith, they inevitably make very serious mistakes. . . . Counsel have been unaware that . . . claims should be preserved; that certain findings by a jury might preclude imposition of the death penalty; or that a separate sentencing phase will follow a conviction. The federal courts are filled with stories of counsel who presented no evidence in mitigation of their client's sentence because they did not know what to offer or how to offer it, or had not read the state's sentencing statute.[139]

Advocates of the death penalty might argue that most errors resulting from deficient lawyering are remedied on appeal. But a sloppy, cursory defense at trial has lasting effects on the defendant's prospects on appeal. Clearly, the appeals process does correct some errors. But the process is far from perfect. There are significant legal barriers to making an appeal based on issues that were not raised in the initial trial. To preserve a claim for later appeal, an attorney must often raise the relevant issue (e.g., admission of improper evidence, failure to admit crucial evidence, composition of the jury) during the initial trial. Otherwise, the defendant may forfeit the right to have the claim considered on appeal. Furthermore, the defendant must show that the lawyer's mistakes were serious enough to violate the constitutional right to "effective assistance of counsel." Recent Supreme Court decisions make it necessary for appellate lawyers to prove that the errors were consequential enough to change the outcome of the case.

Charles Black Jr. has argued that our system of capital punishment is "saturated with discretion," He describes the criminal justice system as a long series of decisions: to arrest or not, to charge or not, to plea-bargain or to go to trial, to seek the death penalty or not, to convict or acquit, to sentence to life in prison or death by execution, on what grounds to appeal, and whether to pardon or commute a sentence of death. He makes the point forcefully:

> Can you really doubt that a process like this, from first to last, is heavily loaded against the poor? Could you really be surprised at the finding that by far the majority of people suffering death are poor? Are you satisfied with that? If you are not, face the fact that there is no way to change it except to do away with the death penalty.[140]

JUSTICE IN BLACK AND WHITE

During the time of slavery there was no pretense of equal justice. Slaves were regarded as property and slave owners could abuse their property in most any way they saw fit. The so-called Black Codes stipulated in law that blacks could be treated far more severely than whites for similar crimes. Prior to the Civil War in the South, blackes could be put to death for a variety of crimes. The rape of a black woman was not considered a crime, but many black men were killed for the alleged rape of a white woman. Blacks could be executed for property crimes such as burglary or arson, while whites were permitted to pay a fine or serve a short jail term. Blacks faced not only harsher punishments but also formidable procedural obstacles: They could not testify in court against whites, and they could not serve on juries.

Unofficial "justice" could be even harsher than that dispensed by the official courts. Recorded lynchings numbered 1,540 during the 1890s, and another 1,951 lynchings took place between 1900 and the end of the 1930s. The yearly number of lynchings often exceeded the number of official executions, and black men were overwhelmingly the targets of these spontaneous killings.[141] At the turn of the century, one commentator summarized the prevailing view of such punishments:

> The frequent atrocity of the crimes committed by negroes of low character, without apparently any particular provocation, is something scarcely to be understood—the adjectives wanton, bestial, outrageous, brutal and inhuman all seem wholly inadequate to express the feeling of utter disgust and abhorrence that is aroused. . . . Southern whites have found the law and its administration utterly unsuited to the function of dealing with negro criminals—hence, the frequent adoption of summary and extra-legal methods of punishment.[142]

Lynchings of black men for the alleged rape of white women were so frequent that in newspaper accounts of the time it was simply reported that a negro man was hanged for "the usual crime." Even in more modern times, blacks have been disproportionately sentenced to death for the crime of rape. An especially thorough investigation by Marvin Wolfgang and Marc Riedel examined 361 rape convictions during the period 1945 to 1965.[143] After controlling for a variety of variables, they found that the best predictor of a death sentence was the race of the offender combined with the race of the victim. Black men convicted of raping white women were the group most likely to be sentenced to death by a shocking margin. Four hundred and fifty-five men were executed for rape between 1930 and 1967 and 89 percent of those men were black. In *Coker v. Georgia* (1977), the Supreme Court ended the death penalty for rape in cases where the victim was not killed.

But that was all a long time ago. Now both blacks and whites are subject to the same laws and members of both groups are routinely sentenced to death for capital murders. Yet there is still a disturbing imbalance. Here are some statistics: At present, the U.S. population is about 12 percent black but the population of death row is 41 percent black;[144] since the reinstatement of the death penalty in 1976, 39.3 percent of the people killed in the execution chamber have been black, and 86 percent of the executions have been people convicted of killing whites, even though roughly half of all murder victims in the United States are black.[145] There have been more than 16,000 executions in American jurisdictions since 1608, yet only 31 whites have been executed for killing a black person, Perhaps such statistics are misleading or inconclusive, but even the most ardent supporters of capital punishment would concede that these striking disparities should make us suspicious.

More important is the pattern of sentencing since the 1976 restructuring of the capital trial. Maybe the problems have been fixed. Unfortunately, the evidence suggests that, despite three decades of legal and procedural tinkering, the death penalty remains capricious, flawed, and discriminatory. Just prior to his retirement in 1994, Justice Harry Blackmun, who had formerly supported capital punishment, concluded that "race continues to play a major role in determining who shall live and who shall die."

Racial bias seeps into the decision-making process at every juncture. It is not primarily the race of the defendant that influences decisions, but the race of the victim. William Bowers and Glenn Pierce looked at 700 homicides and found that offenders whose victims were white were more than twice as likely to be indicted for first-degree murder than offenders whose victims were black. In an examination of over 600 murders, Michael Radelet found that while overall 70 percent of homicides led to first-degree murder indictments, over 92 percent of black offender— white victim murders led to first-degree indictments.[146]

A similar pattern emerges when we examine the decision of whether or not to seek the death penalty. Research indicates that if the victim is white, prosecutors are more than twice as likely to seek a death sentence than if the victim is black, and blacks who kill whites are almost four times as likely to be charged with capital murder than blacks who kill blacks.[147] A study that looked at over 700 murders in New Jersey during the 1980s found that the decision to seek a death sentence was strongly influenced by race of the victim. Prosecutors decided to seek a death sentence for 43 percent of the white-victim murders but only for 28 percent of the black-victim murders. When researchers looked at the race of both victim and offender in combination, they found that prosecutors sought the death penalty in just over half of the black killer-white victim cases, but in only 20 percent of the white killer-black victim cases.[148] In the most sophisticated analysis of the issue, David Baldus, George Woodworth, and Charles Pulaski found that, even after taking over twenty relevant variables into account, prosecutors decided to seek the death penalty five times more often against killers of whites than against killers of blacks.[149]

Only about a quarter of the defendants convicted of capital murder are sentenced to death (although there is tremendous variability from state to state). It is not entirely clear why the other three-quarters are spared. An optimistic inference might be that juries and judges are properly weighing legally relevant criteria and sending only the worst, most barbarous criminals to the execution chamber. There is some evidence to support this inference; several studies have found that the probability of a death sentence is increased when there is more than one victim, when there is another violent felony (e.g., rape), when the victim was a stranger to the offender, and when the murder was especially brutal.[150] Clearly, these are important factors that ought to be considered when making the life-or-death decision. But these are not the only factors that are considered.

Decisions about whether to charge and whether to seek the death penalty occur before the trial begins. It would be comforting to think that the biases that infect those early decisions are somehow corrected during the later stages, during the guilt and penalty trials. Unfortunately, the research shows that later stages only amplify the bias. In a large-scale study of capital sentencing in four states, William Bowers and Glenn Pierce compared the sentences of blacks who killed whites with the sentences of blacks who killed blacks in Ohio, Florida, Georgia, and Texas. In Ohio, the black offender-white victim group was 15 times more likely to receive a death sentence, in Florida they were 37 times more likely, in Georgia they were 33 times more likely, and in Texas they were 87 times more likely.[151] Data from other states led to similar conclusions. For example, even after taking the characteristics of the crime into account, Gross and Mauro found that killing a white person increased the odds of being sentenced to death by a factor of 4 in Illinois, a factor of 7 in Georgia, and a factor of nearly 5 in Florida.[152]

A particularly interesting and consistent finding is that racial bias vanishes when the murder is especially brutal and the defendant has a history of violent crimes. When judging the worst murders, race (of the defendant or of the victim) doesn't seem to matter.[153] Racial bias only creeps in when aggravation is relatively weak and the choice between life and death is difficult. This may be how race finds its way into our system of capital punishment. While some murders are so vicious and violent that race doesn't matter, in less brutal murders both prosecutors and jurors may unintentionally let race influence their decision-making processes. For example, although seldom discussed openly, part of the calculation in deciding whether to try for the death penalty has to do with what some prosecutors call "victim quality." The reasoning is that jurors are more likely to impose a sentence of death if the victim is easy to admire or identify with. It is easier to obtain a death sentence if the victim was a hardworking young mother than if the victim was a drug addict with a long arrest record. It is even possible that the decision not to seek the death penalty is simply a pragmatic calculation made by prosecutors who (correctly) believe that when aggravation is low or moderate, it will be more difficult to obtain a death sentence if the victim was black.

Victim quality is not on any official list of aggravating factors. But jurors, perhaps unconsciously, assess the worth of the victim. Jurors may simply find it easier to identify with victims who are similar to them. Because most jurors in the United States are white, they may find it harder to empathize with black victims. It is also possible that the murder of a white person may subjectively seem more frightening and personally threatening to jurors. If the killer is black and the victim is white, it may have an especially strong impact on white jurors. In those cases where the argument for sending someone to the execution chamber is not overwhelming, similarity between jurors and the victim may come into play, and in some cases it may become the decisive factor.

Racial bias may be *especially* likely in capital cases because they arouse such strong emotions. A dispassionate, rational analysis is exceedingly difficult when confronted with a hideous crime. Also, the concepts that lie at the very heart of the penalty decision (e.g., aggravation and mitigation) are quite slippery. Because the decision must go beyond a mere mechanical weighing of facts, there is plenty of room for bias and prejudice to seep into the process. While racial and other forms of prejudice may exert little influence on factual determinations—understanding the angle of a stab wound or the trajectory of a bullet—the question of whether a defendant should live or die is infused with subjectivity. The complex, value-laden issue of who deserves to die is susceptible to subtle and even unconscious bias.

Several conclusions can be drawn from the research on racial disparities in capital cases: Those who are accused of murdering a white victim are more likely to be charged with a capital crime; those convicted of killing a white victim are more likely to receive a sentence of death; black defendants who are convicted of killing a white person are the group most likely to receive the death penalty; white defendants who murder black victims are the group least likely to receive a death sentence; and the effects of race are most pronounced in southern states like Texas, Georgia, Louisiana, and Florida.[154]

Does the Death Penalty Deter Potential Murderers?

Murder and capital punishment are not opposites that cancel one another out but similars that breed their kind.

—George Bernard Shaw

The theory is simple and self-evident: Fear of the execution chamber will restrain potential murderers. Knowing that they could face the executioner, those who would otherwise kill will stop short of killing. Innocent lives will be saved.

The theory is called deterrence. It has served as a compelling justification for the death penalty since ancient times. The idea is appealing because it is an elaboration of what we know to be true in our own lives: If the potential punishment for a particular behavior is great, we are likely to avoid that behavior. For example, if you work downtown where parking spaces are scarce, you may occasionally risk a $20 or $30 fine for parking illegally. But if the fine is raised to $1,000, only the wealthy will be undeterred. Common sense tells us that the death penalty deters. But common sense also tells us that the earth stands still and the sun moves across the sky. Only after looking at the evidence do we become convinced that we walk on a spinning planet that slowly circles the sun.

As capital punishment became morally troubling to many Americans, the justification of deterrence gained prominence. It offered a seemingly scientific rationale for executions. Supporters of capital punishment were not out for primitive revenge, they were simply discouraging future murders and thereby protecting the public. Quotes from scripture were bolstered by appeals to reason. Even today, for those who favor dispassionate cost-benefit analyses, deterrence provides a coolly logical basis for favoring executions.

For well over a century researchers have been investigating whether or not the death penalty serves as a deterrent. There are now over 200 studies on the topic. The theory of deterrence implies a couple of hypotheses that can be tested by looking closely at murder rates. The first hypothesis is that places with capital punishment should have lower murder rates than places where execution is not an available sanction. The fear created in the hearts and minds of potential murderers should suppress their homicidal impulses. If, for example, one state has the death penalty and another state does not, the death-penalty state should have proportionately fewer killings. This hypothesis has been thoroughly tested.

THE EVIDENCE

One of the earliest studies was conducted by a Massachusetts legislator named Robert Rantoul. In the 1840s, Rantoul compiled statistics on murder and execution rates in several nations over a forty-year period. In 1846 he presented his findings: The deterrent effect was illusory. Indeed, his data revealed a counter-deterrence effect: "Murders have rapidly diminished in those countries in which executions are scarcely known; slightly in France where the change of policy was not so great; while in England, . . . under a milder administration of the law, there has been a change for the better."[168] Since Rantoul's time, hundreds of studies have been conducted to assess the deterrent power of capital punishment. Nearly all of them lend credence to Rantoul's early conclusions.

Critics of this early research countered that the United States is different from other countries. What failed to work in Europe may be effective here. And indeed, the United States furnishes a splendid laboratory for putting deterrence theory to the test. Some states have the death penalty, other states do not. Some states have adopted the death penalty, only to abandon it later. Some states have even adopted the death penalty, abolished it later, only to reinstate it even later. These differences between states enable researchers to conduct multiple tests of the theory. Specifically, the theory predicts that states with capital punishment will have lower murder rates than states without capital punishment. Of course it's a bit more complicated than that, because the states being compared must be as similar as possible. Comparing Oregon, Florida, and Delaware might not be especially informative because these three states differ on several important dimensions. A better test—the test used in the research literature—uses geographically adjacent states, states that tend to share many features including history, culture, and economy. In the 1960s, a sociologist named Thorsten Sellin made just such comparisons. Supporters of capital punishment found no comfort in his findings.

Sellin examined clusters of states that were similar in most respects. He found, for example, that North Dakota, a state without the death penalty, had a lower homicide rate than two similar states that did have the death penalty, South Dakota and Nebraska. Michigan, a non-capital punishment state, had an identical murder rate to Indiana, and a lower rate than Ohio, both of which had the death penalty. Rhode Island, a state that only carried the penalty of life imprisonment, was compared to two death-penalty states, Massachusetts and Connecticut. Rhode Island's murder fate was lower than Connecticut's and identical to Massachusetts's. To be sure, a couple of states without the death penalty (e.g., Maine) had higher rates than comparable states with the death penalty (e.g., New Hampshire). But overall, the states with execution chambers had rates of murder that were significantly higher than states that did not execute murderers.[169]

But maybe things have changed. After all, Sellin's data examined the years 1920 to 1955. It is possible that changes in American culture or the legal system—especially modifications in the trial process since the *Furman* and *Gregg* decisions—have made the deterrent effect more powerful. Several researchers set out to see if deterrence had changed with the times, Ruth Peterson and William Bailey examined homicide rates for a twelve-year period spanning from 1973 to 1984. Comparing similar, adjacent states, they found that the annual murder rate in states with the death penalty was higher than in states that had abolished it. Specifically, the average murder rate in states with the death penalty was 8.64 for every 100,000 people. In states without the death penalty, the rate was 5.35.[170]

Deterrence theory makes other predictions. A second testable hypothesis has to do with the effects, over time, of getting rid of or bringing back the death penalty. If the death penalty is abandoned in a particular state, murder rates should climb because the fear of execution has been removed. Conversely, if a particular place establishes the death penalty or restores it after a long period of absence, then murder rates should fall. The studies described above included this kind of longitudinal analysis of homicide rates when the death penalty was in effect and when it was suspended for a period of years. These analyses revealed no deterrence effect.

In 1983, Richard Lempert looked for a relationship between the number of executions and number of homicides. He included several states over a fifteen-year period. No relationship was found. His conclusion echoed that of earlier researchers: "The death penalty in general and executions in particular do not deter homicide."[171] The conclusions of studies conducted in the United States were confirmed in research conducted abroad. Dane Archer and Rosemary Gartner measured the murder rate in twelve countries and two foreign cities before and after abolition of the death penalty. Eight of the fourteen cases (57 percent) showed a decreased murder rate in the year following abolition, while only five (36 percent) showed an increase. Further, when they examined longer periods of time, there was even less support for the deterrence hypothesis.[172] When looking at this research, it is essential to keep in mind that there are two fundamental public-policy questions: Will abolishing the death penalty increase the murder rate? and, Will reinstating the death penalty cause the murder rate to drop? Based on the research, the answer to both questions is clearly no.

But maybe comparisons between death-penalty states and non-death penalty states are inconclusive. Maybe the paired states were different in a variety of unnoticed and unmeasured ways. Maybe even adjacent states aren't similar enough and researchers were comparing apples and oranges. This basic criticism spawned a new wave of deterrence research. This new wave looked at the effect of the death penalty over long periods of time, and used complex statistical procedures to control for or remove the impact of factors that might influence the number of murders. By taking into account several factors that were known to contribute to murder rates, researchers hoped to purify their comparisons.

One of the first studies to make use of such sophisticated statistical controls was conducted by Baldus and Cole in 1975.[173] Like earlier researchers, they looked at contiguous states. But unlike earlier researchers, they took into account several characteristics known to influence murder rates: unemployment, probability of arrest and conviction, percent of the population between the ages of fifteen and twenty-four, per capita financial expenditures on the police force, and other factors. Even after controlling for all of these factors, no deterrent effect was found. After scores of studies and decades of data analysis, few people found any reason to believe in deterrence. Things looked bleak for deterrence theorists. Then, in 1975, an economist named Isaac Ehrlich came to their rescue.

Ehrlich argued that most of the previous research failed to consider important differences between states. Using a sophisticated statistical technique called multiple regression, he looked at the impact of the death penalty on murder in the United States from 1933 to 1969. Taking into account arrest and conviction rate, unemployment rate, per capita income, population between the ages of fourteen and twenty-four, and other variables, Ehrlich examined what he called "execution risk." This risk was defined as the ratio of executions to convictions for murder. After churning through the data, Ehrlich declared that he had uncovered a powerful deterrent effect.[174]

Ehrlich's findings found an enthusiastic audience. Politicians and policy-makers who supported the death penalty were eager to embrace any research that reinforced their position. And, at the time, Ehrlich's was the only apparently credible study that had managed to detect any deterrent effect. Even better, Ehrlich's findings could be expressed as a pithy slogan: "Every execution prevents seven or eight murders." This lone study supporting a deterrent effect was also cited in the *Gregg v. Georgia* decision of 1976. Balancing the Ehrlich study against the scores of studies that found no deterrent effect, the Supreme Court concluded that "statistical attempts to evaluate the worth of the death penalty as a deterrent to crime by potential offenders have . . . simply been inconclusive."[175]

Because of Ehrlich's highly mathematical approach, only other social scientists could discern the flaws in his research. Almost immediately, critiques began to appear in the research literature. A closer look at the data revealed a striking anomaly: When the last few years (1963 to 1969) were removed from the analysis, the impact of "execution risk" was to increase rather than decrease the number of murders. Other critics pointed out that Ehrlich had failed to include several critical factors in his analysis: rural-to-urban migration, gun ownership, level of violent crime, and length of prison sentences. When these and other key factors were taken into account, the deterrent effect evaporated. The fatal blow to Ehrlich's research came from the prestigious National Academy of Sciences. Their panel (headed by a Nobel Prize-winning economist) reanalyzed Ehrlich's data and came to lite conclusion that the data showed no deterrent effect.[176]

As the evidence against deterrence continued to accumulate, some people suggested yet another explanation for the absence of a deterrence effect: Researchers were looking at the wrong factors. What mattered was not whether the death penalty was are available sanction, but the number of executions that were actually care led out. Maybe it takes an actual execution to instill fear in the hearts of potential murderers, and it is only this fear causes them to refrain from killing. And because it is only actual executions that demonstrate the grave consequences of murder, greater publicity should boost the deterrent effect. According to this line of reasoning, sufficient fear will be felt only when an execution is vivid in people's minds—in the days, weeks, and months immediately following an execution. As the memory of each execution fades in the minds of would-be murderers, the deterrent effect might fade and then finally disappear.

This idea that it is only the actual occurrence of an execution rather than laws authorizing the death penalty) that deters is by no means new. Back in 1935, Robert Dann tabulated the number of murder sixty days before and sixty days after five highly publicized execution. Interestingly, Dann found that the number of murders rose alter each execution.[177] More than forty years later (in 1978), King looked at twenty well-publicized executions over more than a decade. His findings also ran contrary to the predictions of deterrence theory: On average, each execution produced an increase of 1.2 homicides.[178] Supporters of deterrence re-treated a bit farther and suggested that maybe only well-publicized executions generated the effect. But scores of studies failed to support even this more limited prediction. For example, William Bailey conducted an especially detailed analysis of the impact of television publicity on murder rates in 1990. No effect could be detected. Even when the type of publicity (e.g., graphic versus matter-of-fact coverage) was taken into account, there was no discernable impact on murder rates.[179]

Another issue raised by the defenders of deterrence theory concerned the type of murder for which the death penalty was an available punishment. Many studies of deterrence, especially the older studies, have examined total homicide rates. But not all murders are punishable by death. If we make the dubious assumption that murderers know which types of murders are punishable by death, it is possible that only capital murderers are being deterred. Perhaps the deterrent effect is being masked because noncapital murders are included in the analysis. In response to this criticism, researchers have looked at the murder of police officers. This is a useful measure because killing a police officer is punishable by death in every state that permits capital punishment. Further, it has often been argued that the dead: penalty is especially useful for deterring fleeing criminals who are in danger of being arrested. Ernest van den Haag, an outspoken supporter of capital punishment, puts it this way:

> Without the death penalty, an offender having committed a crime that leads to imprisonment for life has nothing to lose if he murders the arresting officer. By murdering the officer . . . such criminals increase their chances of escape, without increasing the severity of the punishment they will suffer if caught.[180]

Despite the apparent logic of Van den Haag's argument, there is no evidence that police officers are safer in jurisdictions that have capital punishment. No deterrence of police murders has been found for the time periods 1919 through 1954, 1961 through 1971, or 1973 through 1984. For the two later time periods, the analyses took into account factors such as poverty, race, unemployment, and urbanization.[181]

The most sophisticated investigation of police killings was published by William Bailey and Ruth Peterson in 1994. They looked at police killings for the fourteen years prior to 1990. Their analysis examined several types of police killings (e.g., on-duty versus off-duty) and took into account several key variables: the total number of executions, the number of executions for police killings, the amount of media coverage of such executions, and the type of media attention given to these executions. They even removed the influence of several variables known to be linked to murder rates (i.e., race, number of people living in cities, number of persons aged sixteen to thirty-four, divorce rate, unemployment, and percentage of the population on welfare). Taking into account a host of relevant factors and using a variety of statistical techniques, these researchers were still unable to locate a deterrent effect.[182]

With respect to the death penalty, deterrence theory points in one direction and the facts point in the opposite direction. The fragile logic of deterrence theory has crumbled under the weight of research evidence. More than a century of experience and more than 200 pieces of research lead to an inescapable conclusion: The death penalty does not deter potential murderers. Confronted with the accumulated evidence, people who once made bold claims about the deterrent power of executions have been forced into a long, slow retreat. As each of their arguments was demolished by the facts, deterrence theorists have found new justifications for supporting capital punishment. One keen observer put it this way: "Proponents [of deterrence] increasingly find themselves affirming more idiosyncratic explanations for the effects they presume the death penalty has, but which research has yet to reveal. . . . With each new set of findings their task becomes more arduous and their arguments become less plausible."[183] The burden of proof falls squarely on the shoulders of those who claim to have faith in the power of deterrence. The conclusion that the death penalty does not deter rests on a mountain of evidence built up over several decades. Anyone who manages to detect a deterrent effect must weigh his or her findings against that mountain.

Research on the lack of deterrence will continue to accumulate. And, occasionally, because of a methodological flaw or a statistical anomaly, or an unusual confluence of events, a researcher will trap the elusive deterrent effect. Later, when other researchers look at the same data, the effect will vanish. The supposed deterrent effect of the death penalty looks more and more like some mythical creature whose existence seems less and less probable. There are still people who long to believe in the myth and, for them, no amount of data will dislodge their conviction. Arthur Koestler's words still ring true forty years later: "The defenders of capital punishment are well aware that the statistical evidence is unanswerable. They do not contest it; they ignore it."[184]

WHY KILLING DOESN'T DETER KILLERS

Perhaps the findings summarized above are unsurprising. After all, the proposition that the death penalty intimidates would-be murderers is based on a thoroughly rational model of human behavior. It assumes that potential killers engage in a dispassionate weighing of the costs and benefits of killing. This assumption is simply wrong. Most murders are crimes of passion—committed under the blinding influence of rage, hatred, jealousy, or fear. To be sure, there are some exceptions, the "hit man" or the terrorist, the calculating husband or wife who kills to collect insurance money. But planned, intentional murders are rare, constituting less than 10 percent of the total.[185]

Who, then, is likely to be deterred by the distant threat of the execution chamber? Probably not the person who acts in the heat of passion or the person whose attempt at robbery goes tragically wrong. Certainly not the insane or mentally disturbed killer or the person whose mind is clouded by alcohol or drugs at the time of the murder. Not the young gang member whose whole subculture exalts macho displays and risk-taking. Not the person who kills spontaneously or accidentally in the midst of an altercation; not the murderer who wishes to be caught; not the criminal who believes he can escape arrest or conviction; not even the cold, calculating murderer who notices that the probability of execution is very low. In his book on death row, David Von Drehle reminds us that

> the reality, with few exceptions, is that murderers are not clear-thinking people. They are impulsive, self-centered, often warped; overwhelmingly they are products of violent homes; frequently they are addled by booze or drugs; and most of them are deeply anti-social. The values and sanctions of society don't concern them. They kill out of mental illness, or sexual perversion, for instant gratification or sheer bloody-mindedness. Some murderers actually seem drawn to the death house.[186]

Deterrence theory owes its intuitive appeal to the fact that when most of us sit back in cool, rational reflection, we reason that the prospect of facing the executioner would prevent us from acting on the urge to kill. But very few people are engaged in rational reflection when they use a knife, a club, or a gun. Besides, most of us do not belong to the small minority of people who will commit a murder. Most of us would not murder even if murder carried a small punishment. We are not the ones who need to be restrained. Not only do we have a well-developed moral sense, we have learned to control our baser impulses. We also consider our lives to be worth living, and we have people we care about. We have a lot to lose.

The theory of deterrence rests on other dubious assumptions. It assumes that capital punishment is *uniquely* deterring, that execution is perceived to be a significantly harsher punishment than life imprisonment without parole. For those few murderers who carefully weigh one possibility against the other, we cannot predict which punishment will be judged to be more frightening. The prospect of living in a cage for decades, surrounded by other dangerous criminals and stripped of all important choices about how to spend your time, is probably at least as terrifying as the thought of being executed sometime in the distant future. As Cesare Beccaria argued, the "prolonged wretchedness" of a life in prison has a greater impact on the human mind than "the idea of death, which men always see in the hazy distance."[187]

Some who believe in the deterrent power of executions despite all evidence to the contrary would argue that we simply need to do the job better. That is, the death penalty could be transformed into an effective deterrent if we increased its severity, certainty, and swiftness. Of course, not much can be done to increase severity. We could turn back the clock and revive the torturous practices of breaking at the wheel, burning at the stake, and boiling in oil. But few Americans would countenance such cruelty, and, in fact, there is no evidence that such practices were any more effective as deterrents. So we are left with the two options of increasing certainty and increasing celerity.

The penalty of death has never been certain. The U.S. execution rate peaked in 1938, when just over 2 percent of homicides resulted in executions.[188] We haven't approached that level of certainty since. A return to that historically high level or even a level ten times higher is not likely to cause potential murderers to believe that the risk of execution is high.

We could, however, compress the length of time between conviction and execution. On average, condemned prisoners wait over eight years for their appointment with the executioner. There is no doubt that, in theory, executions could be swifter. But theory always differs from practice. The price would be high, and the hypothesized increase in deterrence might not even materialize. Our system of capital punishment has evolved over many decades and should not be dismantled in the vain hope that some potential murders *might* be deterred. Questionable attempts to create a deterrent effect must be balanced against our tolerance for error and bias.

The changes in the legal system necessary to boost the deterrent power of capital punishment—simplifying capital trials, dramatically reducing the number of postconviction appeals, increasing the pain caused by executions, increasing the number of crimes eligible for the death penalty—would be draconian, morally unacceptable, and probably unconstitutional. These reforms would also increase the risk of wrongful conviction and execution while failing to reduce the most common capital crime: spontaneous murder committed in the heat of passion.

MORAL RESPONSIBILITY AND FREE WILL

Suppose a man has been convicted of a murder. In a jealous rage, he rapes his ex-wife and then stabs her to death. Clearly, he must be severely punished for his horrible crime. He has shown that he is violent and society must be protected from him. His actions—rape and murder—legally qualify him for the death penalty. But before deciding whether he should die in the execution chamber or live out the rest of his life in prison, we must understand not only the crime, but also the criminal.

Here are four possibilities. First, suppose that he is a young man from a wealthy family who has enjoyed most of life's advantages: loving parents, material comfort, good schools, travel, and interesting experiences. Next, suppose that he is a young man with a brutal past: He and his mother suffered routine beatings from an abusive father throughout his childhood and into his adolescence. He grew up in a poverty-ridden, gang-infested neighborhood and received very little in the way of parental guidance or supervision. Third, suppose that he had an unremarkable middle-class background. He achieved his life's dream of becoming a police officer and was honored several times for his bravery. More than once he saved the lives of innocent bystanders. Or, finally, suppose that the killer is indisputably psychotic and that he had spent much of his life in mental institutions.

The striking differences in the backgrounds of these men raise some disturbing questions. Are all four men equally deserving of death? Are all four equally responsible for their crimes? If not equally responsible, is one of them, say, 90 percent responsible, another 80 percent, 70 percent, or 60 percent responsible? Should background even matter? Does the good service of the police officer count for anything or should all four men be treated the same? Would you be more inclined to show mercy if murderer number one was brain damaged? If murderer number two was a heroin addict? Any assessment of moral blameworthiness must go beyond the act for which a person is on trial. All systems of justice recognize this. That is not to say that the person's crime must be excused, or that the person must not be severely punished. He must be held accountable and he must be punished harshly. It is merely to say that even identical crimes may have very different causes and may be the product of very different life circumstances. We judge, convict, and punish a person. And a person—even a person who has committed a hideous crime—is more than the worst thing he or she has ever done. We are obligated to look not only at the vicious act, but also to struggle to understand the circumstances that produced tile act, the reasons and motives that lie beneath it.

Supporters of capital punishment would argue that this is precisely the kind of information jurors are instructed to take into account when making the life-or-death decision. But the fact that jurors are told to take such information into account obscures the issue of our limited ability to understand the reasons behind someone else's actions. Imagine that you are a juror in a capital case. You have already decided that the defendant is guilty, and now you must decide whether he should be killed or sent to prison for the rest of his life. To decide whether to show mercy, you must make a full and fair assessment of the multitude of factors that led to the murder. To make this assessment, it is first necessary to have the defendant's important life events and experiences laid out before you: his upbringing, family environment, education, formative experiences, the things that shaped his character and behavior. You would also need to know something of his innate, inherited talents, abilities, and predilections. You would also need to have some understanding of how he responded to the events in his life, the impact of his experiences. Of course, it is impossible to know all of this. It is difficult enough to understand the behavior of people we have known for years. Even if we could manage to shut off our feelings of rage and revulsion, it would still be exceedingly difficult to find and consider enough information to allow us to fathom the reasons for a brutal murder. And, as a practical matter, no defendant or public defender can afford to present all the necessary information, and no set of jury instructions can adequately guide jurors in making this morally profound decision. Few defense attorneys even attempt to present sufficient information to make such an assessment.

Despite scientific advances in behavioral genetics and psychology, we are still a very long way from completely mapping out the motives, intentions, habits, interpretations, and situational pressures that propel a particular act of violence. The process is still mysterious. Perhaps if we had complete information and a year or two to sift through the information, we could arrive at a definitive answer to the question, Why did this person commit this terrible crime? But a thorough evaluation of moral culpability is clearly impossible within the constraints of the American courtroom. Some defenders present little information to help the jurors, and even the most careful defenders and prosecutors cannot uncover and present all of the reasons for the violent act. It is simply beyond human understanding. To believe that we can make such judgments is misguided hubris.

At the heart of the matter is an ancient and unresolvable philosophical debate: Free will versus determinism. Without at least an assumption of free will there can be no discussion of ethical behavior or criminal responsibility. Nearly all of us believe in some measure of free will, but we are all partly determinists too. Do you or do you not believe that you are a product of your genetic endowment and your life experiences? If you believe that your behavior is a function of inheritance and experience, you are, at least, a limited determinist, what William James, the great philosopher and psychologist, might have called a "soft determinist." Whereas the "hard determinist" insists that our actions are entirely determined, that no one is free to act differently from the way he or she does act, the soft determinist believes that we possess free will within the constraints imposed by heredity and environment. That, although our actions are not fully determined, our actions are strongly influenced by our conditioning, our values and habits, and the situations we find ourselves in.

In discussing the reasons behind criminal behavior, Stephen Nathanson argues that we must take into account the effort required by a criminal to resist criminal actions and the obstacles to moral behavior encountered by the criminal:

> A person's degree of moral desert is determined by considerations of what could reasonably be expected of him. If a person faces such powerful obstacles to moral behavior that it would require extraordinary amounts of effort to act well, then, though he acts badly, he is not morally to blame . . . different behavior could not reasonably be expected. The causes of difficulty need not be environmental. They could be physical, psychological, or of any sort, but if they make alternative actions extremely difficult or impossible, a person is not fully blameworthy for his deeds, even if they were wrong acts triggered by bad motives.[227]

The philosopher Jeffrey Reiman takes an even broader view suggesting that the larger society must bear some responsibility for the actions of murderers.[228] America spawns more vicious murderers than any other "civilized" country on earth. The social conditions that predictably produce violent offenders (e.g., poverty, routine exposure to violence as a child, access to lethal weapons) are at least partly to blame. It has been said that each nation gets the criminals it deserves. Put differently, a society bears responsibility for violent criminals to the extent that it tolerates social conditions that predictably lead to violence. Until these conditions are remediated, some of the blame rests with the larger community.

Let me be clear: The argument is not that murderers should be excused for their crimes. They must be held accountable and punished severely. The argument is that we cannot possibly fathom the multiple and subtle influences that cause a particular behavior. Instead of pretending omniscience, we should be more humble about our capacity to understand fully why someone commits a horrible crime. We can and should send a dangerous criminal to prison for the rest of his or her life, but we should not presume to judge which people deserve to live and which deserve to die. Our judgments are bound to be faulty.

JUST REVENGE

Beneath the usual justifications for punishing criminals lurks a more visceral and potent motive for the death penalty: revenge. The desire to lash back at those who have harmed us has deep roots in our evolutionary past. It is a powerful human motive that must be taken seriously, but it is not a sufficient justification for killing. Although individually we all feel the primitive urge to exact revenge against those who harm us, collectively we must strive to be more rational, fair, moral, and humane than the criminals who commit the acts of violence or cruelty that we condemn. We all sympathize with a bereaved father who attempts to kill the man who murdered his child. But a group's craving for revenge is far less innocent and immediate, and far less justifiable. A victim's relative who attempts to kill a murderer commits a crime of passion motivated by rage and grief. In contrast, the process leading up to a state-sponsored killing is slow, deliberate, methodical, and largely stripped of human emotion. The anger of families of victims is understandable, hut anger should not be. the basis of social policy. A community's angry cry for killing a murderer is far uglier than the anger felt by an individual who has been wronged by another.

We have all felt wronged and we have all experienced the powerful emotions that drive the hunger for revenge. The urge to see a murderer killed is rooted in the rage and revulsion that most Americans feel when they hear about a horrible, inexplicable murder. We empathize with the victim and the family of the victim and we want to see the murderer pay dearly for his or her crime. In movies, operas, plays, and novels, exacting revenge on those who offend us is often portrayed as emotionally satisfying. But just because the appetite for revenge is real and powerful, that does not mean we should indulge our appetite or build it into our legal system. Justice must take precedence over revenge. Arthur Koestler made this point vividly: "Deep inside every civilized being there lurks a tiny Stone Age man, dangling a club to rob and rape, and screaming 'an eye for an eye.' But we would rather not have that little fur-clad figure dictate the law of the land."[229] Feelings of anger and revulsion at a horrible crime are understandably human and maybe even a healthy indication of concern for the welfare of others. However, even if we accept the legitimacy of anger, anger does not outweigh all other considerations. Feelings of outrage and the quest for revenge do not guarantee that punishments will be fairly or rationally imposed. Anger does not ensure justice; it is an obstacle to justice.

It would be immoral to execute everyone who kills another human being. Every legal system on earth recognizes this. Consequently, every nation with capital punishment must create some method of selecting out those killers who truly "deserve" to die. Because no selection process is perfect, bias, prejudice, and error creep into every system of capital punishment. If the morality of revenge and the morality of the death penalty are to be defended, the defense must be of the death penalty as it is administered in the real world. Too often, defenders of the death penalty argue for its morality in a theoretical, idealized world. The claim that killing is morally justified must be reconciled with disquieting facts: the inevitability of wrongful convictions, the reality of discrimination on the basis of wealth and race, the likelihood that executions increase the murder rate, the reality that millions of dollars must be squandered to bring about a single execution.

Killing is a morally acceptable penalty only if it is essential, and only if it provides substantial benefits that cannot be gained by any other means. Capital punishment is not just a moral abstraction. It is a reality that must be evaluated on the basis of benefits and costs.

WHAT ABOUT THE VICTIMS?

Those who support the death penalty have a ready response to all the arguments against it: "What about the victims?" The question is full of implied meanings: that support for executions is based on selfless sympathy for the victims, that all families of victims of murder are entitled to (and find comfort in) the killing of the person convicted of murdering their loved one, that the abolitionists would be screaming for an execution if their loved ones had been brutally murdered. More fundamentally, the question is an attempt to control and limit the terms of the debate, a demand that we choose sides. The question implies that you must be either on the side of the victim and the victim's family or you must be on the side of the murderer. You must declare your allegiance: Are you pro-victim or pro-murderer?

If by killing a murderer we could resurrect the innocent victim, no one would oppose the death penalty. Unfortunately, there is nothing any of us can do to return the victim to the arms of his or her loved ones. The answer to the question, What about the victim? is not only that an execution will not restore the life of the victim; it is also that a state-sanctioned killing will debase us all and create a new set of victims: the murderer's family.

The wrenching loss of the victim's family cannot be fully appreciated by anyone who has not experienced it firsthand. Their suffering is unimaginable to most of us. "There is nothing to compare with the impact and profound shock of a sudden unexpected death,"[230] according to psychologists. Whereas the loved of people who die from illness may have an opportunity to grieve in advance and say good-bye to the dying person, there are no such opportunities for the families of murder victims When the death is caused not by a tragic accident but by the actions of a murderer, the shock and pain are amplified. The survivors must not only deal with their loss, they must also find ways of dealing with feelings of rage and hatred for the murderer.

It is widely presumed that families of murder victims are uniformly in favor of executions and that execution of the murderer facilitates the healing process. These assumptions may sometimes be true. After witnessing an execution, one relative of a murder victim described the event as therapeutic: "It was spiritual. When he [the condemned man] leaned over for the last time, everything I went there for just lifted off my shoulders. I felt peace . . . I have finality. . . . It was like a miracle of forgiveness."[231] We can only hope that her feelings of peace and forgiveness are lasting.

But the feelings and reactions of those who loved the victim are neither uniform nor predictable. For example, Coretta Scott: King, who lost her husband (Dr. Martin Luther King, Jr.) and her mother-in-law to murder, said that "I stand firmly and unequivocally opposed to the death penalty for those convicted of capital offenses. An evil deed is not redeemed by an evil deed of retaliation. Justice is never advanced by the unnecessary taking of a human life. Morality is never upheld by legalized murder."[232] Some survivors of murder victims have even actively fought to thwart the state's efforts to kill the person who murdered their loved one.

There is at least one national organization—Murder Victims' Families for Reconciliation (MVFR)—comprised of people who have lost family members to violent crime but nonetheless advocate abolition of the death penalty. Their fundamental belief is that "healing happens not by vengeance but by reconciliation—with society, the community, the act of murder itself, and sometimes even with the offender." MVFR's founder, Marie Deans, posed the question, "How can we stand as murder victims, in our pain and sorrow, and give it to someone else's family as well?" She has also written that

> the hundreds of murder victims' families across the country who, to no avail, have pleaded for mercy for those who murdered their loved ones clearly demonstrate that the death penalty has nothing to do with the victims' families. . . . Victims' families simply serve as a cover-up for the fact that our leaders choose to gain votes by reacting to people's fears rather than by honestly responding to society's needs.[233]

Oddile Stern, executive director of Parents of Murdered Children, opposes capital punishment and is "at peace" with the life sentence received by her daughter's murderer. She feels that the execution of a murderer "can never equate to the loss of your child's life and the horrors of murder."[234] Sam Reese Sheppard, whose pregnant mother was murdered when he was only seven years old, calls the death penalty "a hate crime" and believes that "it teaches that vengeance, hatred, and revenge are acceptable values to be cultivated and lived by our society."[235] Indeed, many relatives of murder victims show remarkable compassion and forgiveness:

> There is an old saying: "You would feel different if it happened to you." Well, it did happen to me. . . . But after much thought and many tears I knew that my feelings on capital punishment had not changed. For I knew in my heart that killing is still wrong. . . . He must pay for what he did. But I don't wish him to be punished by death.[236]

For the families of most victims, the long, repetitive process of trials and appeals may even divert them from the task of trying to rebuild their devastated lives. The legal processes leading up to an execution consume many years. Relatives who are determined to bring about an execution must devote a considerable amount of time and attention to the task. They must listen to countless descriptions of the murder; describe their grief front of attorneys, judges, and television cameras; and wait for years while the overburdened legal system makes a final determination. And even if the execution finally comes, they still must go on without their loved one. The long, slow process of trials and appeals, which often requires years of involvement by the victim's family, unnecessarily prolongs the terrible suffering created by a murder. Healing and recovery, according to the National Organization of Victim Assistance, come from "an increased remembrance of the victim—not the murder."[237] The police investigations, trials, appeals, clemency hearings, and meetings with legal personnel dredge up terrible memories time and again. Such events may prolong the mourning process and offer little relief from the pain of loss.

There is another set of victims: the murderer's family. A sentence of death creates additional suffering for the family of the condemned prisoner. The convict is always someone's son, and he is often a brother, a husband, or a father. The relatives of the condemned prisoner—who are often innocent of any wrong-doing—are swept into the widening circle of suffering created by a killing and a counterkilling. Mothers, fathers, sisters, brothers, spouses, and children wait for their loved one to be strapped down and killed by the state. In his moving book, *Shot in the Heart,* Mikal Gilmore describes the pain caused by the execution of his brother Gary:

> One moment you're forcing yourself to live through the hell of knowing that somebody you love is going to die in a known way, at a specific time and place, and that not only is there nothing you can do to change that, but that for the rest of your life, you will have to move around in a world that wanted this death to happen. You will have to walk past people every day who were heartened by the killing of somebody in your family—somebody who had long ago been himself murdered emotionally. You will have to live in this world and either hate it or make peace with it, because it is the only world you will have available to live in.[238]

The shame and stigma of being related to someone on death row is painfully felt by the families of the condemned: "I've found that people can be very cruel when they learn you have an immediate family member on death row. Generally they leave you with the impression they think you are tainted because you are related to a convicted killer."[239] Albert Camus made the point eloquently: "The relatives of the condemned man then discover an excess of suffering that punishes them beyond all justice. A mother's or father's long months of waiting, the visiting-room, the artificial conversations filling up the brief moments spent with the condemned man, the visions of the execution are all tortures."[240]

Families of the condemned and families of the victim share an experience that is similar in some respects:

> The homicide victim dies by sudden, passionate, individual violence, while the condemned prisoner dies by slow, deliberate, and collective violence. The survivors of both must live with the knowledge that their relative died from the intentional acts of others.[241]

Studies of the families of death-row inmates reveal an agonizing mix of emotions: They feel angry that so many people want to see their loved one killed and they become acutely sensitive to how others view the impending execution; they swing between hope and despair as the appeals process progresses; they engage in self-recrimination about what they might have done to prevent the murder; they may be haunted by obsessive thoughts about the murder and the execution to come; they grieve in anticipation of the execution; they worry about the enduring impact the eventual execution will have on them and other family members, especially children. The condemned man's family must live with the loss of someone they love. They must also live with the humiliation and stigma of being related to a person deemed so vile that he had to be exterminated. An execution may or may not bring solace to the victim's family, but it surely enlarges the scope of suffering to include the murderer's family.

It is critical to remember that even in years when executions are relatively frequent, less than 1 percent of murderers end up in the execution chamber. The other 99 percent of families of victims must content themselves with a sentence less than death. This creates yet another problem: Many families will feel cheated because the person who murdered their loved one will never be sent to the execution chamber. Other families will feel cheated if a murderer *is* killed. Jeffrey Dahmer was sentenced to life imprisonment for a hideous string of killings. But after serving only a couple years of his sentence, he was murdered by another inmate. The mother of one of Dahmer's victims was disappointed by his killing. "It's not fair," she said. "His suffering is over now, but we will suffer for the rest of our lives."[242] Instead of executing a tiny percentage of murderers, we could choose to spend some of the money now spent on capital punishment to provide emotional and financial assistance to the survivors of murder victims.

There is another sense in which executions don't serve the interests of the victim's family. Executions often bestow celebrity status on the condemned prisoner and draw attention away from the victims. The victim's survivors often feel betrayed by the courts and the media. You no doubt know the names of some of the worst serial killers, and you may even know the name of some condemned murderer who was recently executed in your state. But do you know the names of any of their victims? As the execution date approaches, a condemned man often becomes the object of sympathy. After all, he is about to be deliberately killed by the state in a carefully premeditated ritual at a specific, predetermined time. The worst murderers seem to enjoy the most notoriety, and their fame increases as their execution day approaches. Many receive bags of love letters and are sought after for interviews. While waiting on death row, John Wayne Gacy, our most prolific serial killer, produced oil paintings that were exhibited in New York and Los Angeles. He had his own 900 number where callers could listen to a twelve-minute statement by Gacy. There have been countless television shows and movies about serial killers, and each time another condemned prisoner is escorted to the execution chamber, his trip is accompanied by a flurry of publicity. One journalist, repulsed by the copious coverage of an execution, observed that the condemned man

> travels to his death on a crescendo of loud, ceremonious trumpets, full-blown biographies of his life and times and meticulous accounts of his final seconds. Yet his victims get barely a mention. Their murderer gets the cameras, headlines and team coverage, they get the fine print.[243]

Reporters and commentators are irresistibly drawn to executions and a significant segment of the American public is morbidly fascinated by the details of the murders, by the life of the murderer, and by the ritual of the execution. It is a tantalizing media opportunity: the drama of last-minute legal maneuvering, the countdown to the killing, the killer's final hours and last words, the reaction of the victim's family, the crowds of protestors and supporters singing and carrying signs outside the prison, the possibility of a bungled execution. Since the days of public hangings, it has never been otherwise. There will always be a depraved curiosity about murderers and executions. The only way to wipe away this ugly sensationalism is to dismantle the execution chambers, justices, the death penalty could be declared unconstitutional once again.

There are events that seem to presage abolition of the death penalty in most democracies. Some of these conditions have been described by Franklin Zimring and Gordon Hawkins; a period when executions become rare or cease entirely, although the punishment is still on the books; political leaders who actively seek abolition *despite* abstract public support for the death penalty; and national leaders who make explicit the link between executions and basic human rights, such as the right to life and the need to withhold from governments the right to kill for political purposes.[249] In other democracies, political and judicial leadership has been crucial. For example, in England, the death penalty was repealed in 1965, when 76 percent of the public favored retention.[250] This pattern holds true for most democracies (e.g., Canada and Germany); public support for the death penalty declines only *after* abolition. To be sure, politicians would rather have public opinion on their side. But usually public opinion is merely a convenient tool—useful when it agrees with the politician's views, ignored when it does not.

The president and state governors, as well as religious, human rights, and medical and legal organizations, could exert the moral leadership that might lead to abolition. Because it is both powerful and politically insulated, the Supreme Court may still be the best hope for full abolition. But even if the Court were to declare capital punishment unconstitutional—as it did in 1972—there might be another backlash against this federal intrusion unless political leaders and abolitionist organizations make the case against executions and help to temper the public's reaction.

THE POLITICS OF KILLING

The death penalty survives because there are benefits associated with it. Two groups receive some benefit from the death penalty: the public and the politicians. For the public, the benefits are largely symbolic and illusory. Capital punishment enables citizens to vent their anger toward violent criminals, to express frustration with the impotence of the criminal justice system, and to satisfy the craving for revenge. Anger and fear are the emotions that energize public support for capital punishment. Social psychologists remind us that "anger is the most positive of the negative emotions, because it is the only one that confers a sense of power.

When politicians argue, angrily, for the death penalty, they may communicate that they are in control, and at the same time arouse a satisfying sense of outrage and power in the voter."[251] Although an occasional execution may be emotionally satisfying for some and inspire a false sense of control, this benefit is purchased at a very high price.

For politicians who routinely invoke the symbolic power of capital punishment, the payoff is more tangible and immediate. By declaring support for capital punishment, ambitious politicians can quickly portray themselves as tough on crime. As Senator Daschle of South Dakota has observed, "We debate in codes, like the death penalty as a code for toughness on crime. . . . He who gets the code first wins."[252] The issue of capital punishment can be easily and effectively exploited for political gain. It has been a key issue in recent presidential elections and state gubernatorial races. Along with other symbolic issues, a candidate's position on the death penalty has been increasingly used to define candidates to voters. Politicians have enthusiastically embraced the death penalty and have frequently proposed that its use be expanded to a host of new crimes. And, in the United States, the death penalty is politicized at the lowest level—the trial level. Prosecutors and judges are elected in most states. For prosecutors who want to become judges, the publicity surrounding a capital murder trial can propel their political careers. They can be seen as anticrime warriors locked in a passionate struggle to send a vicious murderer to his death.

Although all but the most courageous politicians are skittish about proposing alternatives to the death penalty, survey research reveals a broad receptiveness to alternative punishments for murderers. Among the citizenry, there is a deep ambivalence about the death penalty. Juries are hesitant to impose it, and most Americans recognize that discrimination, inequity, and error are an inherent part of the system that sends some prisoners to their deaths. While there is no doubt that Americans want severe punishment for and protection from murderers, that does not mean that the public will settle only for killing them. Politicians have misread or purposely ignored the polls. Americans appear to favor the death penalty only if the alternative is life imprisonment *with* the possibility of parole.

The fight over capital punishment has launched and scuttled political careers. Americans place violent crime at or near the top of their lists of concerns, and the political rhetoric surrounding it is as superheated as it is superficial. Politicians are faced with a dilemma. In a ten-second sound bite they can declare their allegiance to the death penalty and show that they are angry with violent offenders. The argument for abolition takes more time and is more complex. A public declaration of opposition to the death penalty is seen as risky, perhaps even fatal, to a candidacy. Politicians are irresistibly drawn to any policy that appears to offer even a faint promise of turning back the tide of violent crime. In the abstract, the execution chamber is a shining symbol of America's resolve to deal decisively with violent criminals. Politicians gain a potent political weapon in exchange for pretending—in the face of massive evidence to the contrary—that the death penalty can be made to be effective and just.

This cynical manipulation of capital punishment trivializes the public's deep and justified concern about violent crime in America. Unfortunately, the political debate has bypassed a critical discussion of the costs and benefits associated with the death penalty. In the war on crime, abolition has been portrayed as unilateral disarmament.

The policy of capital punishment costs more than just taxpayer dollars and court time. It has a huge social cost: It commandeers and corrupts our national debate over crime and punishment. It lets politicians off the hook. Meanwhile, politicians breathe a sigh of relief because they no longer have to address difficult problems or propose detailed solutions. Instead of a searching debate on how to prevent and respond to crime, candidates simply declare their eagerness for more executions. A productive discussion of the social conditions that spawn violent crime (e.g., poverty, hopelessness, unemployment, domestic violence, access to fire-arms) or effective responses to violence (e.g., enhanced crime detection, certainty of apprehension, rehabilitation, or restitution) is displaced by facile declarations of support for capital punishment. To politicians, the death penalty seems dramatic and forceful, More effective but politically unsexy measures are seldom even discussed. Executions thus become a sideshow designed to divert attention from the crisis in center ring: Although the death penalty appears to be a form of decisive action, it is merely a mask for inaction, an attempt to conceal failure.

The violent crime rate in the United States is several times higher than those of other Western nations. A probing debate about how to prevent and reduce violent crime is desperately needed. Instead, by focusing on the executions of a few individual murderers, we divert precious attention and resources from treating the causes of crime. Constructive reforms that carry the potential to reduce violent crime remain untried or are quickly abandoned. While funding for education, family support services, early intervention, and treatment programs dries up, tens of millions of dollars are squandered to preserve the penalty of death.

The death penalty is public property. We own it. Executions are carried out in our names, at our expense. Our political leaders owe us full disclosure of its costs and consequences. It is irresponsible to be willfully ignorant of how it is administered, to diligently avoid the troubling realities. The job of political leaders is to challenge or defend social policies as they are expressed *in practice.* Realities must take precedence over abstractions. If a policy harms public safety, wastes taxpayer money, and systematically discriminates, elected representatives are ethically obliged to change or abandon the policy.

Unencumbered by the facts, people scream for executions from a safe distance. Voices of opposition are effectively silenced because candidates and journalists are afraid to challenge what is viewed as an extremely popular policy. This silence produces a one-sided, one-dimensional debate, which only serves to strengthen abstract support of the death penalty. The public is led to believe that only soft-headed bleeding hearts could oppose executions and that evidence on costs and benefits is ambiguous or inconclusive.

THE ROLE OF THE MEDIA

Despite the high murder rate in the United States, few Americans are murderers or victims of murder or friends and family of either group. Thankfully, for most of us murder is an abstraction, a terrifying but remote possibility. Because of this lack of personal experience with murder, most Americans rely on the mass media for information about its prevalence. In many studies Americans vastly overestimate murder rates.[253] This overestimation effect is especially strong for heavy TV viewers.

This is not surprising. The mass media pours out a steady stream of violence. We can all switch on our TVs and watch thugs, perverts, rapists, terrorists, and serial killers any night of tile week. The simplified and stereotyped portrayals of crime in Newscasts and fictional programs create deep misconceptions and great fear. As fear and anxiety grow, the public becomes increasingly receptive to any policy that has even a remote chance of pushing back the perceived tidal wave of violence. It is at this point that the media and politicians enter into an implicit and destructive partnership: The fear instilled by the media is soothed by politicians who propose the death penalty as a simple and decisive solution to violent crime. As Glenn Pierce and Michael Radelet have argued, "In terms of political strategy, media-promoted stereotypes of criminals and crime are invaluable vehicles for politicians advocating capital punishment. A one-dimensional policy such as the death penalty seems justified if the crime problem it addresses is also one-dimensional and simple. If, on the other hand, crime is a highly complex and diverse phenomenon, an extraordinarily limited policy such as the death penalty is of little relevance."[254] The media presents a distorted, sensationalized, and excessively violent picture of life in America. Fear of violence fuels support for the death penalty, and politicians are delighted to capitalize on this fear.

The death penalty is the triumph of symbolism over realism. To say that public support is largely symbolic is not to say that hearts and minds cannot be swayed by new, compelling information. Attitudes are resistant to change but they are not unchangeable. If information about the costs and consequences of the death penalty became widely publicized, there might be a sizable shift in even abstract support. So far, the accumulated evidence against capital punishment has been relegated to the back pages. For the most part, the mainstream media confines its coverage of the death penalty to executions and political campaigns. As the number of executions increases, expanded coverage is reserved for botched executions or those involving infamous murderers. It is simply not the kind of coverage that stimulates probing discussions.

AN ALTERNATIVE TO KILLING: LWOP+R

According to Amnesty International, "The alternative to the death penalty, like the alternative to torture, is abolition."[255] But that would happen to convicted murderers if there were no more execution? There is already a realistic alternative to killing them: Life imprisonment without parole plus restitution (LWOP+R). If we tore down the execution chambers, people convicted of what are now capital crimes would receive an automatic sentence of LWOP+R. They would be forced to live out their lives within prison walls and would never be eligible for parole. In prison, they would he required to work to defray the costs of their own confinement, and a portion of their earnings would go to a victim's relief fund. Americans seem ready to embrace this alternative. As we have seen, detailed surveys of attitudes toward the death penalty show that Americans favor LWOP+R because it reduces the cost of incarceration, provides some form of restitution to victims, and is more likely to teach murderers to accept responsibility for their crimes.[256]

A sentence of LWOP has several advantages over a sentence of death. First, it takes effect as soon as the sentence is handed down. When no execution is at stake, the number of appeals is vastly reduced. Second, the community can rest assured that the murder's fate is sealed and victim's loved ones can begin to rebuild their devastated lives. Third, the convict sinks into the anonymity of a gray penitentiary instead of becoming a tragic celebrity battling to foil the state's efforts to kill him. Finally, LWOP is a harsh punishment by any measure. Perhaps some people feel that a life spent in prison, with or without hard labor, is too lenient a punishment for killers. A little imagination and a visit to any overcrowded American penitentiary should be sufficient to any dispel that misconception. Murderers sentenced to LWOP would suffer all the pains of prison life: a bleak, barren environment; loss of control over all but the most trivial decisions loss of contact with family and friends; crushing boredom; and a grinding fear of other inmates and prison guards. This sense of fear and vulnerability would only grow as the prisoner ages and the prison fills up with younger, stronger inmates. All this without any hope of release. LWOP is the death penalty in passive form: God, not the state, decides when the inmate will die in prison.

If prisoners serving a sentence of LWOP were required to work, part of what they earned from prison labor could be contributed to a victims' assistance fund. This fond could be used to provide services and to ease the financial hardships on victims' families. Obviously, neither executions nor restitution payments nor any other form of punishment can ever begin to "repay" the victims' survivors. Prisoners are typically paid very little for their labor, so for any one prisoner the amount of money contributed to a victims' fund would be small. Still, a lifetime of labor multiplied by thousands of condemned prisoners could yield significant savings in the cost of incarceration, and could create a significant pool of money for victims' families. By adding an element of restitution to the sentence of convicted murderers, we could show that we despise murder but we respect human life.

It is not unrealistic to believe that the prisoners now condemned to die can be trusted to work. In Texas, doomed inmates are already working for the state. Some work as janitors or orderlies, but most work in the death-row garment factory. For more than a decade, death-row prisoners classified as "work capable" have been making sheets, towels, uniforms, diapers, tote bags, pants, and shirts. They sit behind sewing machines or cut up fabric according to state specifications. These inmates wield knives, scissors, and other potentially lethal tailoring tools. The garments made by the inmates are sold to state agencies and the profits are used to reduce the costs of imprisonment. There have been no serious violent incidents in the factory, and even minor infractions occur less than once a month.[257] There is a long waiting list of men who want to join the workforce, not to make money—they are paid nothing for their labor—but for the opportunity to socialize, to spend more than three hours a day outside their cells, and for the chance to prove that they are capable of useful activity. "The work program gives me a reason to get up in the morning," said one death-row prisoner. "If I were in segregation, I would probably sleep all day just trying to forget. It gives me a sense of dignity, doing something to completion."[258] There are also benefits for prison personnel. Prison guards report that working makes the inmates less dangerous. According to the president of the Association of State Correctional Administrators, "We know that inmate idleness is one of the precursors of inmate violence and other prison problems."[259]

Dangerousness

Some people argue that murderers should be killed because they might harm or kill inmates or prison personnel. After all, murderers have already been convicted of vicious crimes, and, since they will never be released from prison, they have nothing to lose. While it is true that a corpse can't commit further crimes, there is no evidence to suggest that inmates serving life sentences for murder are any more dangerous than the general prison population.[260] Although well-publicized serial murders come easily to mind, very few murderers kill more than once. Indeed, there is much evidence to suggest that "lifers" are far better behaved than the general prison population.[261] One survey of wardens found that lifers "are not a management problem" and that, instead, "they are a stabilizing influence in the institution."[262] Inmates vary in their adaptation to prison. Some murderers continue to be dangerous in prison; others are tamed and broken by the experience. Many murderers are weak and cowardly men who pulled a trigger during the commission of a robbery. Once they are placed in a prison cell they no longer pose a threat. The converse is also true: Some who enter prison for nonviolent offenses become murderous while in prison.

Lifers, like any other inmates, can be disciplined for any violation of rules. They can be confined to their cell, placed in isolation, or their minimal privileges can be revoked. Lifers recognize that the prison will always be their only home. They strive to create a predictable, secure environment because there is no prospect of release and there are heavy penalties for misbehavior. Past behavior on the outside is simply not a reliable predictor of behavior in prison. In fact, the only people in a good position to judge the dangerousness of inmates are correctional workers. In a system without capital punishment, local prison administrators would be allowed to decide which inmates pose security risks. These administrators would be granted the latitude to decide which prisoners should be placed in the limited number of high-security cells.

Because jurors are reluctant to impose a death sentence and a substantial number of death sentences are vacated on appeal, an LWOP+R sentence would be swifter, surer, and more final. The uniquely long and complex process of capital appeals would not be necessary. There would also be far more equity: Everyone convicted of aggravated murder would receive the same punishment regardless of race or wealth. Mistakes would still occur (although the chance of uncovering mistakes would be greater), but we would never again kill the wrong person or torture someone with the threat of execution.

The Message We Send

Much of the appeal of the death penalty lies in symbolism. But what message is sent by occasionally killing a killer? Killing is an odd way to show that killing is wrong, an odd way to show that society is just and humane. We intend to send the message that murderers will be killed and thereby to deter people who are contemplating murder. We intend to get revenge. Yet, despite our intentions, we also send the message that killing is an acceptable way of solving the problem of violence, that a life should be extinguished if we have the power to take it and the offender has taken a life. We lend legal authority to the dangerous idea that if someone has committed a depraved crime, we should treat him or her as a nonhuman who can be killed without remorse.

We could choose to react differently. We could refuse to respond to killers with a killing of our own. An execution is an endorsement of revenge, a statement that fear and anger ought to be granted full expression even when they decrease public safety. Blinded by the urge for revenge, we support a corrupt system of punishment. To preserve the primitive satisfaction gained from killing the occasional murderer, we are willing to tolerate an arbitrary, costly, discriminatory system that sometimes kills an innocent person. Renunciation of the death penalty would send a clearer, more constructive message: that we will not debase ourselves by killing, that the government should not have the power to kill its citizens, and that we are willing to forsake eye-for-an-eye revenge in favor of a fairer, cheaper, more humane alternative.

In part, the death penalty is a response to fear and social turbulence. As a leading scholar has pointed out, "It has flourished in America with the institution of slavery, with racial strife during Reconstruction, and with economic adversity at the time of the Great Depression, especially in the regions where these conditions were most keenly felt."[263] In contemporary America, where fear of violence has soared, executions reassure us that we are at least doing something. The morality play of trial and execution enables the public to believe that our legal system is, at least occasionally, capable of taking decisive action. The public ritual of arrest, conviction, sentencing, and execution are meant to reassure the public and give expression to their anger.

Unfortunately, the reality is that instead of protecting society and serving the ideal of justice, the death penalty harms public safety and contributes to injustice.

We do not allow executions to be broadcast on network television, or even on pay-per-view. The spectacle of televised executions would offend our collective sensibilities as a civilized people and expose executions as shameful and anachronistic rituals. The solution we endorse in the abstract is less appealing when it becomes a flesh-and-blood matter. When we kill a prisoner, we do it at night with only a small group of witnesses looking on. Few are allowed to see the prisoner strapped in, few get to see the needles inserted in his arms, few get to watch him die, few get to view the corpse. We take pains to hide the identity of the executioner, and we conduct the killing in an isolated wing of the prison. We have even tried to make the act of killing as palatable and "painless" as possible. Executions are now passionless bureaucratic rituals stripped of anger or excitement. They are the most methodical, cold-blooded, premeditated form of killing. To soothe any pangs of conscience, we remind ourselves of what the murderer did, and as the rage and revulsion rise up in us, we once again feel that executions are justified.

The influential anthropologist Bronislaw Malinowski argued that cultures turn to magic when knowledge and reason fail.[264] Other anthropologists have pointed out that executions are not unlike ancient human sacrifices. Both are wrapped in ritual: the last supper, the reading of the death warrant, the last walk, the visit with clergy, weighing and measuring of the doomed man. But the most fundamental similarity is that both are irrational attempts to alter mysterious and frightening forces, attempts by state officials to demonstrate that they are still in control. The killing of prisoners persists not because it stems the tide of violent crime, but because, like human sacrifice, it creates the comforting illusion that the state is taking action. Executions are acts of desperation, admissions of failure. Like human sacrifices, executions do not appease the gods, ward off the forces of evil, or restore social order. After the corpse has been carried from the execution chamber, we are less safe and less humane.

The United States is still bucking the worldwide trend toward abolition, a trend that is especially strong in open, democratic societies where there are ample opportunities to debate the utility and morality of different criminal sanctions. There is a strong, though not steady, tendency for punishments to become less-harsh as societies evolve and moral sensibilities mature. Social upheaval, rising crime rates, or political demagoguery can slow, but not halt, this progress. Eventually, torture, killing, and the infliction of unnecessary suffering will come to be seen as morally repugnant. Suffering that serves no constructive purpose will come to be viewed as morally wrong, as will punishment that is inequitably applied. As societies mature, punishments are evaluated on the criteria of certainty, utility, humaneness, and fairness of application, not on hollow symbolism.

In Conclusion

Capital punishment is a failed social policy. As we begin the new millennium, we should abandon this relic of the barbaric past. Killing was once a public spectacle designed to terrify the masses and to demonstrate the fearsome power of the state. Today, we would find such spectacles vile and repugnant. If we want to be seen as a truly civilized country, we should not permit premeditated legal killing. No legal system is capable of deciding who should live and who should die in an infallible, evenhanded way. We should not pretend that ours can.

It is easy to support capital punishment in the abstract. It involves little thought and much emotion. It is far more difficult to support the death penalty as reality—a penalty that squanders taxpayer money and court time, a penalty that is routinely discriminatory, a penalty that increases violent crime and poisons our public discourse. In spite of evidence and history, supporters of capital punishment claim that all these problems can be fixed, But it is the reality that must be defended, not some fantasy world of ideal justice.

Support for the death penalty requires a sort of unthinking sentimentality. It requires an irrational faith that the government can select out those who should die without prejudice or mistake. It requires a belief that legal killings will magically suppress illegal killings. Most of all, it requires that we turn away from the facts and stubbornly refuse to look back.

U.S. Departmentuf Justice
Office of Justice Programs
Bureau of Justice Statistics

CAPITAL PUNISHMENT, 2011 - STATISTICAL TABLES

Tracy L. Snell, BJS Statistician

At yearend **2011, 35** states and the Federal Bureau of Prisons held 3,082 inmates under sentence of death, which was 57 fewer than at yearend 2010 (figure 1). This represents the eleventh consecutive year in which the number of inmates under sentence of death decreased.

Four states (California, Florida, Texas, and Pennsylvania) held more than half of all inmates on death row on December **31, 2011.** The Federal Bureau of Prisons held 56 inmates under sentence of death at yearend.

Of prisoners under sentence of death at yearend, 55% were white and 42% were black. The 387 Hispanic inmates under sentence of death accounted for 14% of inmates with a known ethnicity. Ninety-eight percent of inmates under sentence of death were male, and 2% were female. The race and sex of inmates under sentence of death has remained relatively unchanged since 2000.

Among inmates for whom legal status at the time of the capital offense was available, 40% had an active criminal justice status. Less than half of these inmates were on parole, about a quarter were on probation, and the remaining inmates had charges pending, were incarcerated, had escaped from incarceration, or had some other criminal justice status.

Criminal history patterns of death row inmates differed by race and Hispanic origin. More black inmates had a prior felony conviction (72%), compared to Hispanic (64%) or white (62%) inmates. Similar percentages of white (9%), black (8%), and Hispanic (6%) inmates had a prior homicide conviction, A slightly higher percentage of Hispanic (31%) and black (30%) inmates were on probation or parole at the time of their capital offense, compared to 23% of white inmates.

Figure 4.1   Status of the death penalty, December 31, 2011

Executions during 2011		Number of prisoners under sentence of death on 12/31/2011		Jurisdictions with no death penalty on 12/31/2011
Texas	13	California	705	Alaska
Alabama	6	Florida	393	District of Columbia
Ohio	5	Texas	301	Hawaii
Georgia	4	Pennsylvania	207	Illinois
Arizona	4	Alabama	196	Iowa
Florida	2	North Carolina	158	Maine
Mississippi	2	Ohio	142	Massachusetts
Oklahoma	2	Arizona	130	Michigan
Missouri	1	Georgia	96	Minnesota
Delaware	1	Louisiana	87	New Jersey
South Carolina	1	Tennessee	87	North Dakota
Virginia	1	Nevada	81	Rhode Island
Idaho	1	Oklahoma	63	Vermont
		Mississippi	57	West Virginia
		Federal Bureau of Prisons	56	Wisconsin
		21 other jurisdictions*	323	
Total	43	Total	3,082	

*New Mexico repealed the death penalty for offenses committed after July 1, 2009. As of December 31, 2011, two men were under previously imposed death sentences.

Source: Bureau of Justice Statistics, National Prisoner Statistics Program (NPS-8), 2011.

Table 4.1   Capital offenses, by state, 2011

State	Offense
Alabama	Intentional murder with 18 aggravating factors (Ala, Stat, Ann, 13A-5-40(a)(1)-(18)).
Arizona	First-degree murder, Including pre-meditated murder and felony murder, accompanied by at least 1 of 14 aggravating factors (A.R.S. §13-703(F)).
Arkansas	Capital murder (Ark/Code Ann. 5-10-101) with a finding of at least 1 of 10 aggravating circumstances; treason.
California	First-degree murder with special circumstances; sabotage; train wrecking causing death; treason; perjury in a capital case causing execution of an Innocent parson; fatal assault by a prisoner serving a life sentence.
Colorado	First-degree murder with at least 1 of 17 aggravating factors; first-degree kidnapping resulting In death; treason.
Connect/cut	Capital felony with 8 forms of aggravated homicide (C.G.S. § 53a-54b).
Delaware	First-degree murder (11 Del, C. § 636) with at least 1 statutory aggravating circumstance (11 Del. C. § 4209).
Florida	First-degree murder; felony murder; capital drug trafficking; capital sexual battery.
Georgia	Murder with aggravating circumstances; kidnapping with bodily injury or ransom when the victim dies; aircraft hijacking; treason.
Idaho	First-degree murder with aggravating factors; first-degree kidnapping; perjury resulting in the execution of an innocent person.
Indiana	Murder with 16 aggravating circumstances (IC 35-50-2-9).
Kansas	Capital murder (KSA 21-5401) with 8 aggravating circumstances (KSA 21-6617, KSA 21-6624).
Kentucky	Capital murder with the presence of at least one statutory aggravating circumstance; capital kidnapping (KRS 532.025).
Louisiana	First-degree murder; treason (La. R.S. 14:30 and 14:113).
Maryland	First-degree murder, either premeditated or during the commission of a felony, provided that certain death eligibility requirements are satisfied.
Mississippi	Capital murder (Miss, Code Ann, § 97-3-19(2)); aircraft piracy (Miss, Code Ann, § 97-25-55(1)).
Missouri	First-degree murder (565.020 RSMO 2000).
Montana	Capital murder with 1 of 9 aggravating circumstances (Mont. Code Ann. § 46-18-303); aggravated kidnapping; felony murder; aggravated sexual intercourse without consent (Mont. Code Ann. §45-5-503).
Nebraska	First-degree murder with a finding of at least 1 statutorily-defined aggravating circumstance.
Nevada	First-degree murder with at least 1 of 15 aggravating circumstances (NRS 200.030, 200.033, 200.035).
New Hampshire	Murder committed in the course of rape, kidnapping, drug crimes, or burglary; killing of a police officer, judge, or prosecutor; murder for hire; murder by an Inmate while serving a sentence of life without parole (RSA 630:1, RSA 630:5).
New Mexico[a]	First-degree murder with at (east 1 of 7 aggravating factors (NMSA 1978 § 31-20A-5).
New York[b]	First-degree murder with 1 of 13 aggravating factors (NY Penal Law §125.27).
North Carolina	First-degree murder (NCGS §14-17) with the finding of at least 1 of 11 statutory aggravating circumstances (NCGS § 15A-2000).
Ohio	Aggravated murder with at least 1 of 10 aggravating circumstances (O.R.C. secs, 2903.01, 2929.02, and 2929.04).
Oklahoma	First-degree murder in conjunction with a finding of at least 1 of 8 statutorily-defined aggravating circumstances.

State	Offense
Oregon	Aggravated murder (ORS 163.095).
Pennsylvania	First-degree murder with 18 aggravating circumstances.
South Carolina	Murder with at least 1 of 12 aggravating circumstances (§ 16-3-20(C)(a)).
South Dakota	First-degree murder with 1 of 10 aggravating circumstances.
Tennessee	First-degree murder (Tenn. Code Ann. § 39-13-202) with 1 of 16 aggravating circumstances (Tenn. Code Ann, § 39-13-204).
Texas	Criminal homicide with 1 of 9 aggravating circumstances (Tex, Penal Code §19.03).
Utah	Aggravated murder (76-5-202, Utah Code Annotated).
Virginia	First-degree murder with 1 of 15 aggravating circumstances (VA Code §18.2-31).
Washington	Aggravated first-degree murder,
Wyoming	First-degree murder; murder during the commission of sexual assault, sexual abuse of a minor, arson, robbery, burglary, escape, resisting arrest, kidnapping, or abuse of a minor under 16 (W.S.A. §6-2-101 (a)).

[a]New Mexico enacted a prospective repeal of its capital statute as of July 1, 2009. Offenders who committed their offenses prior to that date are eligible for the death penalty.
[b]The New York Court of Appeals held that a portion of New York's death penalty sentencing statute (CPL 400.27) was unconstitutional (*People* V. *Taylor,* 9 N.Y.3d 129 (2007)). As a result, no defendants can be sentenced to death until the legislature corrects the errors in this statute.

Source: Bureau of Justice Statistics, National Prisoner Statistics Program (NPS-8), 2011.

Table 4.2   Demographic characteristics of prisoners under sentence of death, 2011

Characteristic	Total yearend	Admissions	Removals
Total inmates	3,082	80	137
Sex			
Male	98.0%	93.8%	99.3%
Female	2.0	6.3	0.7
Race[a]			
White	55.3%	48.8%	57.7%
Black	41.8	46.3	42.3
All other races[b]	3.0	5.0	0
Hispanic origin[c]			
Hispanic	14.0%	14.1%	7.3%
Non-Hispanic	86.0	85.9	92.7
Age			
18–19	0%	0%	0%
20–24	0.9	11.3	0
25–29	4.3	21.3	3.6
30–34	11.0	13.8	8.8
35–39	14.8	18.8	16.1
40–44	17.9	10.0	13.1
45–49	16.8	10.0	18.2

(Continued)

Table 4.2   Demographic characteristics of prisoners under sentence of death, 2011 (*Continued*)

Characteristic	Total yearend	Admissions	Removals
50–54	14.7	8.8	16.8
55–59	9.3	1.3	8.8
60–64	6.4	2.5	6.6
65 or older	3.8	2.5	8.0
Average age			
Mean	45 yr	37 yr	47 yr
Median	45	36	47
Education[d]			
8th grade or less	13.6%	13.0%	16.5%
9th-11th grade	35.3	33.3	40.0
High school graduate/GED	41.9	37.0	32.2
Any college	9.2	16.7	11.3
Median education level	12yr	12 yr	11 yr
Marital status[e]			
Married	22.3%	22.1%	19.4%
Divorced/separated	20.1	14.3	21.0
Widowed	3.0	7.8	3.2
Never married	54.6	55.8	56.5

Note: Detail may not sum to total due to rounding.

[a]Percentages for white and black inmates include persons of Hispanic or Latino origin, which may differ from other tables in this report.

[b]At yearend 201, inmates in "all other races" consisted of 24 American Indians, 41 Asians, and 26 self-identified Hispanics. During 2011, 1 Asian and 3 self-Identified Hispanic inmates were admitted.

[c]Calculations exclude count of inmates with unknown Hispanic origin: 325 total yearend, 9 admissions, and 14 removals.

[d]Calculations exclude count of inmates with unknown education level; 534 total yearend, 26 admissions, and 22 removals.

[e]Calculations exclude count of inmates with, unknown marital status; 357 total yearend, 3 admissions, and 13 removals.

Source: Bureau of Justice Statistics, National Prisoner Statistics Program (NPS-8), 2011.

APPENDIX
Law Enforcement Careers

LAW ENFORCEMENT CAREERS

The following career paths will enable you to enter law enforcement either at the local, state or federal levels. Read each description to develop a point of view on whether your career selection is right for you.

BAILIFF

Bailiffs are law enforcement officers who are responsible for maintaining order and providing security in courtrooms. Also called marshals or court officers, their duties vary depending on their location, but typically include enforcing courtroom rules, opening court by announcing judges' arrivals, guarding sequestered juries, delivering documents, taking custody of offenders, and calling witnesses to the stand and presenting the oath. The educational requirements for bailiffs can also vary depending on their location. Some local and state law enforcement agencies require at least a high school diploma or GED, while others require some college and law enforcement or military experience. Others prefer bailiffs to have an associate's or bachelor's criminal justice degree. However, for employment on the federal level, a bachelor's degree and related work experience is a requirement for entry-level positions. In addition to the minimum education requirements, bailiffs may also be required to complete a formal training program that includes instruction in topics like custody and security procedures, use of firearms and chemical sprays, self-defense, CPR, and first aid.

The U.S. Bureau of labor Statistics (BLS) reports that jobs in this field are expected to increase eight percent between 2010 and 2020. The rising demand is expected to be a result of the growing population and the need to replace retiring employees. The BLS also reports that the median annual salary for court bailiffs was $38,570 in 2010. The lowest 10% earned $18,980 or less, while the top ten percent earned $66.400 or more.

If you are interested in pursuing a career as a bailiff, you are encouraged to contact local and state law enforcement agencies, courts, and schools with criminal justice programs to connect with internship resources. In addition, you may consider applying to attend one of three 12-week internship sessions sponsored by the Federal law Enforcement Training Center. The program is open to criminal justice seniors and graduate students.

As part of your preparation for a bailiff career, you may enjoy exploring subjects like law enforcement systems, community policing, and critical incident analysis.

BORDER PATROL AGENT

Border patrol agents are the law enforcement officers of the U.S. Customs and Border Protection (CBP) within the Department of Homeland Security (DHS). They are primarily responsible for patrolling the Mexican and Canadian international land borders and the coastal waters surrounding the Florida Peninsula and the island of Puerto Rico to detect, prevent and apprehend terrorists, undocumented aliens and smugglers of aliens at or near the land border. Working with other law enforcement officers, they help to facilitate the flow of legal immigration and impo tation of goods while preventing illegal trafficking. To qualify for the GL-5 level, the lowest rank, you mu t have at least three years of general work experience that demonstrates your decision-making and ability o maintain composure in potentially dangerous situations. A four-year degree may be substituted if you d n't have the required background experience. Although there is not a requirement that your degree be in a articular field, a bachelor degree in criminal justice may help to give you a competitive edge. Once hired, bor er patrol trainees must attend a 58-day training program at the Border Patrol Academy. During the training yo 'll receive instruction in both border patrol and federal law enforcement subjects. Federal law enforce-m ent subjects include communications, report writing, and ethics and conduct. Border patrol-specific training includes instruction in areas like immigration and nationality law, border patrol operations, physical training, and Spanish.

Since knowledge of Spanish is critical as many of the persons border patrol agents come into contact with speak only Spanish, trainees are tested for Spanish speaking skills within the first two weeks of training at the academy. If you cannot pass the exam, you will have to complete eight weeks of Spanish language training in addition to your basic training.

The employment rate for this field is expected to grow by 7% between 2010 and 2020, as predicted by the U.S. Bureau of Labor Statistics. In addition, heightened security concerns regarding American border safety and illegal immigration has resulted in a need for qualified applicants, therefore, individuals who are bilingual or have law enforcement or military experience are expected to find the best job opportunities. According to the U.S. Bureau of Labor and Statistics, the average annual border patrol agent salary was $55,010 in 2010.

The U.S. Customs and Border Protection (CBP)'s Career Interns program is available to collegiate juniors and seniors. Career interns who successfully complete the educational requirements, and the career or degree-related work experience totaling 640 hours, will be considered for conversion to a permanent position upon completion of the program.

If you are in a criminal justice career as a border patrol agent, you may consider taking classes like homeland security and terrorism, crime prevention, and policing in context.

BOUNTY HUNTER

Bounty hunters are individuals who execute warrants by locating, apprehending, and transporting fugitives who have forfeited their bail by failing to appear in court. Bounty hunters are also sometimes referred to as bail enforcement agents, fugitive recovery agents, or bail fugitive investigators. Although there are not any specific education or training requirements to become a bounty hunter, several schools offer online and video training courses that may help you prepare for a career as a bounty hunter. However, you may consider pursuing a criminal justice associate's degree to gain a fundamental understanding of criminal behavior and the law, and especially the statutes in your state. For example, you should know your rights and limitations as a bounty hunter as it relates to the use of force or firearms. Additionally, you may also consider becoming trained in the areas of safety and self-defense. The U.S. Bureau of Labor Statistics anticipates a 21 percent employment growth for bounty hunters through 2020, due to an increasing demand for security and safety. Although the U.S. Bureau of Labor Statistics, reports the median annual salary for bounty hunters as $42,870 in 2010, bounty hunters are typically independent contractors, and they typically earn a commission of between 10 to 25% of the bond. Therefore, the annual earnings for bounty hunters are dependent on the number cases taken and a person's apprehension success rate.

Licensing requirements vary by state. For example, in Connecticut, potential bounty hunters must meet several requirements, including submitting copies of driving records, credit reports, high school or college transcripts, and letters of reference. Candidates must also complete a minimum of 20 hours of approved criminal justice training. On the other hand, Louisiana only requires potential bounty hunters to complete at least eight hours of training to qualify for licensing and to wear clothing that identifies their profession once they are licensed by the state.

Students thinking of becoming bounty hunters typically take courses like constitutional law, criminal procedure, or criminal investigation.

CORRECTIONS OFFICER

Correctional officers work in the penal system, which is the corrections and rehabilitation segment of the criminal justice system. Corrections officers are responsible for maintaining security within prisons. Their duties can include supervising inmates, conducting cell searches, restraining inmates, and preventing assaults, insurgences, and escapes. The basic education requirement for corrections officers is a high school diploma or a general education development (GED) certificate. However, some state and local agencies may require applicants to have some college credits. In many cases, military and law enforcement experience can be substituted for education. If you would like to work in corrections on the federal level, you will need to possess a bachelor's degree. According to the Federal Bureau of Prisons, a bachelor's degree in criminal justice or a related subject is a hiring requirement for correctional officers in federal prisons.

In addition to the academy training that most agencies provide to new corrections officers, there is usually also on-the-job training. New recruits typically shadow a more experienced officer for several weeks or months, and they receive training in the legal limitations and boundaries of their position. Lastly, many agencies also offer new recruits training in the use of firearms and self-defense to ensure their safety when working with inmates. On the federal level, corrections officers are required to go through 200 hours of formal training during their first year of employment, and to keep up with changes and developments by participating in annual in-service trainings.

The job outlook for correctional officers is relatively fair, according to the BLS. Between 2010 and 2010 the employment of corrections officers is predicted to grow by five percent, which is slower than average. However, there will continue to be a demand for corrections officers due to population growth and prison overcrowding. The BLS also reports that the average annual salary for corrections officers who worked in jails in 2010 was $39,040, while the average annual salary for corrections officers working in federal prisons was $54,310.

The majority of internships for corrections officers can be found on the federal level. The Federal Bureau of Prisons operates a Pathways Internship Program that offers students career exploration and development opportunities. Successful completion of the program can improve your eligibility for permanent positions once you complete your degree.

Students interested in a career as a corrections officer typically take courses like criminology, criminal behavior, and corrections and rehabilitation.

CRIME SCENE INVESTIGATOR

Crime scene investigators, also called forensic science technicians, process crime scenes to collect, identify, classify, and analyze evidence. They work with the police to help apprehend individuals suspected of criminal activity. Crime scene investigators can also be critical to a prosecutor's case since their crime reports and testimony can either help convict or acquit suspects in criminal cases. The educational requirements for crime scene investigators vary by location and employer. Many crime scene investigation careers require a bachelor's degree in either forensic science or a natural science, like biology, with an emphasis on criminal investigation, or a criminal justice degree with a background in science. Others may require a criminal justice degree with some background in science. Smaller or rural agencies may hire applicants who have a high school diploma or GED equivalent. Because they require extensive on-the-job training before working independently, newly hired crime scene investigators must complete on-the-job training in the form of an apprenticeship. During the apprenticeship they are paired with more experienced investigators to learn proper methodology and procedures for collecting and classifying evidence. Additionally, criminal investigators who work in a crime lab must complete DNA-analysis training, which can last for 6 to 12 months, while firearms analysis training can last up to three years.

According to the U.S. Bureau of Labor Statistics, employment of crime scene investigators is forecasted to grow by 19% through 2020. The increased use of forensic evidence in court cases accounts for the projected increase in the number crime scene investigator positions that will become available. BLS also reports that the average annual salary of crime scene investigators was $51,570 in 2010. Actual salaries vary depending on location, degree level, and experience, which may account for the fact that the lowest 10% in the field earned less than $32,900, and the lop 10% earned more than $82,990 in 2010.

Typically, students interested in exploring crime scene investigation careers are able to gain practical experience by participating in internship programs sponsored by, or by securing summer employment with, a local, state, or federal law enforcement agency. Crime Scene Investigator Network offers students resources associated with education and careers in crime scene investigation, including internship listings.

Students interested in studying crime scene Investigations may find taking classes like blood patterns and crime scenes, crime scene photography, and foundations of criminal investigation interesting and helpful.

CRIMINAL PROFILER

Criminal profilers create psychological profiles of criminals to identify behavioral patterns, which can help officers isolate their searches to suspects who fit a particular profile. Criminal profilers examine crime scenes, interview witnesses and victims, and analyze crime scene evidence to gather the information needed to create a psychological profile. They may work within a local, state, or federal law enforcement agency, and they may be called upon to give expert witness testimony in a court case. Education requirements for criminal profilers are not clearly defined, however, it is recommended that if you are interested in becoming a criminal profiler that you obtain at least a bachelor degree in criminal justice, psychology, or behavioral science. Other possible educational pathways can include pursuing a double major in psychology and criminal justice, or getting a criminal justice bachelor's degree and a master's degree in psychology or forensic psychology. The Behaviors Science Unit (BSU) of the Federal Bureau of Investigation (FBI) offers basic behavioral science training seminars to various groups including domestic and international law enforcement officers, U.S. military and intelligence officers, new agents, and academic personnel, when appropriate. The training includes topics such as bio-psycho social aspects of criminal behavior, applied criminology, death investigation management, and juvenile crime and behavior.

According to the Bureau of labor Statistics, the job outlook for criminal investigators is expected to be 3% between 2010 and 2020. Job opportunities for state and federal criminal investigators are expected to be competitive due to greater opportunities for growth and higher salaries. The BLS also reports that the job outlook for psychologists is 22% during the same time frame, however, since criminal profiling is a small occupation, there is expected to be intense competition for the positions that will come available during the decade.

The mean annual wage for criminal investigators and detectives, according to BLS, is $68,820, while the average annual wage of psychologists is $68,640, which may give you an idea of what the average salary is for a criminal profiler.

The FBI's Behavior Science Unit offers full-time unpaid internship opportunities during the spring and fall semesters to qualified undergraduate, graduate, and post graduate students interested in exploring careers in criminal profiling.

As you consider your educational pathway to pursuing a career as a criminal profiler, you may consider taking courses like sociology of deviance, psychological factors of crime, and crime, deviation and conformity.

CRIMINOLOGIST

Criminologists typically work in local, state, and federal law enforcement agencies. They are responsible for studying and analyzing the behavior and methods of criminals, in order to determine what motivates them. Once criminologists have identified criminal patterns, law enforcement uses the information to assess potential criminal situations, and to predict (and prevent) additional crime. Entry-level criminologists usually hold a bachelor's degree in criminology, sociology or psychology, However, many federal and private industry employers prefer that criminologists hold at least a master's degree in behavioral science or a closely related field of study, Choosing to pursue a master's degree from one of the top criminal justice graduate programs may take you up to two years to complete, but having an advanced degree can definitely give you a distinct advantage when competing for jobs in your field. According to the U.S. Bureau of Labor Statistics (BLS), the employment growth rate for criminologists is expected to be 18% between now and 2020, Even though individuals with advanced degrees will enjoy the best career opportunities, bachelor's and master's degree holders should do well in fields such as criminal justice, public policy, or victims services.

National salary data on PayScale.com indicates that criminologists can typically earn between $38,986 and $61,079, with a median annual salary of $46,464 as of February 2013, As a recent bachelor's graduate, you can expect to generally start out toward the lower end of the pay range, and increase as you gain experience, certifications, and specialized training during the course of your career.

There are a wide variety of criminologist internships available to students enrolled in both on-campus and online criminal justice degree programs. Many internships are available through local, state, and federal law enforcement, corrections, victim services, and rehabilitative agencies. However, your school can be a good source for arranging internships also.

There are not any licensing requirements to enter the criminologist field. If you are considering pursuing a career as a criminologist, courses like correctional philosophy, psychological factors of crime, and meta-analysis in criminal justice are typically the types of classes enjoyed by others in your field.

CUSTOMS AGENT

Customs border and protection officers, or customs agents, are federal law enforcement officers of the U.S. Customs and Border Protection (CBP) and the Department of Homeland Security (DHS) responsible for enforcing U.S. customs laws for every item or individual that enters or leaves the country. They are present at every international airport, seaport, and land border crossing to ensure to detect and confiscate smuggled goods, prevent individuals without legal authorization from entering the country, and to ensure import duties are paid. To qualify for the entry-level rank of GS-5, the lowest rank, you must have at least three years of general work experience that demonstrates your ability to interact well with people and to learn and apply information. If you do not have the required professional experience, a bachelor's degree may be an acceptable substitute. Once hired, as a customs agent trainee, you are required to attend a one-month training program at the Federal Law Enforcement Training Center (FLETC). During your training you'll receive instruction in basic law enforcement skills, cross-cultural communications, entry and control procedures, and U.S. customs import and export laws. If you are selected for duty in area requiring knowledge of Spanish, you may receive an additional six weeks of language training if you do not pass a Spanish proficiency test.

According to the U.S. Bureau of Labor Statistics, the employment rate for this field is expected to grow by 7% between 2010 and 2020. Additionally, heightened security concerns regarding illegal immigration, terrorism, and gun trafficking has resulted in a need for qualified applicants, therefore, if you are bilingual, or have law enforcement or military experience, it is expected that you should have the best employment opportunities.

According to the U.S. Bureau of Labor and Statistics, the average annual border patrol agent salary was $55,010 in 2010.

The U.S. Customs and Border Protection (CBP)'s Career Interns program is available to undergraduate juniors and seniors, as well as students enrolled in criminal justice graduate programs. Career interns who successfully complete the educational requirements, and the career or degree-related work experience totaling 640 hours, will be considered for conversion to a permanent position upon completion of the program.

If you a considering a career as a customs agent, you may enjoy taking criminal justice courses like psychology of criminal behavior, drugs and crime, and deviance and social control.

FEDERAL SPECIAL AGENT

The role of federal special agents falls under the law enforcement category of the criminal justice system, but instead of being assigned to a single geographic area, the entire country is their jurisdiction. As the nation's primary investigators, they are responsible for enforcing over 300 federal statutes and investigating criminal activities that threaten national security.

To meet the educational hiring requirement for a federal special agent, you must have, at minimum, a bachelor's degree from an accredited college or university and at least three years of professional work experience. You must also be able to pass physical, medical, and psychological exams in addition to a series of lie detector tests.

Along with the basic educational requirements, federal special agents must undergo an intensive 20-week training at the FBI Academy in Quantico, Virginia. The training includes classroom and practical instruction in areas like national security investigations, interviewing, and criminal investigations.

Although BLS reports that the expected job growth for investigators in general will be 7%, it is also expected that federal special agent positions will remain competitive due to a higher rate of pay, opportunities for inter-agency transfers, and greater room for advancement and promotions. According to Payscale.com, the median salary for a federal special agent is $68,619.

The Federal Bureau of Investigations (FBI) offers several 10-week summer internship opportunities to junior and senior undergraduate students interested in learning about FBI operations and exploring career opportunities with the Bureau. Students may work at one of 56 field office locations, FBI headquarters in Washington, DC, or the Criminal Justice Information Services Center in West Virginia.

If you are a student interested in federal special agent career opportunities or pursuing an online criminal justice degree, you may enjoy taking class like fundamentals of law, forensic science, or investigative and intelligence techniques.

GAME WARDEN

Game wardens are commissioned peace officers who patrol the lands and waterways of their communities to enforce fishing, hunting, and boating safety laws. Game wardens may patrol borders as part of their state's homeland security initiative, investigate environmental crimes, and conduct search-and-rescue operations in a state's lakes and rivers. They also educate the public regarding environmental laws, assist other law enforcement agencies with apprehending criminals, and render aid during natural disasters, such as floods and hurricanes.

Game wardens typically have to meet specific hiring criteria, however, the requirements can vary greatly by state. Some states require candidates to have a high school diploma or general education equivalent (GED), while other states require game warden candidates to have a bachelor's degree from an accredited college or university. Some hiring preference may be given to people with previous law enforcement experience.

Once hired, game warden cadets are required to attend a game warden training academy typically at the state's game warden training center for, depending on the state, 18 to 36 weeks. During the training, they receive instruction in various subjects including wildlife and natural resource management, boat operations, defensive tactics, water rescue, homeland security, use of firearms, and law enforcement curriculum and tactics.

According to BLS, there will only be 400 new game warden positions will be created between 2010 and 2020, which is roughly a five percent growth between 2010 and 2020. Jobs for game wardens should remain competitive since state and federal agencies typically offer higher pay and more opportunities for advancement than local agencies. In addition, BLS also suggests that candidates who are bilingual, or who have law enforcement or military experience will find the best opportunities in federal agencies. The U.S. Bureau of Labor Statistics (BLS) also reports that the median annual salary for game wardens in 2010 was $49,730.

There are several types of internships offered on the federal level by the U.S. Fish and Wildlife Service, The fish and game departments in most states also have their own internship programs, as well. For example, Trinity River NWR offers the Student Conservation Association (SCA) internship to college students interested in conservation. In addition to receiving a work assignment, interns also receive a weekly stipend, a place to live during their internship, and transportation for work. In addition, students who satisfy the terms of their internship also receive an academic scholarship through the SCA Program.

If you are a criminal justice student interested in pursuing a career as a game warden, you may enjoy taking courses like public safety operations, wildlife management, and occupational crime.

LAW ENFORCEMENT OFFICER

Law enforcement officers are responsible for maintaining public safety, preventing criminal activity, and apprehending criminal offenders within their jurisdiction. They also work with other agencies within the criminal justice system by helping to ensure violators are prosecuted by testifying in court, interviewing victims, and locating witnesses to crimes. Most police departments require applicants to have a minimum of a high school diploma or equivalent, and some agencies require at least a criminal justice associate degree. However, you should have a bachelor's degree or higher if you want to move up the ranks within a police department.

Before being sworn as a law enforcement officer, you must attend basic training at a police academy that, depending on your agency and location, may last from 12 weeks to over a year. During basic training, you will receive classroom and hands-on instruction in areas that will help you be successful as a law enforcement officer, such as community policing, use of force, self-defense, and ethics.

According to the U.S. Bureau of Labor Statistics, the overall job outlook for law enforcement officers is favorable. On the local level, the expected rate of employment growth is 7%, however, most municipal agencies experience high turnover rates that can create job opportunities for qualified applicants. On the other hand, it is estimated that the outlook for federal law enforcement officers will continue to be competitive because of higher salaries and more opportunities for advancement. BLS also reports that the average median salary for law enforcement officers in 2010 was $53,540.

College students studying criminal justice may apply to anyone of the 12-week internship sessions held three times a year by the Federal Law Enforcement Training Center. The program is open to criminal justice seniors and graduate students. In addition, many local police departments have cadet programs, which allow qualified individuals who have not meet the hiring age requirement to gain work experience and receive training that prepares them to transition to a law enforcement officer position once they become eligible.

There are not any licensing or certification requirements for becoming a law enforcement officer. If you are considering becoming a cop, you may enjoy taking constitutional law and sociology. You may also consider taking a foreign language if you will be working in an urban area with diverse populations.

MILITARY POLICE

Military police are charged with the duty of protecting the lives and property of enlisted personnel by enforcing military laws and regulations. They are also responsible for controlling traffic, preventing crime, and responding to emergencies on military bases. Similar to their civilian law enforcement counterparts, military police perform patrols; interview witnesses, victims, and suspects in investigations; conduct crime scene security processing; and arrest and charge criminal suspects. All branches of the Armed Forces require their members to be high school graduates or have equivalent credentials, such as a GED. However, if you are interested in becoming an officer, you will typically need to have a bachelor's or master's degree to qualify for officer training. To join the Army's military police, you must first take the Armed Forces Vocational Aptitude Battery (ASVAB). The ASVAB helps determine your suitability for certain occupations, and your score determines the types of training programs that may accept you. If you are accepted, you will then have to participate in a 20-week job training program in addition to the on-the-job training in police methods you will receive.

During those 20 weeks, you will receive classroom and field instruction. Topics that are covered include basic warrior skills and use of firearms; traffic and crowd control; investigating and collecting evidence; military/civil laws and jurisdiction; and arrest and restraint of suspects.

According to the U.S. Bureau of Labor Statistics (BLS), the job outlook in the military should be very good. Although the number of active-duty personnel may decrease due to wars and regional conflicts, overall the size of the Armed Forces is expected to remain constant between now and 2020. In addition, as personnel move up the ranks, retire, or leave the service, there will be an increased need to fill entry-level positions.

The average base salary for an Army military police sergeant is $29,380. However, according to the Army, that salary is supplemented by $24,580 worth of benefits, including a housing and food allowance, special pay, health care, and tax advantages, making the net income for a military police sergeant around $53, 960.

There are various internship opportunities available for students who participate in a Reserve Officer Training Corps (ROTC) program at their college or university, however, there are no internships available specifically for military police. Additionally, there are not any licensing requirements to meet prior to enlisting in the Armed Forces.

Although a degree is not required to become a military police officer, taking courses like police and society, criminal investigation, and theories of crime and deviance as part of a criminal justice degree can help prepare you for a variety of opportunities in this niche.

PAROLE OFFICER

Parole officers work with individuals who have been released from prison or jail and are serving parole until their actual sentence release date. The role of the parole officer is to aid in the offender's rehabilitation and help them avoid returning to prison. Parole officers accomplish this by providing offenders with resources, such as family and substance abuse counseling, job training, or educational programs to help them re-enter society and change their behavior patterns to reduce the risk of recidivism. State and federal corrections and justice departments most often employ parole officers. To enter the field, you must have a bachelor's degree in criminal justice or a related field. Federal parole officers are typically required to have at an additional year of graduate-level studies in areas like social work, sociology, or counseling. Specialized parole officer education can typically include coursework in interviewing and counseling, juvenile processes, parole terminology, case law, adult criminal justice systems, statutes, fines and restitution, and court reports and presentations. These kinds of courses can help new parole officers gain tile knowledge and develop the skills they need for success in their career.

As large numbers of existing parole officers are expected to retire within the next few years, there will be more new openings for qualified applicants, making the job outlook for parole officers solid. According to BLS, employment of parole officers will grow at a rate of 18% between 2010 and 2020. Parole officer salaries vary depending on experience, education, and location. The BLS reports that the median annual salary for this field was $47,200 in 2010.

Internships in this field provide students studying criminal justice the opportunity to gain working knowledge of the parole process and the day-to-day responsibilities of a parole officer. Typically, interns are allowed to handle many of the basic parole officer functions, including verifying offenders' employment and residence information, assisting with offender background investigations, maintaining files and records, and entering information into the agency's computerized database.

There are not any specific licensing requirements for parole officers. However, most states require parole officers to attain some form of certification once they have completed training and probationary programs.

Criminal justice students focusing on parole officer education may enjoy courses like race, gender, class and gender in a correctional context, or administration of community-based corrections programs.

POLICE DETECTIVE

Police detectives are un uniformed officers who collect evidence, investigate criminal activity, conduct interviews of suspects, witnesses, and victims, and arrest suspects. Typically, police detectives start out as patrol officers, so the entry-level criteria for detectives is the same as it is for cops. Also, like uniformed police officers, detectives are often called upon to testify in court to support a prosecution's case against an offender. They also help district attorneys by ensuring the evidence they collect and the confessions they receive are admissible in court.

Police detectives must complete a few years as a patrol officer before being eligible to take a written examination that qualifies them to become detectives. Having a criminal justice degree may help you earn a higher salary as an officer, and may give you a competitive advantage when applying for detective and other promotions.

According to the U.S. Bureau of Labor Statistics (BLS), there were 119,400 criminal investigators and police detectives in the U.S. in 2010, and most of them worked for local police departments and the federal government. The BLS predicts that job opportunities in most local police departments will be good, but there will be a lot of competition for police jobs in state and federal agencies. The BLS also reports that in 2010 the median annual salary for detectives and criminal investigators in the U.S. was $68,820.

If you are considering pursuing an associate's or bachelor's degree in criminal justice, you may find taking courses like criminology and public policy, police administration, and criminal investigation interesting and beneficial.

PRIVATE INVESTIGATOR

Private investigators are non-law enforcement detectives who conduct surveillance, find facts and information, and analyze and present their findings as it relates to their clients' personal, legal, and business matters. They provide many services, including tracing missing persons, conducting background checks, and investigating suspected criminal activity. In many cases, their investigation can overlap with a criminal investigation being conducted by law enforcement officers. They may also be called upon to share their findings with the authorities and to testify in court. Although most private investigators have some college credentials, most firms do not have formal education requirements, and private investigators typically learn on the job.

In addition to learning how to collect data, private investigators need to acquire industry-specific knowledge to succeed in their field. For example, investigators may need to study accounting, finance, business management, and fraud prevention to be effective as corporate investigators. Or, they may choose to go into criminal investigations, which would call for a degree in criminal justice, criminology, or law enforcement.

The Bureau of labor Statistics predicts the best opportunities will be found in entry-level investigative work for people with previous law enforcement or military experience. The job outlook for private investigators is still quite positive, in general. There were 34,700 private investigators employed in 2010, and BLS predicts the field will experience a 21 percent increase in growth by 2020, which is faster than all other occupations are expected to grow. The anticipated growth stems from increased security concerns and the increased demand to protect confidential data and property from theft and exploitation. According to BLS, the average median pay for private investigators was $42,870 in 2010.

Although there are no formal educational requirements, most states require private investigators to become licensed. The licensing requirements vary significantly from state to state. For example in Texas, the Texas Department of Public Safety requires that an individual has at least a year of work experience with a registered licensed security company and completion of five levels of security and investigation training to qualify for a private investigator license. However, in Florida, Florida Department of Agriculture and Consumer Services Division of Licensing, only requires that an applicant complete the first 24 hours of an approved 40-hour course to satisfy the training requirement.

Students interested in private investigations may be also interested in courses like policing, investigative function, and organized crime in America.

PROBATION OFFICER

The terms probation officer and parole officer are often used interchangeably, however, the two positions are actually different. Probation officers work with offenders who have been convicted of a crime, but were granted probation in lieu of jail time, and parole officers work with offenders who have served jail time. Probation officers develop and implement rehabilitation plans that include home and work visits, counseling referrals, and overseeing drug tests and electronic monitoring to ensure the offender doesn't endanger anyone or themselves. Except for in very small or rural areas, probation officers typically work with either adults or juveniles, but not both. Typically, agencies require probation officers to have a bachelor's degree in corrections, criminal justice, or another closely related field. However, if you don't have related work experience, you may be required to have a master's degree in criminal justice or corrections as a substitute for experience. In general, some states require probation officers to complete a training program sponsored by the state before seeking certification, and others require an on-the-job probationary period of six months to one year before being allowed to take a certification exam. In addition to college courses, probation officers can participate in professional development training that helps to develop skills in areas like social perceptiveness, inductive reasoning, judgment and decision making, problem sensitivity, and maintaining interpersonal relationships, all of which can help probation officers do their jobs well.

According to the U.S. Bureau of Labor Statistics, (BLS), the employment growth rate for probation officers is expected to be 18% through 2020, which is average for all occupations. It is also predicted that the job outlook for probation officers will remain stable due to a large number of the workforce that will retire in the coming years. Also, the acceptance of community-based corrections programs has led to decreased sentencing, which also increases the need for probation officers.

The BLS also reports that the median annual salary for probation officers was $47,200 in 2010, however, the upper 10 percent earned more than $80,750. Because actual salaries vary depending on experience and education, it may be worth the investment to pursue a master's degree in criminal justice or a similar subject to increase your earning potential.

Probation officer internships can provide criminal justice students with the opportunity to gain practical experience. Interns are usually assigned tasks related to low-level offenders, like verifying offenders' employment and residence information, assisting with offender background investigations, maintaining files and records, and entering information into the agency's computerized database.

There are not any specific licensing requirements for employment as probation officers. However, most states require probation officers to attain certification once they have completed training and probationary programs.

As a criminal justice student interested in a career as a probation officer, you may consider taking courses like theories of crime prevention, criminal justice ethics, or juvenile delinquency.

SECURITY OFFICER

The security officer's role in the criminal justice system is to deter criminal activity, enforce laws, and to monitor all levels of activity to protect properly against theft, defacement, fire, and other forms of illegal activity. Security officers accomplish this by monitoring alarms and surveillance cameras, controlling access to specified areas, interviewing witnesses in case of court testimony, and detaining criminal offenders for the police. In most cases, employers require security officers to have a high school diploma or a GED. Employers who hire armed security officers, however, typically give preference to applicants who have completed some criminal justice coursework or who have law enforcement experience. For the most part, you do not need to have any specific training to qualify for a security officer position, as most employers provide on-the-job training to new officers. The specific type and amount of training you may receive varies and is dependent on the type of security work you are hired to do. ASIS International, an organization of security practitioners, has developed training guidelines that recommend 8 to 16 hours of on-the-job training in addition to 8 hours of annual training. In general, training typically covers emergency response protocol, first aid, public relations, detention of suspects, and report writing.

The guidelines also recommend annual firearms training for armed officers as required by the state in which they work. If you are interested in becoming an armed security officer, your training will be more rigorous and involve training in use of force and weapons retention. You may also be tested periodically in the use of firearms.

Industry sources indicate that as concerns about terrorism and crime continue to rise, the need for the protection of people and property will also rise. In fact, the U.S. Bureau of Labor Statistics expects the employment rate for security officers to grow by 19% between 2010 and 2020, which translates to around 195,000 new positions becoming available during that time frame. Although many people are drawn to the field because of the low training requirements and part-time employment positions, the field experiences a great deal of turnover, which will create additional job opportunities. Security officers with related experience, such as a background in law enforcement or a criminal justice degree, will be the most competitive and secure the best prospects.

The average median wage for security officers is $23,920, however, the top 10% of security officers earned $41,680. If you have professional experience and more education, it can translate into a higher pay rate for you. Taking classes like public safety operations, criminal justice ethics, and police community relations can help to give you a competitive edge in the job market.

Security officers are required to be licensed in most states. Although specific requirements vary by state, in general, you should be at least 18 years of age, pass a criminal background check, not have a history of drug use, and complete the required amount of training. Also, if you want to become an armed security officer, attaining a firearm license is a separate process. In some states, the licensing agency is the Department of Public Safety, and in others it is the Division of Licensing. It is advisable that you check with the state in which you will work to verify the specific agency and requirements for your situation.

If you are considering pursuing a security guard career, classes like police function, criminal justice ethics, and police and society may be of interest to you.

SOCIOLOGIST

Sociologists working in the criminal justice system study how social influences affect individuals and groups, especially in the context of the social forces related to crime and delinquency. They also examine how criminal justice agencies and institutions affect people's lives. The findings of their sociological studies can help lawmakers and law enforcement develop, implement, and evaluate public and crime control policies. Generally, the entry-level educational requirement for sociologists is a masters' degree, If you are interested in becoming a sociologist within the criminal justice system, you may consider earning a bachelor's degree sociology with a specialization in criminal justice and a master's degree in sociology to prepare for a sociologist career. According to the U.S. Bureau of Labor Statistics (BLS), the employment growth rate for sociologists is expected to be 18% between now and 2020. It is expected that the growth can be attributed to the use of sociological research in policy development, and in the research of social issues, problems, or programs. BLS goes on to report that the median annual salary of sociologists was $72,360 in 2010.

As a recent graduate, you should expect your actual salary to vary, depending on your degree level, years of relevant experience, and geographical location. For example, the lowest 10% of sociologists earned less than $44,000, while the top 10% earned close to $130,000 in 2010.

There are a wide variety of internships available to undergraduate and graduate students of criminal justice who want to explore sociologist careers. Typically, most sociology and criminal justice oriented internships are available through local, state, and federal law enforcement agencies, juvenile justice departments, adult corrections agencies, and criminal law organizations.

There are not any licensing requirements for becoming a sociologist. If you are considering pursuing a career as a sociologist, courses like current social problems, sociology of crime and punishment, and structure factors in crime are typically the types of classes that may be enjoyed by other students in your field.

SUBSTANCE ABUSE COUNSELOR

Substance abuse counselors in the criminal justice system typically work with either adult or juvenile offenders and their parole or probation officers to provide assessments, education, and treatment plans to help offenders recover drug and alcohol addiction. Substance abuse counselors also provide group and individual counseling to inmates, offenders on probation, parolees, and the families of the offenders. Depending on the type of work, state regulations, level of responsibility, and the counseling setting, the educational requirements for substance abuse counselors can range from a high school diploma or equivalent to a master's degree. However, substance abuse counselors working in private practice must have a master's degree and a state license to practice counseling. As part of the licensing requirement, you will need to complete 2,000 to 3,000 hours of supervised clinical experience. That is a substantial time commitment, as it will take you anywhere from one year to 18 months to complete the required number of hours working 40 hours each week. If you work part-time, it may take you even longer. According the BLS, the employment of substance abuse counselors is expected to grow by 27 percent through 2020. They speculate the fast rate of growth will be due to the criminal justice system's attempt to curb offender recidivism by requiring substance abuse treatment as part of an offender's sentence, or in lieu of jail time.

The BLS also reports that the average annual salary for substance abuse counselors was $38,120 in 2010. However, salaries are determined by location, education, and experience. For example, the lowest 10% of substance abuse counselors earned less than $25,000, while the upper 10% earned over $60,000. Therefore, earning a master's degree in counseling, criminology, psychology, or a related subject could be a very good investment in your career.

Students pursuing an associate's, bachelor's, or master's degree should be able to secure internship opportunities through hospitals, human and social services organizations, mental health outpatient centers, and residential substance abuse and mental health facilities. Schools with criminal justice programs may also be able to help you connect with criminal justice professionals to arrange substance abuse counseling internship opportunities within the context of corrections.

Licensing is required for substance abuse counselors in private practice. Specific licensing requirements vary from state to state, however, general requirements include holding a master's degree, completion of 2,000 to 3,000 hours of supervised clinical experience, and a passing score on a state-approved licensing exam. Additionally, the requirements for substance abuse counselors who do not operate in private practice are also different. Therefore, it is recommended that you contact your state's regulating board and your state's licensing board to verify the actual licensing requirements for your state.

In addition to mandated licensing, substance abuse counselors may also seek voluntary certification. The certified criminal justice professional (CCJP) credential, also known as certified criminal justice addiction professional certification, is for criminal justice professionals who provide treatment services to adult and juvenile drug offenders. If you have a criminal justice degree, it may be possible to apply your bachelor's or master's degree towards the certification's education requirements. Becoming certified demonstrates professional competency in your field.

If you are interested in pursuing a career in substance abuse counseling, you may also be interested in taking courses like drugs and crime; alcohol, drugs, and society, and sociology of crime and punishment.

TRANSPORTATION SECURITY ADMINISTRATION OFFICER

Transportation Security Administration (TSA) officers are security guards responsible for protecting people, property, equipment, and freight at airports, seaports, and rail terminals. Their primary duties include screening passengers and baggage for weapons, explosives and illegal items; guarding vehicles to ensure nothing is stolen during loading or unloading; and watching for criminal activity. The hiring requirements for TSA officers include a high school diploma or GED and at least one year of security-related work experience. TSA officers must also pass a background check, drug screening, and physical exam. TSA officer candidates are required to complete a basic training program that includes at least 40 hours of classroom instruction and 60 hours of on-the-job training to achieve initial certification as a check point TSA officer. Students interested in pursuing supervisory TSA officer positions are encouraged to consider completing a criminal justice associate degree for a more competitive edge. According to the U.S. Bureau of Labor Statistics (BLS), employment of TSA officers is anticipated to grow by 10% through 2020, which is about average for all occupations. The average median salary for TSA officers in 2010, as reported by BLS, was $37,070.

The Transportation Security Administration (TSA) offers several paid and unpaid internship opportunities in its various operation areas, including transportation security, management, administration, and professional services to undergraduate and graduate students. As a criminal justice student, you may consider taking courses like criminology, theory and practice of crime prevention, and terrorism.

LEGAL CAREERS

From paralegal to judge, the legal careers listed below will expand your understanding of legal paths you can take. Some require advanced degrees, but many are viable alternatives post-graduation.

ATTORNEY (DEFENSE)

Defense attorneys are lawyers who specialize in representing or advocating for the accused in criminal court cases. They are usually either hired by individual clients or by the government as public defenders. To become a lawyer, you typically need to complete at least seven years of full-time study after high school, which includes a four-year undergraduate degree and three years of law school. Earning a Juris Doctor (J.D.) degree from a law school accredited by the American Bar Association (ABA) and passing your state's bar exam should allow you to practice law in your state. Before you can begin your studies, most law schools require you to take the Law School Admission Test (LSAT), which measures your aptitude for the study of law. LSAT scores are usually a determining factor in law school admission, so it is important that you prepare for the exam. In law school, you will study subjects like civil action, criminal procedure, legal research and writing, property law, criminal law, and constitutional law. You may also choose a specialization, such as family or corporate law, while in law school.

The U.S. Bureau of Labor Statistics (BLS) forecasts a 10% growth in the employment of defense attorneys between 2010 and 2020. However, even with the 73,600 new jobs expected to be added during that timeframe, competition is expected to be strong due to economic factors and budget constraints potentially negatively affecting hiring trends.

According to BLS, the average annual salary of defense lawyers was $112,760 during 2010. The actual income of a new defense attorney income can vary depending on factors such as whether you open your own practice, work for a large law firm, or work for the government as a public defender.

Typically, law students are able to gain practical experience by participating in internship programs sponsored by their schools, or by securing summer jobs in a variety of legal environments, including law firms, corporate legal departments, and government agencies. In addition, agencies like the U.S. Department of Justice offers several paid and unpaid internship opportunities in its management offices, litigating divisions, legal and policy offices and investigatory and law enforcement offices to undergraduate and graduate students.

Specific procedures vary by state, but in general, attorneys must become licensed by passing the written bar exam upon completion of law school. Since the exam is administered through each state, you must pass the bar in each state you would like to work. Some states also require attorneys to pass ethics exams and other state-specific tests.

Students considering becoming defense attorneys typically enjoy courses like the law of deprivation of liberty, law and science in criminal justice, and evidentiary issues in criminal justice.

ATTORNEY (PROSECUTOR)

Prosecutors are licensed lawyers who are either elected or hired to represent local, state, and federal governments in criminal cases against individuals or groups charged with criminal activity. They work closely with law enforcement officers, participate in criminal investigations, interview witnesses and victims, present evidence in court, and help to determine the punishment or settlement criminal defendants should receive. To become an attorney, you typically need to complete at least seven years of full-time study after high school, which includes a four-year undergraduate degree and three years of law school. Earning a juris doctor (J.D.) degree from a law school accredited by the American Bar Association (ABA) and passing your state's bar exam should allow you to practice law in your state. Before you can begin your studies, most law schools require you to take the law School Admission Test (LSAT). The LSAT measures necessary qualities to succeed in law school, such as reading comprehension, logic, reasoning, and analytical thinking skills. Admission to law school competitive and the test scores are usually a determining factor in law school admission, so it is important that you prepare for the exam. During the first half of law school, you will learn fundamental aspects of the law such as civil procedure, legal research and writing, property law, and constitutional law. In the second half of law school, you may choose a specialization, such as tax or criminal law.

According to the U.S. Bureau of Labor Statistics (BLS) forecasts a 10% growth in the employment of prosecution attorneys between 2010 and 2020. The growth is attributed to the continued need for prosecution lawyers in federal government to prosecute civil and criminal cases on behalf of the United States.

According to BLS, the average annual salary of defense lawyers was $112,760 during 2010. During the same year, the lowest 10% earned less than $54,130 and the top 10 percent earned more than $166,400. Your actual income as a new prosecution attorney income will vary depending on factors such as size of agency, government level, and geographic location.

Law students have a variety of internship opportunities to choose from to gain exposure and practical experience. You can participate in internship programs sponsored by your school or secure a summer job in a variety of legal environments, including law firms, corporate legal departments, and government agencies. Also, the U.S. Department of Justice offers undergraduate and graduate students several paid and unpaid internship opportunities in its litigating divisions, legal and policy offices, and investigatory offices.

Although specific procedures vary by state, in general, attorneys must become licensed by passing the written bar exam upon completion of law school. Since the exam is administered through each state, you must pass the bar in each state you would like to work. Some states also require attorneys to pass ethics exams and other state-specific tests.

Students interested in becoming prosecution attorneys typically enjoy courses like the law and the legal system, constitutional criminal procedure, and legal foundations of the trial process.

COURT REPORTER

Court reporters are critical to the field of criminal justice because they are able to create verbatim and accurate transcripts of legal proceedings, meetings, depositions, and speeches. Their responsibilities include ensuring legal records are complete, accurate, and secure. Most court reporters receive their education at either a community college or vocational school. The programs are varied, depending on the transcription method learned, so the amount of time it takes to complete training can be from six months for a certificate to two to four years for an associate's degree. Additionally, court reporter training programs usually include English grammar and phonetics, legal procedures, and legal terminology courses. Court reporters are also required to meet on-the-job training requisites upon completion of a training program. Certified court reporters are also required to complete online training and continuing education classes to maintain their National Court Reporters Association (NCRA) certification. Lastly, licensed court reporters must also meet their state's licensing continuing education requirements as well. The U.S. Bureau of Labor Statistics predicts that the employment of court reporters will grow by 14% by 2020. The anticipated employment growth is attributed to the increased use of court reporters outside the traditional legal setting. Court reporter services are currently being used for closed captioning on the Internet and on television. In addition, court reporters with real-time captioning experience and Communication Access Real-Time Translation (CART) will have the best job prospects.

In 2010, there were approximately 22,000 court reporters working in the U.S., and over half worked in state and local government. The median annual wage for court reporters was $47,700 that same year.

There are internship opportunities for court reporting students wanting to gain practical experience by applying their classroom knowledge to real-life situations. Your school should be your first point of reference for approved work sites if you need to complete an internship for graduation. However, court reporting agencies like AccuScript, Inc. offer working and student internships that allow students to explore careers as freelance court reporters and to help students transition smoothly from court reporting student to professional court reporter.

Court reporting students may find taking courses like business and professional writing, introduction to law and the legal system, and basic computer skills for legal professionals useful.

JUDGE

Judges commonly preside over trials or hearings regarding nearly every aspect of society on the municipal, state, and federal levels. They ensure proceedings are orderly and fair. Judges also interpret the law and apply precedent with the objective of protecting the legal rights of both the prosecution and the defense. They also give directions to the jury in a jury trial, or they rule on a defendant's innocence or guilt in trials without a jury. For the most part, judges are required to have a law degree. Earning a law degree usually takes seven years of full-time study after high school that includes four years in undergraduate studies and three years in law school. Most judges have years of experience working as an attorney before being elected or appointed into judgeship. All judges in each state must go through some form or training or orientation. Judicial training is provided by agencies such as the National Judicial College, the Federal Judicial Center, the American Bar Association, and the National Center for State Courts. Continuing education courses are also required by most states, and can vary in length from a few days to a few weeks. Also, federal administrative law judges are required to be lawyers and to pass an exam administered by the U.S. Office of Personnel Management.

According to the Bureau of Labor Statistics, very little change is expected in federal and state judgeships because each new position that comes available due to death, retirement, or expiration of term must be authorized and approved by state or federal legislature. Therefore, employment of judges is expected to grow by seven percent through 2020, which is slower than average for all occupations. In 2010, the median annual salary for judges, magistrate judges, and magistrates was $119,270, while the average salary for administrative law judges was $85,500.

There are not really any internships for judges, as the individuals typically appointed or elected into judgeships have considerable law experience from working as attorneys. However, for students interested in criminal justice internships, the U.S. Department of Justice has a listing of the paid and unpaid internship opportunities available in several agencies.

There are not any licensing requirements specific to the position of judge; however, most judges are required to be licensed to practice law. Since many judges were lawyers before they became judges, they already hold a license.

Students interested in pursuing a career as a judge typically enjoy courses like the specific problems in law and social control, capital punishment, and juvenile justice.

PARALEGAL

A paralegal (or legal assistant) works in private law firms or government agencies. Depending on their experience and education, paralegals can perform many of the same tasks an attorney would. Paralegals help lawyers prepare for hearings, trials, depositions, and meetings. Additionally, paralegals may also investigate the facts of a case, draft pleadings and motions, or conduct legal research.

According to the U.S. Bureau of Labor Statistics (BLS), it is projected that employment of paralegals will grow by 18 percent between 2010 and 2020. This growth is attributed to things like law firms cutting costs by using more paralegals to reduce overhead, and corporations hiring paralegals as part of an in-house legal system to avoid the high cost of having law firms on retainer.

Competition for jobs is expected to remain strong, but paralegals who are formally trained, have experience, and who are specialized will have the best job prospects. Aundrea mentioned that freelance paralegals face a different set of challenges in the fact that, even though they have the freedom to be their own bosses, they don't spend as much time doing actual "paralegal work"—this is because they have to balance their roles as paralegals with being entrepreneurs.

The BLS also reports that the average annual salary of paralegals was $46,68 in 2010, while the lowest 10% earned less than $29,460, and the top 10% earned in excess of $74,870. Actual salaries vary, depending on geographic location, degree level, professional experience, and the size of your employer.

Most paralegal training programs will offer you an opportunity to participate in an internship in which you can gain practical experience by working in a corporate legal department, a public defender's or attorney general's office, a law firm, or a nonprofit legal aid organization. Internships typically are for several months, and can sometimes lead to a permanent position.

There are not any licensing requirements to become a paralegal, however, most employers expect paralegals to seek voluntary certification through the National Association of Legal Assistants (NALA). If you are considering a career as a paralegal, you may enjoy taking courses like introduction to criminal justice, courts and criminal justice, and legal foundations of the trial process.

CPSIA information can be obtained at www.ICGtesting.com
Printed in the USA
LVOW02s1602040115

421250LV00002B/2/P

9 781465 247872